Joe Fedison

YOU CAN GET THE TRUTH

YOU CAN FIX THE WORLD

www.YouCanGetTheTruth.com

YOU CAN GET THE TRUTH - YOU CAN FIX THE WORLD

You Can Get The Truth Books
PO Box 1839
Absecon, NJ 08201
www.YouCanGetTheTruth.com

ISBN-13: 978-0-9858258-0-5
ISBN-10: 0985825804

First Edition

To my son Joey,

As an only child of a single parent I know it hasn't always been easy for you. You are a great son and I am proud to be your father. My wish is that this book will bring you a world of happiness, hope and purpose.

Love,
Your dad

Contents

PREFACE

Growing up, whenever I heard a statistic or "so called" fact in the news, I just assumed it must be true. It's in the news, why would reporters lie? As I became older, some of these "facts" didn't make sense and even though I had no proof, I was thinking of the questions that could be asked to verify the details.

In college I began to notice some of the challenges in the world, that appeared to be easy to solve, were reported as difficult situations that we were stuck with. Watching television day after day, I find it hard to believe I am the only one who sees this. Am I the only one frustrated by the issues being debated, spun and attacked that have solutions, where even the best word spinner could not deny them?

So as I watch, I am waiting for the reporter, interviewer, or government investigative panel to ask the obvious questions that could get right to the bottom of the issue. They could expose the truth, the problem would be solved and we could move on to the next challenge. Unfortunately, the right questions are rarely asked and all I can think is, "How can that be?" And I truly believe I am not the only one who feels there may be a problem here.

Every once in awhile I would discuss these issues with my friends and was puzzled to discover that some of them see it and some of them don't. I realized that when people are presented with undeniable proof, they still may not believe you. Maybe this is the reason why you can have a problem with a definitive solution and have millions of people on opposite sides of the issue. How can that be if it has already been solved? It's either right or wrong, there are no sides. My first thought is that I am glad these people are not in charge of making major decisions for the entire country. Then I think maybe they are and maybe that is the problem.

I can't tell my friends what to think. I can't tell you how to feel about certain situations or issues. Most of the time it doesn't matter, because you probably aren't the one making decisions that affect everyone else. The problem arises when decision makers have all the facts and proof in front of them and choose to make a bad decision. That decision then adversely affects other people directly or indirectly, either now or in the future.

It seems simple to me. If someone is in a position of making decisions for you, wouldn't you expect them to follow a few basic rules, especially if your money pays their salary? The first rule is they should tell the truth. Another rule would be, if their decisions cost you money, they should get the best value for that money. This list of rules could go on, but the last one should be: If their decision doesn't make sense, then you are allowed to question them before they make a mistake. Why does this even have to be said? It is common sense and I am sure you won't find too many people who would disagree with these rules. You will actually find people who claim this is how it works, but I could find others who can prove it doesn't.

I always had a knack for finding the truth, I thought it was easy. You find out what the problem is, learn what the facts are and then use common sense and logic to prove whether it is right or wrong, true or false. Sometimes this wasn't enough to get to the truth. The reason is because some people don't want you to know the truth. I learned how to add a few extra steps that made it nearly impossible for someone to lie to me. I realized, through discussions with my friends, that not many people approach problem solving the way I do. I am the person you didn't want to get in to a discussion with, because I was constantly fact checking and questioning your reasoning. I just wanted to be told the truth when having a conversation. The benefit to me was being able to make a mental list of who to believe when they spoke to me and who not to believe. What if you could do this when faced with financial or medical decisions? Ever heard of someone being lied to about their finances? What if you knew who was lying and who was telling the truth? Would that make your life easier?

I was the middle child of three boys and one of the ways I could compete with my older brother was to try to be smarter and excel in school. I developed a passion for learning early on and tried to read everything and anything that was around me. By my teenage years I had developed a basic knowledge on multiple subjects and began to question people when I thought something didn't sound right. Unfortunately, this didn't go over well with my father. For some reason he chose to make up facts, and sometimes words, when imparting his authority on me. It came that day when I finally said, "That doesn't make sense." I remember one time getting a dictionary to prove my point. Ironically I was right, but it probably wasn't the smartest move at the time. A lot of times these "discussions" did not turn out well, but I was tired of someone not telling me the truth. Just tell me the truth, even if the truth is, "I don't know." That is all I ask for.

Sometimes, when I proved my point, my father would resort to the trump card. When I said, "Why", his simple answer was, "Because I'm your father." As I grew older, that answer was never good enough. I remember asking, "What does that mean?" How does you being my father make your statements correct? It doesn't make sense. My son was born in 1994 and I have been a single parent since 1996. I have never used the excuse, "Because I'm your father." As much as I butted heads with my father, I guess I should be thanking him. If he didn't make sense of the world the way he did, then I would have never had the motivation to learn how to expose the truth the way I do.

Over the years I became better at exposing the truth. Ironically, I only used it in certain situations. I still had the belief that, if you had a title or a position then you must know what you are talking about. So I believed what the "experts" told me, until I started proving them wrong. And then it finally sunk into my thick skull. That is when I realized that people like to state what they "think" or want to be true, they don't always base their decisions on facts, and sometimes they will lie. It is difficult to navigate through life when people don't give you the right answers to your questions. Again, all I wanted was people to tell me the truth. I am capable of figuring out what to do from there. If I made a mistake, at least I knew it was my fault.

The problem is how do you get the "experts" to tell the truth, when they either don't know it or don't want you to know it? Who in their right mind is going to admit fault when they are trying to keep a secret? And that became my quest. How do you get people to admit the truth, even when they don't want to? I thought I had the answer several times, but when I tested it, I didn't get the result I was expecting. After multiple revisions, I finally came up with a formula that worked. Then I spent 18 months putting it down on paper. It is an evolution of how I thought throughout my life. The toughest part was not being able to refer to someone else who has done similar work, because I couldn't find any examples. I knew the foundation of how it worked, but putting it on paper was more involved than I expected. Writing it also opened my eyes to other techniques, which evolved through trial and error. Several ideas I had at the beginning have changed and several of them were removed completely.

The end result is I have written a book that will fix the world. This book doesn't detail the problems of society nor does it analyze the effects of bad decisions. It is a "How To" guide that shows exactly what needs to be done to fix any problem that has a solution. It is written so anyone can use the techniques described and it doesn't require a college degree, money, or political connections. Readers will learn simple methods for exposing the truth, finding solutions to most of the world's problems and implementing them today, not ten years in the future. These are bold statements and I don't expect you to believe me, so read the book and prove me wrong.

This book is not designed to stir up a big debate or to give people the opportunity for their fifteen minutes of fame, me included. It is written for people who want to do something, but never knew how to do it. It is written to open your eyes to the solutions that are available right now and to motivate you to fix the problems they solve. The techniques in this book revolve around exposing the truth in the quickest way possible.

So if there is a way to expose the truth quickly, why are we waiting? If there are two sides to an issue, instead of hearing each side sell their reasoning, let's just go prove it right or wrong and move on. Why does it seem like this never happens? Right now there is a big debate about natural gas drilling in Pennsylvania. One side says it is safe and the other side says it has already polluted the water source for thousands of people. I don't know who is right or wrong, but why can't we get a camera crew and few biochemists to test the water and tell the world what the truth is? Is it really that hard? Trust me, we are smart enough to make our own decisions once we know all the facts, which means once we know the truth.

As a young child I thought I would be a scientist who would make great discoveries and save the world. I remember spending most of my money on science books and electronics kits. In fourth grade I got a microscope for Christmas and the first question I asked my mom was could I get a slide with cancer on it so I could find a cure. Fast forward to now and I am not a scientist, but like a lot of people, I still want to save the world. So maybe I won't find the cure for cancer, but I truly believe I have found a way to fix almost everything else.

When fixing problems, there is power in numbers. What would happen if several million people had the skills to expose the truth about issues that plague our country and the world? It's not the same as one person confronting their Mayor. When everyone knows there is something wrong and they begin exposing the truth, then the lies will no longer work and the status quo will change. That is what this book is about.

With this power you will be able to change the current landscape of our society. I would like to request that your first goal should be to stop the financial havoc that has a strangle hold on Middle America and the rest of the world. I have outlined a plan in this book to accomplish that. Once it is done and people can breathe again, then we can go ahead and fix the other problems.

So I have a plan. I have written it in this book. There is no doubt this plan will work. The only variable is "when" it will work. It could work right now. There is absolutely no logical reasoning why it can't. Whether you believe me or not, you will not be able to deny the truths this book will deliver.

INTRODUCTION

"Hell, there are no rules here - we're
trying to accomplish something."

Thomas Edison

I believe we can easily make the world a better place and we don't need any scientific breakthroughs to do it. We have everything we need right now. There's enough energy, enough food, enough land, enough water and there is certainly enough money. The only thing we are lacking is enough truth.

There are simple solutions available right now to fix most of the problems in our world today and this book shows how to do that step-by-step. This book is designed to teach people methods for exposing the truth and fixing problems. There are many books that expose scandals, conspiracies and corruption, so the truth is already out there. You will learn how to take the next step, using what they found out and fixing what is wrong.

If you are the casual reader I welcome you, but if you picked up this book, I am suspecting you will do more. Maybe you already have. Maybe you are one of the millions of people who just can't take the lies anymore and you have tried to make things right or you could be someone who wants to do something, but just aren't sure how to do it. You might even be a leader of a large organization or movement that has hundreds of thousands of people who already know how to make things happen. Whichever one you are, this book will deliver the tools to accomplish your goals.

I have created a method that anyone can use to expose the truth and fix problems. I was not taught this method and I don't believe you will find it written in any other book. It is built on logic that makes sense to me and I believe it will make sense to you when you read it. The methods I have developed make the term "Brutally Honest" seem like it should be in a nursery rhyme. I hold no punches. Not because I want to hurt people's feelings by proving them wrong. It is because our world needs people to tell the truth and that needs to happen now. So if you are a person who will be humiliated by someone exposing your lies, which coincidentally adversely affected millions of people, I am not going to lose too much sleep over that.

The goals of this book are as follows:

1. Get you to understand that just because some people have a position and a title doesn't always mean they are qualified or they possess the integrity to do what's right.
2. Show you how to prove what I am saying is either true or not. I don't want you to believe it just because it is written in a book. I want you to learn how to find the facts for yourself and make your own decisions.
3. Teach you how to craft questions so you can expose the truth and produce immediate results.
4. Outline solutions that are available right now to fix huge global challenges, which when enacted could begin to turn the economy around within 6-12 months.
5. List a variety of other issues that may have solutions and provide a few questions that should be asked by people who can take the lead and fix those problems.
6. Motivate you to stand up for what is right.

The first five parts of this book are setup to teach you the process of exposing the truth step-by-step. At the beginning of each part there is a "mini" flowchart. This flowchart is a snapshot of what you should understand from that section. When you reach PART 6, you will see how all five "mini" flowcharts fit together to create the "Problem Solving Process." There are additional enhancements in the chapters that follow that, but this is all you really need.

The purpose of this book is to teach the method and to have people use it. Therefore I don't want to slow anyone down who wants to learn the techniques as quickly as possible. In the first five parts I have written the summary first and titled it, "What You Will Learn". If you agree with the summary and understand the premise of any chapter, you can quickly move on to the next. There are parts of this book that can be used as an ongoing reference guide and therefore having the summary first will help you find information much faster.

PART 6 has detailed instructions on how to apply the "Problem Solving Process". PART 7 introduces the "Problem Solving Method", with instructions and guidelines. PART 8 provides templates you can copy, which are designed for you to fill in the answers for a particular truth exposing encounter. In PART 9, I have gone over in detail what I believe to be the underlying problem of our current economy, then I presented a plan that can be used right now to fix that problem in PART 10. PART 11 is written for people who believe that Executive Compensation is out of control and they want to do something about it.

In PART 12 I have touched on multiple areas that should be addressed. In some cases I have written a few sentences and in others I have gone in to more detail outlining exactly what to do. This is to show you how this method for exposing the truth can be used in nearly all scenarios. I want you to realize that if there is a particular problem you want fixed, then this book will show you how to do it, even if I didn't mention it here. PART 13 are final thoughts that didn't belong in any other section.

Throughout this book I use the terms "right thing" and "wrong thing" or "good" and "bad". Here is what I mean when I refer to these terms:

- **Right Thing (Good):** When someone who makes decisions that affects others, who they may not even know, it should be expected that they do it morally, ethically and without criminal activity. It is done for the better good of society as a whole.

- **Wrong Thing (Bad):** Making decisions that adversely affect others, knowing that they were wrong. Taking bribes, not telling the truth, suppressing data or information, getting even and getting things they do not deserve.

In this book I write about fixing problems. For the sake of future discussions, when I use any form of the word "fix" as it applies to solving problems, it means: When a solution is enacted that benefits the society as a whole; even though some people won't like it, they cannot prove it to be wrong.

When I say "they" or "them", it means anyone who is on the wrong side of an issue trying to convince everyone else they are on the right side (this will become more evident as you read on).

For items listed in this book, I have used numbers (1, 2, 3, etc.) and bullets (●). For the most part, numbered lists are meant to follow a specific order and lists that are bulleted can be used in any order.

I believe that people do the best with what they have. This means that if you push anyone into a corner there aren't many options left. When it comes to providing food and shelter for their family, sometimes people make bad choices. These are not the people I am talking about when I refer to people doing the wrong thing. I am talking about the person who more than likely pushed those people into the corner.

Using the techniques outlined in this book will allow you to get right down to the truth. You will notice there is no "sugar coating", it is direct and to the point, and a person's feelings have been removed from the equation. Emotion does not change whether data, recalling events or research are true or not, it has nothing to do with it. When financial institutions reported false data and pensions plans lost millions, do you think they worried about retiree's feelings?

When it comes to solving global challenges, tact, political correctness and making friends are optional. You don't have to be a skilled communicator who understands the human psyche in order to expose the truth. If you are a great speaker and want to use those skills to make friends, be my guest. I am willing to bet that when you bring a hidden truth to the public light, the people you are exposing aren't going to want to be friends.

I want to make one fact clear. The problems that I discuss in this book are caused by a relative few and I understand that most the people in the world are doing what's right. If there is a statement about a particular profession or industry, please don't take offense to it personally. Sadly though, I can't think of any industry or profession that hasn't had some type of corruption or scandal. This book is not directed at any person in any profession who does the "right thing". You know who you are and you also know who the "other" people are. I know that the good people of the world outnumber the bad people of the world by a large percentage and that is exactly what I am counting on. This book is about fixing problems, I applaud you if you have integrity and are committed to doing the right thing, but I did not write a book on how to fix what is right.

It doesn't matter if you are a teenager or in the twilight of your life. The methods in this book are based on simple logic that anyone can use and sometimes all it takes is a little bit of courage. So be prepared, you are about to learn some of the most effective skills and strategies for exposing the truth that have ever been written on paper.

PART 1:

A PSYCHOLOGY FOR SOLVING PROBLEMS

What You Will Learn

This section is written to give you a background to understanding the reasoning that is used throughout this book. The information is not new, it is just written in a way that shows the power each concept has for exposing the truth and fixing problems.

Chapter 1: It IS Simple
- We should focus on problems that can be solved now.
- Use the same rules you follow in your own life:
  - If there is a solution to a problem – you use it.
  - If something is broken – you fix it.
  - If something is not known – you find it out.
  - If someone is not doing the job – you find someone else who can.
- Are you willing to accept truths that may not coincide with your current beliefs?
- Fixing problems begins with asking questions that expose the truth.

Chapter 2: A World Of Problems
- There are global problems that affect everyone.
- There are people who have researched and discovered solutions to many of the world's problems. They have written books, essays, done interviews and made documentaries.
- There are other problems that could be solved if people were permitted to uncover the truth.

Chapter 3: Don't Believe Everything You Hear
- Just because people are elected or hired to fix problems doesn't mean they can or will.
- There are people in the world who deliberately keep problems from being solved.
- Just because you read a statement or heard a statistic on the news doesn't mean it is true.

Chapter 4: The Proof Is Knowing The Truth
- It is easier to expose the truth when you know what it is.
- If you want to be part of the solution you should know what you are talking about.
- Don't believe anything I say, prove it to yourself. From now on, be your own judge.

Chapter 5: The Power To Fix What Is Wrong

- You have a right to have your own thoughts and to make your own decisions.
- You have the right to question people who make decisions that affect your life directly or indirectly, either now or in the future.
- The reasons people don't ask questions when they think something is wrong:
  - They forgot they had the power to question and act on their own decisions.
  - They were never told the truth in the first place, so they accepted the circumstances.
  - They knew there was something wrong, but didn't know what to do.
- The reason why solvable problems persist is because enough people don't know the truth.
- When the truth is globalized the demand for change is stronger than the lies that hide the solutions.

Problem Solving Process - PART: 1

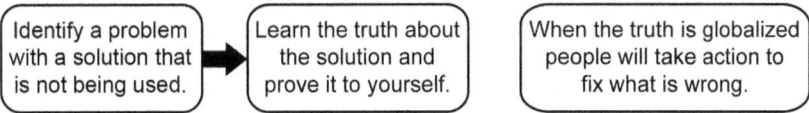

| Identify a problem with a solution that is not being used. | → | Learn the truth about the solution and prove it to yourself. | When the truth is globalized people will take action to fix what is wrong. |

This is the first part of the "Problem Solving Process", which states there are problems with solutions that are not being solved. You need to know the truth or be able to find the truth. The best way to fix a problem is to expose the truth and globalize it.

So now the question becomes, "Why don't people know the truth about the world's problems?" This will be answered in PART 2.

Chapter 1: It IS Simple

> *"All truths are easy to understand once they*
> *are discovered; the point is to discover them."*
>
> ## *Galileo Galilei*

Galileo Galilei put it in writing over 450 years ago. For the most part he was talking about science, but his quote holds true for all issues. How can you understand anything if you don't discover the truth? Whenever something is unknown, the quest for the truth begins by asking questions. What would happen if? How long will it take? Why did it end up like this? Therefore the key to understanding anything is to discover the truth and that is accomplished by asking the right questions. If you ask the right questions that lead to the truth, then you know what caused that event or problem. If you know what caused a problem, then all you have to do is ask the right questions to discover how to fix the problem. This is why I say it is simple.

When I was younger, I recall famines in Africa that were broadcast all over the news. They would show images of children starving to death and I thought how terrible that was. I also thought, "Why is this happening, can't you just put seeds in the ground and grow food?" I remember people telling me, "It's not that simple." I would just look at them and say, "Why, food doesn't grow in that part of the world?" I was told the famine was caused by over population, government policies and crop failures. So I asked why would you have children if you cannot feed them, why would the government make bad decisions for its citizens that kill them and why don't leaders have a plan in case there is a crop failure? It just didn't make sense to me. As I got older I realized there was more to that problem then I understood. Yes, there are simple solutions, but I didn't know the whole truth.

Even though there are global problems that appear to have simple solutions, there are usually other reasons why they aren't being solved. One of the reasons is because you cannot get enough people to agree on what the right solution is. Another reason is that certain problems just don't have any solutions right now. Either way, these types of problems cost people money and time and there never seems to be a solution. So the simple person inside of me says, "Why don't we focus on problems that could be solved right now if everyone knew the truth?" I am not talking about daily problems involving neighbors, family or the workplace. I am talking about global issues dealing with energy, finance, health and government where the truth can easily be discovered if someone asked the right questions.

You might think problem solving isn't simple, but what if it is? We use simple rules of problem solving in our own lives every day.

- If there is a solution to a problem – we use it.
- If something is broken – we fix it.
- If something is not known – we find it out.
- If someone is not doing the job – we find someone else who can.

People use these rules for their lives and simultaneously believe they wouldn't work on the world stage. Have you ever had a difficult problem where someone told you the solution and you used it? Did anything ever break and you fixed it? Did you ever figure out something that you didn't know? Did you ever have someone do something for you that wasn't right, so you found someone else to do the job? All of these examples involved two important factors. At some point you needed to ask a question and then you needed to know the truth. Once that was accomplished you were able to fix whatever was wrong.

Are You Willing To Accept The Truth

Think about how you react to new information. Are you willing to accept truths that may not coincide with your current beliefs? Are you willing to be honest with yourself? The truth is that all of the information in this book is public knowledge and record, there is nothing secret here. The problem isn't proving it, the problem is whether or not you can look at the facts and honestly admit that it either makes sense or doesn't make sense. I am not trying to sway the public for my personal benefit. My plan is to assist anyone who wants to change things for the better by supplying the tools they need, in the hopes that some of them succeed. The good news is we don't need to fix every problem; just a few major ones will change the world immensely. I guarantee it.

The first step to fixing world problems is to find out the truth by asking the right questions. This is common sense and people already know this. So why aren't the problems being fixed? The main reason is because people have been led to believe that solving the world's problems is difficult and complicated. What if that wasn't true? This is where I will start to lose some of the readers and it is not based on intelligence, money or political affiliation. The reason is, it is hard to believe something different than your current beliefs. There is nothing wrong with this; we all do it. So I am asking you to read on and not believe me. I want you to prove it to yourself.

Chapter 2: A World Of Problems

I don't want to be the bearer of bad news, but unless you are in total denial, there are plenty of people who continue to point out the ever growing problems in our world today. Not that you need anyone to point them out, you can just look around for yourself. Any time you want to see how bad things are, just Google words and phrases such as: fraud, embezzlement, environment, sex scandal, lawsuit, wrongful death, or just search white collar crime. Add any of those search terms to any of the following industries or institutions and see what comes up. That will get you to the tip of the iceberg.

Health Care	**Lobbyist**	**Politics**	**Construction**
Wall Street	**Military**	**Energy**	**Telecommunications**
Government	**Religion**	**Education**	**Pharmaceutical**

This is just a quick list to prove a point, I am sure you could add more. If you want to find out what professional journalists found, just Google Investigative Journalist and you may find problems you didn't even know existed.

Coincidentally, this list represents multi-billion dollar industries, yes even religion. Religion has created a multitude of millionaires over the last 3 decades. There are religious dating sites, television evangelists who fly around in private jets, and religious lobbyist (go tally their coffers). I even remember being solicited for a Christian mortgage, which returns over 80,000 results if you Google it.

Just for the record, people aren't against religion; they are against the people who ruin religion for everyone else. Need proof? Go ask this question to people from different religions: "If you could practice your faith without anyone telling you how, would you care if someone else practiced a different faith as long as it didn't affect you?" Do you think that is what "religious freedom" is all about? The same reasoning holds true for capitalism. People aren't against capitalism, they are against corrupt capitalism. That's the problem in a nutshell and people are well aware of it.

There are enough books, articles, reports, data, and commentary for you to research on the subject of what is wrong. I don't think I have to convince anyone that the world could be a better place. I just wanted to setup a starting point for the rest of this book, which is there are problems in this world that affect all of us directly or indirectly. Some of these problems will never have a definitive solution that everyone can agree on, but there are issues with common sense solutions that pretty much everyone would agree on. Wouldn't it be better to work on problems that have solutions and affect most of us, instead of using the same time and resources to debate issues that will never be solved?

Go to the political section of any bookstore and you will find plenty of books that detail what is wrong with the world. Many of them are considered propaganda, designed to sway your views via emotion and aren't based on facts, but there are plenty of authors who researched a real problem or event and presented it in a logical, truthful manor. This is one way for you to find the truth about problems in our world. The work has already been done. Oddly, some of these books spell out exactly how the problem could be fixed. Some of them even prove criminal activity that was never punished. The facts and data are so clear that no one could deny the authors research. This is an example of how knowing the truth doesn't always fix the problem.

There are also problems that can be solved, although the solution is not yet available. This happens when a problem arises, but the information cannot be accessed to prove what happened. If you cannot look at the facts then how do you know the truth? Even when there are laws created to expose the truth, someone figures out how to sidestep them. The ultimate tool used by people to hide the truth is claiming they have secret information. Some businesses load up on lawyers who do what they can to keep the truth from being exposed. Why are so many businesses afraid of the truth? I can only think of one reason why people withhold information; they don't want you to know what is really going on.

Chapter 3: Don't Believe Everything You Hear

The main goal of this chapter is to make sure you understand that just because statements are made by people who appear to know what they are talking about, doesn't mean those statements are correct. If you hear something that doesn't sound right, the first question you should think of is, "What if they are wrong?" This doesn't mean you don't respect the person or you are calling them a liar. It means you are not sure and you need more information to make an intelligent decision. If you get more information and you find out they were right, did anyone get hurt? On the other hand, have you ever made a decision that turned out bad because someone gave you information that was incorrect? When making important decisions it is always better to take a second look and get more information if needed. This rule also applies to major decisions that affect the world.

Companies and governments spend millions of dollars getting information out to the public. Sometimes they have something that will benefit people and sometimes it isn't a benefit, but there is no other choice, and sometimes they know it isn't a benefit, but they want to convince you otherwise. It is the last reason you need to be concerned with. You should take notice whenever a company or the government goes out of their way to convince you that what they are doing is right. One of the "red flags" is if you see different news outlets saying exactly the same thing, which usually means that information was fed to them. There are more details about this method of deceiving the public in PART 3 of this book.

People get caught up in trusting others just because they have an official title, important job, or they said something on television. One thing has nothing to do with the other. You might have an expectation or believe that is the way it should be, but there is no guarantee that anyone at anytime will not tell a lie. You have to understand that what is seen in the public eye isn't always reflective of what goes on behind closed doors. Even when terrible decisions are made that adversely affect millions of people, they can usually justify why they did it. There is always a reason for people's actions, it is known as the truth and that's what we are after.

I think I was like most people. I believed that those who make decisions affecting our lives are doing so in our best interest. They attained their position by getting a higher education, working hard and gaining the experience necessary to make the best decisions. At no time did I think they were not qualified to be in whatever position they were in. Making decisions that affect other people's lives is important, so why would anyone hire a person if they couldn't do the job? When I heard these "important" people make statements on television, claiming all the reasons why we had to do something, I just believed them. Until they proved me wrong.

Whenever I would hear something that didn't make sense, I started asking questions in my mind. These are the same questions you can ask yourself:

- Is there any logical reasoning that says I have to believe everything I hear?
- Is it possible that even though someone has good intentions, they can still make the wrong decision?
- Is it possible even good people can have bad information and make the wrong decision?
- Is it possible that bad people want me to believe something that isn't true?

You don't have to stop believing every statement you hear. You don't have to look at every official as if they are lying to you. You have to be smart and think for yourself. If something doesn't make sense to you, there is probably a good reason. There is enough evidence in the world that proves people make bad decisions all the time. Sometimes it is because the person is in a position of authority, but they don't have the credentials required for that job. They try to make the right decisions, but sometimes they don't. This is what happened when Hurricane Katrina hit. Other times people make bad decisions because they were influenced by money or other benefits. The point is you don't always know at first, but you should always be on your guard.

The truth is no one is right 100% of the time. It is easy to research past decisions made by governments, the military, big business, small business, scientists, police officers, school teachers, clergy and the average citizen that were wrong and adversely affected the lives of others. It happens every day of every week. When someone gives you reasons for their decision, is it guaranteed they will tell the truth? So why does it seem so farfetched that an expert or a person with an official title can make the wrong decision?

Thankfully some of these wrong decisions don't affect you or me directly, but some of them deal with global issues that change our lives in a split second. It happens when someone says yes or someone says no: should we drill that well, should we go to war, should we pass this bill, should we tell them the real test results, should I commit insider trading, should I lie about the facts, etc. The number of these decisions is limitless and when they are wrong they have the power to devastate people's lives.

You don't have to be a genius with three PHDs to know when something doesn't sound right. Just because someone graduated from an Ivy League school doesn't mean they are making the right decision. It is a good prerequisite, but it is not a guarantee. If this is true, and I know it is, who says you can't tell when something is wrong? Who says you can't speak up and say, "Enough! Show me why." Then you say, "Look, I am not trying to attack you. This is a major issue and certain elements don't sound right, so all I want to do is find the truth."

One of the major challenges I had early on in my life was that whenever someone spoke to me I believed them. I made life changing decisions based on what others said. Isn't that how it works? When you don't understand something you ask someone else. They give you the answer and then you base your decisions on what they said. It took me a while to realize that not everyone is going to give you the right answer. There are several reasons of why this may be. One is that they just don't know the right answer, but they want to appear to be intelligent. Another reason is that they don't want you to know what the truth is. They could also believe they are telling you the right answer, but the definitions in their head are different then the definitions in your head. So, even though they gave you the sincere truth (according to them), it still wasn't correct for your situation and therefore would affect any decisions you made based on it. Not everyone is trying to lie to you, but you still need to know the truth.

Hopefully you will agree that not everything you read or watch on television is going to be true, even if the person has a big title or is an expert in their field. I am not saying that everyone is liar, but if it doesn't sound right to you, don't you have a right to question it? Thankfully, this is happening everyday by socially conscious people who are saying, "That is wrong and I know it is wrong", and then they take the next step and do something about it. We need more people doing this, because some of the checks and balances we have in place are not doing the job.

Remember, the goal isn't to try and prove everyone wrong all of the time. The goal is to find the truth and fix problems. If all the facts were available all of the time, I believe people are smart enough to make their own decisions.

Chapter 4: The Proof Is Knowing The Truth

This is a very important chapter. If you know something is absolutely true or false, there is nothing anyone can say or do to make you think differently. One of the biggest challenges I see with people today is their willingness to believe almost anything without needing any proof. I can understand how this happens, because I used to be the same way. You grow up and just expect people of authority to tell you the truth. When someone makes a statement, who is supposed to have the right answers, it is natural to assume they are right. Especially if it is a government official with a job description that includes protecting the general public. There should never be a need to have to find out if they are telling the truth.

It is not just governments; it is every industry and every profession. We are constantly bombarded with less than true information, which is designed to hide what is wrong with their message, and we believe it. That unquestioning belief is what they count on. It gives them the ability to make any statement as if it was fact, without being challenged. That is an incredible power and has been used successfully to convince people that something is right when it really is wrong. Look up any scandal and you will find the way it began was by convincing someone that "what was wrong is right" and that person was unable to prove it or didn't even try.

There is a lot of information presented in this book and I am not expecting you to believe any of it. It is important that you learn how to prove things for yourself. No one is going to fool you if you know the truth. How hard is it to prove something is right or wrong? The good news is that 99% of the information you will need is readily available to the public via the Internet. There are other ways to research the facts, but the Internet is the most efficient. It is fast, easily accessible and covers pretty much ever subject and issue known to date. The Internet has become one of the great equalizers, giving anyone the power to research facts and debunk myths.

Looking up facts on the Internet is sometimes like a puzzle. You are given a few clues and now you have to research it and either prove or disprove the argument. There is a good chance that when you research you will find a lot of information on a topic supporting both sides of the argument. That means some of the information you find on the Internet is going to be wrong. This is done on purpose.

It is known that people like you and me will be searching for the truth and a way to combat that is to present the lies as if they were the truth. This can be done through "experts" who tell a different story to discredit the truth and sway the masses to their way of thinking. The term used for this is disinformation, which means intentionally false or inaccurate information that is spread deliberately. Therefore you will have to learn how to decipher what is fact and what has been written to hide the facts.

There are plenty of ways to detect disinformation on the Internet. Below are some of the techniques that I have used. If you want to learn more on this subject just Google: disinformation, how to find the truth or any similar phrase.

1. Find who owns the website:

It is no secret that organizations will put up websites designed to throw researchers off the track. Be diligent. One clue is to see who owns the website. This is fairly simple. Go to Google and search "whois", multiple sites will come up. You may have to try 2 or 3 before you get the result. Once you get on the whois site all you have to do is type in the domain of the website you are researching, i.e. yahoo.com and it will give you the contact information for that website. NOTE: This is sometimes not available if the owner pays more to have their information hidden from the public, but it does work most of the time. Now just do a little research on the owner and see if there is a connection to the content. In other words, are they benefiting from the information they are offering you?

2. Research the author of the article:

Google the author's name, see if they have written similar articles supporting the article you just read. Add the word democrat or republican to their name search and see if this information is politically motivated. Find out if they were compensated to write their article and then find out who paid them.

3. Find collaborating stories:

Check to see if other stories have been written about the same subject. Do they come to the same conclusion? Are the authors credible?

4. Check news sources outside of the United States:

This has become tough over the last decade because even international news sources are being bought up in order to spread a single message globally, but speak to any foreign visitor to the U.S. and ask them a simple question, "Do you get the same news that we get in the US?" You will be surprised by the answer. Just Google "non U.S. news" and you will find other sources that may tell a different story.

So when you look at specific scenarios in this book and go to the Internet to research, just ask yourself, "Does this make sense?" It is that simple; please just use your own brain. Why do you have to be told what is right or wrong? Wouldn't it be better if you could find the truth on your own?

Throughout this book I have noted particular words that you can search on the Internet to find the answers for a particular topic. You might be able to find more than I did. You might even think of better words. That's the point. I am not here to tell you to do this my way. I just want to show you what is possible when it comes to finding the truth.

Know What You Are Talking About

Cliché as it may sound, knowledge is power. You should know something about what you are talking about. In our "digital" era, knowledge is easy to obtain. You don't have to go to college or read every book on a particular subject, although that couldn't hurt. All you need is the ability to ask logical questions, either to the right person or simply on the Internet.

If you go back in history you can find countless wrong decisions that affected millions of people. Some of them happened because one person made a claim and the other person had no way of proving or disproving it, so it was just accepted as fact. Now they make commercials where two people are arguing about whether something is true or not and in a split second one of them has accessed the information on their smart phone. With this type of power and access to information I am still amazed how people don't question other people when they think something is wrong. Just look it up on your smart phone and show them what they are trying to tell you is wrong.

What about when a group of people get so fed up that they decide to take action. One of the forms of action is protesting, it happens all over the world and sometimes it does induce change. If you took part in a protest, wouldn't you want your efforts to amount to something positive instead of being the reason for its failure?

One of the tactics used by someone who feels threatened by a group of protestors is to find one person that doesn't even know why they are protesting. You see this happen on the news. They bring a camera crew to the protestor's rally and interview multiple people until they find the one that has no clue why they are there. Then that is the clip that is shown across the news media to let the world know that this protest is just a bunch of idiots who have nothing better to do than protest, they don't even know why they are there. Don't be that person.

So before you speak up, why not take a few minutes to understand why you are speaking up. Why not write a few notes so you are prepared when someone puts you on the spot. At least answer one question, write it down and keep it in your pocket. That question is, "Why am I doing this?" Even if the news reporter is trying to find a real story, at least you can give them a real answer. If you organized the protest maybe you should print up thousands of notes that state why people are there and pass them out to the protesters. There's a simple solution.

The way nations have controlled their citizens in the past, and still today in some countries, is to limit information and education. Thanks to a little thing called the Internet it is becoming harder and harder for people in power to do this. As of the writing of this book, the Middle East is in turmoil mainly due to the Internet, with Facebook and Twitter leading the way. When people are able to discuss issues, they start realizing they are not the only ones who feel a certain way. Sometimes it is as simple as, "Why are we doing all of the work and they are getting all of the benefits?" So the point is knowledge isn't only facts and data, it is knowing what is really going on in the world and not just believing something because you read it somewhere. In the Middle East, the ruling parties constantly put out news propaganda that stated everything was fine and that uprisings would not last. Thanks to the ability to access information, people were able to find the truth and make their own decisions about the messages they were hearing.

It is a lot easier to prove your point when you know what your point is. The argument becomes more powerful when you actually know the facts behind your cause. All it takes is a few minutes on the Internet and maybe writing some notes down on an index card. Wouldn't it be worth it, if that was the reason for fixing a major problem? The few people who are ruining everything for the rest of us are betting on the fact that you won't be informed. The reason is simple, they know they are outnumbered and there is no way they can control billions of people who know the truth.

Chapter 5: The Power To Fix What Is Wrong

If you live in the United States, you live in a country that was founded on the premise of freedom, which includes the right for you to think the way you want. Just because someone wants you to agree with them, doesn't mean you have to, especially if you know they are wrong. You have basic rights that give you all the power you need.

1. Do you have the right to have your own thoughts?
2. Do you have the right to make your own decisions?
3. Do you have the right to know the truth when making a decision?
4. Do you have the right to act on your own decisions?
5. Do you have the right to question other's decisions that affect you?

I know it's common sense, but sometimes in a fast paced world where we don't have time to think, it is good to be reminded of what we already know. Nobody can tell you what to think or what decisions to make (within the limits of the law). This is important to understand because the quality of your life comes down to the decisions you make or the decisions that are made for you.

People have a right to their own thoughts, which means they have a right to believe whatever they want. They also have a right to change their minds about any of their beliefs at any time. You can try and convince someone that your belief is the right way, but they may or may not agree. When groups have different beliefs for the same issue and there is no way to factually prove who is right, the methods in this book will not work. This book is designed to expose the truth, not to change people's beliefs. If they have a belief and they changed it because someone exposed the truth to them, that is different. Most people only "believed" a certain way because they never knew the truth in the first place.

1. Examples of beliefs (there is no right or wrong):
    a. Teenagers shouldn't date before the age of 16.
    b. We shouldn't put up windmills because they are an eyesore.
2. Examples of truths (they can be proved by fact):
    a. If you fail all of your classes in high school you will not graduate.
    b. Getting better gas mileage will save you money.
3. Examples of beliefs that people can change when they learn the truth:

a. Parents used to give their children over-the-counter cold medicines they believed to be safe. The FDA no longer recommends giving these drugs to children under 6 years old. People believed they were doing the right thing for their children, the truth was exposed and they changed their beliefs.

b. In the United States, men used to believe that women could not do the same jobs as them. It was frowned upon if a woman tried to have a "professional" career. Women proved men wrong, the truth was exposed and men now believe differently.

The world can be fixed by exposing the truth in Examples #2 and #3 above. What slows progress down is when people try to fix Example #1. They want to convince people to believe what they think is right and since it is just a belief there is no right or wrong. That is why you see these types of issues debated for months, years and decades without ever coming to a solution the major majority can agree on. Do not get caught in this trap. Solve the problems that can be fixed now.

I don't think anyone can argue that when you need to make a decision it is better to know the truth before you act. Has there ever been a time when someone convinced you into making a decision, but later on you found out they didn't give you all the facts and you ended up on the short end of the stick? Did you want to make that decision blindly, without all of the information necessary? If you had a choice to make decisions based on facts or to blindly accept the decisions from others, which would you choose? These are common sense questions that have definitive answers everyone can agree on. So why are so many important decisions made without knowing all of the facts or consequences?

People in the United States have the right to have their own thoughts and to make their own decisions. Through the perversion of politics, these basic rights have become clouded in a way that appears we are making our own decisions, when in fact the major ones are being made for us. I just read that the United States pledged support to Afghanistan until the year 2024. I wonder if that was a decision a majority of Americans would agree with. Did anyone even get the option to ask, "By the way, who is paying for this and can I ask a few questions before you make that commitment?" This is an accepted practice, because our system is setup in way where we entrust others to make those important decisions on our behalf. Their job is to make decisions based on our best interests. They include decisions affecting energy, health care, foreign policy, financial policy and how our tax dollars are spent. This system would work fine if the influences of power and money were not involved.

In some countries, one of the decisions made by its citizens is to elect people who make decisions for them. Sometimes this works and sometimes it doesn't. Based on public polls of the American people, you can argue that it hasn't worked for a long time, but we still have a right to make our own decisions and act on those decisions. So that means you have the right to change decisions that others made for you. It is just a decision. As much as you may be told something is set in stone, it really isn't. If enough people demand that something must change, it will.

So if people have the right to change decisions that are wrong, what is stopping them? I can think of three reasons:

1. They forgot they had the power to question and act on their own decisions.
2. They were never told the truth in the first place, so they accepted the circumstances.
3. They knew there was something wrong, but didn't know what to do.

These are three problems you will no longer have after reading this book. Sometimes the decisions that are made for you are wrong. Do you just have to accept the consequences of someone else's poor judgment?

I am totally convinced that people are fed up and are searching for the formula that will fix what is wrong with our world. I believe with the right tools they will be successful because of the following:

1. There are more good people in the world than bad.
2. Right is always better than wrong.
3. People want to know the truth.
4. Good people will act against what's wrong when they know the truth.

So that's it, all we need is the truth. What if there was a way to get to the truth on just about every issue out there? What if it could be done so simply and effectively that no one would be immune? What if you could learn how to accomplish that? It's difficult when only one person knows the truth, because they can be discredited with a few false news stories about them or their "theories". Try to convince the world that 5 million people don't know what they are talking about, that is a little tougher.

Knowing the truth can increase the pressure that eventually results in fixing the problem. It is based on a simple theory, which is when everyone knows the truth you can no longer convince them otherwise. When that happens something has to change. There are more and more examples where the truth is being pushed into the spotlight, even against the status quo. This happened with the delay of the vote on the SOPA and PIPA bills. You can Google it to find out the details, but the story is that public outrage formed because the truth came out and millions of people wanted it fixed. Guess what, politicians backed away. There was also a backlash fueled by the Internet against Susan G. Komen for the Cure, which resulted in a resignation. So don't tell me it isn't possible. When the masses know the truth, they will take action.

Beware. Once you start questioning the status quo you will definitely hit resistance. They might even say you hate America…you are not a patriot… just pay your increased taxes, gas prices and food bills, and don't rock the boat. When that happens remember, people don't hate America, they hate the people who ruin America for the rest of us.

Americans aren't upset when a company sells a good product for a fair price and makes a profit. Americans don't mind working hard and they appreciate the fact that they have the opportunity to do what they want. What they don't understand is that in the land of plenty, there seems to be so little left over for them. When they look at some of the people that have the most, it appears they didn't earn what they have. There is even proof that some of them just took it, they didn't deserve it. That's what Americans are upset about.

PART 2:

AT THE ROOT
OF PROBLEMS

What You Will Learn

In PART 1 you gained a basic understanding of how you should think when approaching problem solving. This section details how a relatively few people are able to convince millions that what they are doing is right, even though it is wrong.

The problem with our world today is that people have found ways to get things they didn't earn or deserve and are adversely affecting others in the process. This undeserved success is achieved and sustained through: Lies, Misleading Messages, Limited Consequences, Inadequate Oversight and the Suppression of Real Solutions. You need to understand how these 5 elements support "undeserved success", because they are exactly what need to be fixed and that is what the Problem Solving Process will do. They are the root of the problem. There are other factors, but these are the ones that can be fixed. Knock these legs out and there will be nothing left to stand on.

Chapter 6: Undeserved Success
- In order to fix any problem you have to find what the initial cause was and eliminate it.
- The problem with our world today is that people have found ways to get things they didn't earn or deserve and are adversely affecting others in the process.
- The first step to obtaining undeserved success is to suppress the truth and the only way to accomplish that is to lie.

Chapter 7: Lies - Call Them What They Are
- You need to learn how to filter the lies that affect you and not focus on the ones that don't.
- One of the main attributes necessary to get things you don't deserve is the ability to make a lie appear to be the truth.
- People have lied in every profession, what stops any of them from telling a lie now or in the future?

Chapter 8: Messages – A Lie Appearing True
- The use of misleading messages is the legal way of not telling the truth.
- It is known that people will believe a message if it is presented to them in an authoritative manor.

- Misleading phrases are added to messages to make people believe that everyone is onboard and it is based on fact. The phrases include: "A study was done", "In a poll taken", "An anonymous source" and "Americans say".
- People are paid big money just to create messages that are designed to manipulate the public.
- Anyone can call themselves an expert, that doesn't mean they are.

Chapter 9: Limited Consequences For Bad Behavior
- As long as people believe they are immune to criminal prosecution the deterrent of committing a crime has diminished.
- When someone breaks the law they have to pay the consequences. There is no special treatment for social status and wealth when it comes to crime.
- Limited consequences for bad behavior reinforce people's ability to attain and sustain undeserved success

Chapter 10: Protection Agencies Not Protecting
- The U.S. has a history of companies committing offenses against the general public.
- There are literally thousands of government agency employees with the sole purpose of protecting the best interest of the American public. These agencies include: SEC, FDA, CDC, EPA and OSHA.
- Protection Agency employees need to be held accountable for their role in any decisions that purposely and adversely affected others.

Chapter 11: Real Solutions Being Suppressed
- There are a number of solutions to some of the world's greatest challenges and for some reason the majority of the world doesn't even know they exist.
- Companies do not want to lose their market share and they are willing to suppress solutions to accomplish that. The public will always choose the better option if they know it exists.
- Companies spend billions of dollars a year creating messages that assure you there are no better options, even when there are.

Problem Solving Process - PART: 2

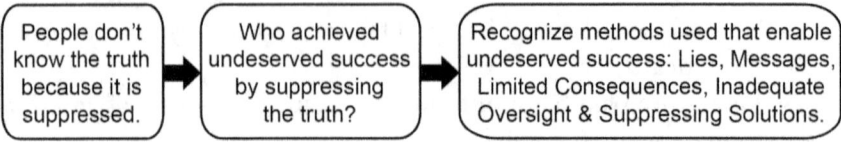

| People don't know the truth because it is suppressed. | → | Who achieved undeserved success by suppressing the truth? | → | Recognize methods used that enable undeserved success: Lies, Messages, Limited Consequences, Inadequate Oversight & Suppressing Solutions. |

Every day you are bombarded with messages that are designed to get you to believe something without knowing the entire truth. The main reason is that if you knew the truth, you may not agree with what they are selling you. If you do not agree with what they are selling you, then you might not buy their product (message). If you don't buy their message, then they don't have control over you and if they don't have control over you, then they don't have control over your money.

If you want to fix the world, then start speaking the truth and force people who make decisions affecting your life to do the same. When everyone knows the truth, no one can hide or profit from the lies. You are always going to have people who try to get things they don't deserve; you just have to make it difficult for them by eliminating their support system.

Chapter 6: Undeserved Success

So what is it? How can a few people convince billions of people that they should live a sub-standard life when a better life is available for everyone? You have to hand it to them; it is quite a feat when you think about it. What kind of network do you have to put together that will suppress the truth, proliferate the lies and have most of the world accept it? Then they add the icing on the cake, this network is setup to protect its own. When one of them gets caught, the punishment rarely matches the crime.

What is it that makes a person want to oppress other people anyway? Do you think they wake up each day and say, "How can I ruin their life today?" I don't think that is the case. It is probably the opposite, "How can I make my life better today?" That goal is okay. The problem arises when the person who says that realizes they don't possess the skills, experience, education, talent or whatever else they might need to become successful. It might even be that the time is not right or the world doesn't want what they consider success.

Now they have a dilemma. They want a better life, but they don't currently have what it takes to get it. They are at a crossroad. They can choose to learn new skills, they can get an education, or they can figure out how to get it another way. Unfortunately, "the other way" has become very enticing. The rewards are pretty good and the consequences can be limited if you spend your rewards in the right places. There is one more factor involved with this equation and it is probably the reason why the whole world doesn't take this route. In order for someone to be successful by bypassing the work, it usually means that someone else is going to have to pay for that person's success. Sometimes it in monetarily and sometimes it is not.

Ask a hundred people what causes the problems in the world and you might get a hundred different answers. The reason is because most of the answers are actually the result of the underlying cause. In order to fix any problem you have to find what the initial cause was and eliminate it. You can narrow down most of the world's problems to one basic cause. It is at the root of the problem when a decision maker has a choice. They say yes or no, left or right, good or bad and in the split second it takes to decide, millions of lives become affected.

Sometimes those decisions are right, but when they are purposely wrong it is because:

The problem with our world today is that people have found ways to get things they didn't earn or deserve and are adversely affecting others in the process.

That's it. I know it sounds too simple, but think about it. Think of all the corruption and scandals of the last decade and then think what would have happened if the above sentence did not play a part. It is true in politics, business, war, and is the basis of nearly all crime. If people never found a way to "beat the system", would you ever be taken advantage of? Examples include: CEOs taking millions in stock options as they run their company into the ground, brokerage houses selling packaged securities and then betting against them, countries draining resources from other countries, leaders brutally suppressing their people because they know they could never win a fair election, corporations taking shortcuts to boost profits even though it destroys the environment or causes irreversible health damage and the list can go on and on. It is because they found ways to get things they did not deserve – they took the route of least integrity.

There are many examples of "people finding ways to get things they do not deserve" throughout history, but unfortunately it has grown exponential in the last decade. There are times when people get caught, but rarely go to jail for the criminal offense. They pay a big fine to the government (do you ever wonder where all that fine money goes) and they let out a statement of "Oh, I didn't know." It is swept under the carpet and they go on with business as usual.

I am not saying that people don't make honest mistakes, they do. When that is found out to be the truth, don't most people understand? If you eliminated the dishonest mistakes the world would be a much better place. If you were able to fix the mistakes, you can fix the world.

Think about the following questions:

- Do people sometimes make mistakes? YES
- If a mistake was already made, does it mean there are no other options? NO
- If it is possible, shouldn't we fix those mistakes? YES

Just to make one point clear, there is nothing wrong with someone having an idea, creating a product or service and selling it for a profit. That is what makes the United States great, it is the essence of capitalism, as long as people know the truth and have a choice of whether or not to spend their money buying that product. The choice is the difference. Even in a volatile economic environment anyone can still create their own "rags to riches" story. They just don't want their money taken by people who don't deserve it.

Of course there will be people who say what about lottery winners or people who inherit wealth, they didn't deserve that. If I was in front of them I would probably just role my eyes, but since I am not, here is the answer: those people did not find a way to get something they didn't deserve. If someone inherits money or wins a lottery it did not affect me. Even if I bought a lottery ticket, I had a choice.

So how does one achieve undeserved success and more importantly how does one sustain it? In the same way that the cause of the problems is a simple concept, the way undeserved success is obtained is just as easy to understand. The first step is to suppress the truth and the only way to accomplish that is to lie.

Chapter 7: Lies - Call Them What They Are

For the purposes of this book, which is to expose the truth and fix problems, there are lies that just don't concern me and for the most part do not concern you. There is a difference in lies and here is a simple explanation.

1. You hit a ball, break a window and claim it was someone else. You said you didn't take the car across town and you did. You claimed you were the faster skier that day and you weren't. Honestly, I really don't care. Know why? Because none of these lies affect me or my family directly or indirectly, either now or in the future.

2. On the other hand, you cheat on your exam and now have an important government job that you cannot handle. You skim money off the top of an investment fund and falsify the data to hide it. You write false articles about foreign policy that later leads to war. These lies lead to decisions that I have no say in, but affect me and my family. These are the lies that need to be found out and the people who create them need to pay the consequences.

There is a lot going on in the world and probably in your life. You need to learn how to filter out what doesn't affect you. If someone lies about something that has nothing to do with you, why would you care? Better yet, why would you waste valuable time and resources when there are other critical issues? The point is, when it comes to someone lying, you have to decide whether or not it adversely affects you or does it just not matter. Before you speak up, ask yourself, "How does this affect me?" If it does, then by all means, make a stand and be heard.

So why do people lie in the first place, knowing it will adversely affect others? Think about it, if you could have everything you ever wanted, would you lie for it, even if people died, became ill or lost their family fortunes? Let's make it less dramatic. If you could get something that you wanted, but didn't deserve it, would you lie for it? Maybe you would, maybe you wouldn't.

Do you ever get tired of hearing about good people who worked hard most of their lives, followed all the rules and then were cheated out of their American dream? Not because they went out and gambled it away, became an alcoholic or committed a crime and spent it all on lawyers. No, it's worse. One morning they woke up and found out the retirement fund they had been investing in for 20-30 years just lost 70% of its value and they owe more on their home than it is worth. Some people even awoke to find their retirement fund was part of a scandal, where one person decided to take everyone's money. To make matters worse, the world is becoming more expensive to live in. The price of oil has shot up and now energy has become a major part of their decreasing budget. Their health insurance premiums are exploding, food costs are rising, property taxes keep going up and the only thing that isn't growing is their income. Does this sound familiar, maybe a situation you are caught up in? I know these issues are not front page news, but there are millions of Americans hanging on a thread financially and some people still want you to believe that nobody saw it coming and it couldn't be avoided. Is it possible someone is lying?

One of the main attributes necessary to get things you don't deserve is the ability to make a lie appear to be the truth. Whether it is a misleading statement, omitting important facts or producing bias research; to a lot of people that is called lying. Here is the definition for lying: the telling of lies, or false statements; untruthfulness.

What is wrong with the truth? Do you feel good when you find out someone has lied to you? What if they lied to you and that lie affected your way of life immensely; you lost your home, your health deteriorated or a loved one even died. Now how do you feel about that lie? If you don't like it, what makes you think anyone else would like it, in this or any other country?

I am pretty sure most people do not want to be lied to. So why is it done so much in our society today and why is it so rarely punished when it comes to issues that affect millions of people? It is almost as if the "lying" flood gates have opened. It has been done in every profession of every industry at every level, right up to the President of the United States. Go through the following "short" list and mark all of the professionals where you can guarantee not one of them ever lied: Doctor, Lawyer, Clergy, Fireman, Policeman, Teacher, CEO, Colonel, General, Board Member, Dentist, Accountant, Investment Banker, President of the United States, Congressmen, Judge, Thief, Rapist, Murderer, Arsonist, Bank Robber, Pimp, Prostitute, Drug Dealer, Drug User, etc. When it comes to lying, they all belong in the same category. If someone's lie affects another person adversely, I am sure that person would have preferred the truth.

If there are people in every profession that have lied in the past, what stops any of them from telling a lie now or in the future? Nothing! On the day that you are reading this section, yes right now, someone in one of those professions is knowingly telling a lie that will affect more than one person adversely. They are telling this lie because they are unable to get what they want without deception.

Once the lie is started, the next step is to convince the world that it is the truth. The goal is to make people believe it is the best or only choice available and everyone is in the same boat. They need you to believe it is a shared sacrifice and messages are created to validate that.

Chapter 8: Messages – A Lie Appearing True

Have you ever watched the news and sit back in disbelief of the actions of people in this and other countries. You hear so-called experts explain why things are the way they are and cringe at their reasoning. A lot of times what they say doesn't even make sense. Sometimes you wonder if they even believe it themselves; it is totally illogical and the worst part is no one questions them. Why is it, when there is a major decision that will affect millions of people, you rarely see either side of the issue definitively prove their point. They will quote some study or expert and cherry pick the data, but you rarely get all the facts. Why don't they show us the facts and data in their entirety? What if the message is misleading or completely false, wouldn't the facts help to prove that?

As for misleading messages, you need to be afraid when you hear the same exact words over and over again from different media outlets. This is directly from every political and PR game book. They create one message and send it out around the country so everyone is saying exactly the same thing. After a month of being inundated with the same message, people believe it to be true; even if it makes no sense. If they have to repeat the same message thousands of times, that probably means there is something wrong with the logic and if you had time to think about it, you might just figure it out. The truth is they don't even care if you believe it or not, all they need is a small majority and that validates the message in a democratic society.

Instead of directly lying they create misleading messages, which is the legal way of not telling the truth. An example of this is something you can see on the news. News agencies show a video clip and have a voice-over of what is happening in our current world. When you watch and hear this, do you expect the video clip to match what is being said? When watching this news clip, would you think the video clip is weeks, months or even years old, even if they were talking about a current crisis that may affect you?

This is done when they report on storms (the weather) and foreign news, especially war related. They replay the same violent clips over and over making different statements about the violence on different days. Someone should go to the news agencies and ask them why they want to mislead us. Why do they show images that aren't for the story they are telling us? Is that news? In advertising, would that be similar to "bait and switch", showing one thing, but actually giving you something else. Why do news agencies care about swaying our thoughts on important world issues, why don't they just tell the truth? I know, hard for you to swallow. Again, don't believe me. Just Google: press lies, media lies, fact checkers, spin and propaganda. There should be a website that constantly scores news channels for truthfulness. Then the public can decide if they want news or lies.

Unfortunately, most of the people do believe the messages. Here's irony: your friends will question every little thing you do and you have to spend time proving you are right, but when it comes to misleading news messages that even sound ludicrous, they just accept them as truth and move on. Maybe it goes back to some of their core beliefs. Maybe it has something to do with trusting authority, their job is to protect us and who would hire someone that would take advantage of us. That is exactly what the perpetrators are banking on. They know this truth about human nature and continuously exploit it. They know that most people will believe a message if it is presented to them in an authoritative way.

So people go on with their lives with the belief that, when messages appear official then they are obviously true. People just trust, sit back and believe that the current status quo has specific logical reasons that could not be avoided. What do you think? Is it possible we would be better off if it wasn't for the bad decisions that leaders and experts have made in the past? Can you think of any "Official" decisions that, if were made differently, would have changed our world immensely? Why don't they inundate us with that message?

There is an industry that earns billions of dollars a year creating messages. They know if something is said long enough, in an associative way, the human brain will learn to believe it as fact, this is Advertising 101. So whenever they need to sway your thinking from logical to illogical they will construct a message using specific words and may even associate it with something emotional (your life, terrorism, your kids and religion are some of the favorites). This message gets pushed through media outlets, which repeat them over and over. If it didn't make sense the first time, how does it make sense the 100th time? As stupid as it sounds (because we can't be fooled... right) it works. It works every single day. Not because they created something great, just because they convinced you that their lies are the truth.

38

Messages are crafted in a way to sound true, but are really stretching the truth. So you have to listen to the words that are being used. One of the techniques is using words such as, "Up to..." or "As much as..." and putting them in front of whatever they want to claim as being a fact. It looks like this, "Up to 40 Percent of Americans May Get Swine Flu Over Next 2 Years." That is an actual statement, Google it. This is ludicrous, so I am going to use it. Did you know that up to 3 billion people have read this book? Did I lie? No, you're reading this book, so that is at least 1 person and 1 is up to 3 billion. Did I scare you with my facts?

Start listening to the news and you will hear these phrases crafted into messages. What could be the reason for telling people that 40% of Americans may get Swine Flu? Some people believe it is a scare tactic that is designed to make the public get vaccinated. Do you remember SARS? The problem is that the media is used as a tool to allow disinformation that is cleverly disguised as the truth.

A way to enhance the message is to make it seem like everyone is onboard. They use phrases like: "Americans say", "There are a group of people", "An anonymous source", "It is common belief" and my all time favorites: "A study was done", "In a poll taken", and "A member of (university, council, organization, etc.). All that needs to be done is to add these words to any statement you want the public to accept as truth, whether it is or not. These few words are cleverly designed so that they technically aren't lies. Other ones include: "It's been said" (by who), "I believe" (who cares, stick with the facts), "Possibly" (really, I am possibly a genius), and "Countless" (countless what).

For example let's use "Americans say". The reality is all you need is two Americans to validate whatever it is you are stating and now your statement is the truth. How about this, "Americans say that aliens live at the North Pole." This is a true statement; the only problem is it sounds like it means the entire American population believes aliens live at the North Pole, which we know every American does not believe that. Watch the news and you will see these tactics used in business, politics, war mongering and world affairs, just to name a few.

I have another one for you, "An anonymous source has stated that Americans are about to embark on a campaign to force public officials to do what is right for the people or they will vote them out of office. Experts explain that the plan doesn't just involve elected officials." This is a true statement and I hope this book is one of the reasons why.

I am not saying that every message that is sent out through the media is incorrect, but I am saying a lot of them are misleading and are designed to sway your thoughts to benefit someone else.

People are paid big money just to create messages that are designed to manipulate the public. This is how it works:

1. **ISSUE:** Pick an issue that has common sense solutions that you don't want to offer to the public, because it would reduce the profits for that sector: Energy, Health Care, Financial, etc.
2. **MESSAGE:** Put together a PR plan to sway the masses into believing there are no other solutions than the ones you have or at least show how your solution is the best.
3. **DEPLOYMENT:** Spread the message through the news media using spokespeople, studies, research and then lobby to enact laws that protect the message.
4. **RESULT:** The general public now believes they have been given the best option and adjust their lives to that outcome. Whether it is paying more for food or gas, going to war, the proliferation of pharmaceuticals or the negative campaigns that scare you in to not using something that is actually good for you. The facts are still out there and anyone could look them up, but the message is so strong that most people just accept it as truth and do not feel the need to prove or disprove it.

This method has worked so well that, in some cases, there are no longer better options. Some of the messages have been repeated so many times that even the perpetrators now believe them to be true. Our country is totally convinced there are logical reasons beyond our control as to why gas prices are so high. That's what happens when you have enough money to create a huge message campaign and then validate it with so-called expert testimony.

REMEMBER: Sometimes governments, organizations, companies or entire industries create false or misleading messages to sway the masses away from the truth. I challenge anyone to prove that this statement is false.

Beware Of The Expert

Do you think all the data that is reported everyday is correct? If it was, then there would be no need for the corrections that are made weeks, months or even years later stating they made a mistake. How do you make a mistake on collecting data? It either is or it isn't. Most of the time it is just about tallying numbers: home sales, inflation, GDP, durable goods, etc. You just get the data and compare it to previous data; I would imagine that high school students could do that. Nevertheless, they come out the following month and adjust last month's data downwards, thus making this month's (weak) data look better than it really is. I know I am not the only one who sees this happening. I could understand if they didn't have all of the data, but then again how hard is it to get it and why don't they just hold the report back or say it is flawed?

Aren't these supposedly well educated experts who have experience in their fields? If not, why are they creating reports and sometimes recommendations that affect the rest of the world? So if these experts are constantly correcting their data then there are only two conclusions to make: 1. They are not experts and 2. Someone isn't telling the truth.

In either case, why should they be believed now or any time in the future? Don't just tell me some statistic or data about my health, the environment, war, politics, education, immigration, etc...show me. And if I don't believe it, do I have the right as an American citizen to challenge and question it? All people want is the truth. If your conclusions sound faulty there is probably an easy fix. Re-tally the data and stream the entire process over the internet so ANYONE can watch and verify. That should be no problem, unless there is something to hide.

What about experts who report on research conducted in their field? I would have to believe that these experts went to college and maybe even have a post graduate degree, which seems like a fair assumption for an expert. So how do these intelligent people get something wrong even after they had access to review the data?

You probably know the answers, but here are a few from me:

- They just aren't that smart.
- They were given the information by someone else, and even though it didn't make sense, they didn't verify it before delivering it to the public as truth.

41

- They received an incentive to deliver the information, even though they knew the data was falsified.
- They didn't realize the impact of their harmful actions on the rest of the world and they rationalized by convincing themselves that they aren't the problem.

The point is simple, not every expert is a liar, but some are. The ones who lie are doing so because they are benefitting from validating someone else's lie. I don't know who is worse, the lying expert or the TV reporter who doesn't question their lies.

Chapter 9: Limited Consequences For Bad Behavior

As long as people believe they are immune to criminal prosecution the deterrent of committing a crime has diminished. What gives people immunity in a society that functions on laws and consequences? There are several factors involved and most of them deal with money and who you know.

- Family Connections
- Political Connections
- Law Enforcement Connections
- Government Agency Connections
- Fraternal Connections

There is also the person who may not have any connections or money at first, but they still find a way to achieve undeserved success by employing the belief of limited consequences. They think they are smarter than everyone else, or at least the people who are policing them. Therefore they believe they will not get caught and will not have to pay the consequences. Ironically, this is the same belief that even the most dangerous criminals have.

By having "immunity" some people feel invincible and that is amplified through a cycle of undeserved success. They get away with a small crime and that builds their confidence to do more. The payoff is tremendous and the possible consequences appear to be negligible, even though there are agencies to stop it.

In the United States there is an epidemic of people who think they can cheat their way to the top because they believe the consequences are limited. There is proof that this starts at a young age, usually the mid-teens. High school students have been caught paying other students to take the SAT for them. These payments have gone as high as $3000 per test. I think they should question the person who gave the student the $3000 needed to pay off the test taking imposter. A spokesperson of one cheater stated the reason this happens is because kids see corporate executives cheating their way to success, why can't anyone else? That's a bad sign of the times.

What happens to the students that don't get caught? They get accepted to a top-rated college where they don't have the educational background to succeed. How are they going to pass their tests and get a degree? The same way they got there, they already have a successful model of how to achieve undeserved success. There is also a good chance they become friends with other people who have used the same model. They cheat their way through college and get a business degree with a good GPA. Some of them didn't even need it, because the connections they have would have gotten them the job they were looking for anyway.

When this happens, what are the consequences for everyone else?

- This person may not know what to do in a crisis that affects you and your family.
- They may take shortcuts since that is how they learned to succeed.
- Someone with the education and skills did not get the job they worked hard for and didn't take any shortcuts.

Now this person is in a position of authority, with the ability to make decisions that affect your life and they do not have the necessary education or background. If you have ever seen a top official or executive speak and make statements that appear ludicrous and unintelligent, they probably are. The reason is because that person does not know what they are talking about.

Another case of mid-teen limited consequences is when they commit a criminal offense and nothing happens. This includes theft, drug possession, drug trafficking, driving under the influence and even vehicular homicide. The teen commits the crime and because their family is wealthy and has the right connections, they get off completely or maybe serve community service. Is there any reason why the consequences for breaking the law should be based on how much money you have or who you know?

Now the teen has been taught an important lesson. Even if you commit a crime there is a good chance you will get away with it. It tells them they are immune to even criminal prosecution from law enforcement agencies. Sometimes the person believes they are invincible, nobody can touch them. As they go through their career they befriend like-minded people. Is it possible these are the people who were in charge when the stock market melted down in 2007-2008?

44

There were so many white collar crimes during the 1st decade of this century, it made you wonder what happened to the checks and balances. What happened to all of the criminals? Some got caught, very few got punished, and most of them got away with it. There were times when the punishment was equal to a slap on the wrist and included a fine 1/10 of the money they profited from the crime.

When someone breaks the law they have to pay the consequences. Isn't that one of the basic beliefs of a civil society? There is no special treatment for social status and wealth when it comes to crime. Not just some of the time, all of the time. Not just the person who isn't on the "inside", everyone. The current climate of stealing money and using it to buy your freedom has got to end and the people accepting those payoffs need to be subjected to the consequences also. When it comes to people who were defrauded of their money, the person who did it should pay every dime back, I don't care if it takes the rest of their lives. How does paying a small fine and going to jail help the person that lost their retirement fund? Here's the answer, it doesn't it.

Here's a scary reality. What do you do about crimes committed by the enforcement agency in charge of watching over our best interests? Who is watching them? Are these the same people who cheated on their SAT, cheated their way through college and then were given this position of authority?

This is the result of limited consequences for bad behavior, which reinforce people's ability to attain and sustain undeserved success. The deterrents are in place. The problem is they are not doing the job they were originally created to do, which is protect the best interests of American citizens.

Chapter 10: Protection Agencies
Not Protecting

The U.S. has a history of companies committing offenses against the general public. These are crimes that affect people's lives dramatically and we know it.

- Did companies ever dump toxic waste into the environment that adversely affected people?
- Did anyone on Wall Street ever commit insider trading that adversely affected people?
- Did anyone in Government ever commit a felony while in office?
- Did any company ever try to sell food to the public that was unsafe for human consumption?

These are some of the reasons why people said there needs to be a way to check up on the offenses of others. The government responded by establishing agencies designed to protect the people. These agencies created rules and hired people to make sure the rules were upheld. There are literally thousands of government employees with the sole purpose of protecting the best interest of the American public. Sometimes it works and sometimes it doesn't. You can research examples on the Internet of when these agencies have failed the public and unfortunately some of the reasons came down to money.

United States protection agencies include: SEC (Securities and Exchange Commission), FDA (Food and Drug Administration), CDC (Centers for Disease Control and Prevention), EPA (Environmental Protection Agency), and OSHA (Occupational Safety and Health Administration). The FDA is funded by the firms it is authorized to watch over (a little conflict of interest). For the most part, these agencies were originally created to protect us against ourselves, not from foreign threats.

Here are a few agency mission statements that can be found on each official website:

- SEC: The mission of the U.S. Securities and Exchange Commission is to protect investors, maintain fair, orderly, and efficient markets, and facilitate capital formation.
- EPA: The mission of EPA is to protect human health and the environment.

- FDA: The FDA is responsible for protecting the public health by assuring the safety, efficacy, and security of human and veterinary drugs, biological products, medical devices, our nation's food supply, cosmetics, and products that emit radiation.

If those three agencies alone did exactly what their mission statement claims, the economic landscape of the United Sates would look completely different then it does now. Sometimes these agencies are called upon when there is crisis and the government puts a commission together to find out the truth. Agency employees testify to prove or disprove allegations. The questions they are asked should be designed to expose the truth. Even if they are not asked the right questions at a hearing, someone should track them down and ask them at their office. We deserve to know the truth. If they aren't telling the truth, being fair, or doing their job then they shouldn't have that job.

This same conclusion should hold true when an agency official tries to pass the buck by stating it was "someone" else. Find out who that someone else is and bring them in to testify. If this happened all the time you would see less people using this "crutch" to achieve their undeserved success. Another group that should be questioned are the "shadow" messengers, people in government agencies that are told what statements to make to the public. They may know they are wrong or they may not know, but ignorance is not a defense. Isn't that what we've been told?

Chapter 11: Real Solutions Being Suppressed

Did you ever watch a show or read an article about someone who discovered a solution to a universal problem and you thought wow, now we don't have to worry about that any more. Then a couple of years later you notice that it was never talked about again or you find out that just a few people are actually using the solution. It works and does what it claims, so why isn't the whole world benefitting from it?

There are a number of solutions to some of the world's greatest challenges and for some reason the majority of people don't even know they exist. Sometimes the solution gets in to the main stream 5, 10 or even 20 years later. Why is that? Is it because when someone solves a problem there is no need for more research and development, the problem was fixed, so they moved on and forgot to tell everyone else? What about advancements in technologies that make the original solution outdated and more costly? If this is the case, then you can understand why some corporations don't want advancements in their industry, because that could decrease their customer base.

I have a personal example for a major problem that affects millions of people and it has a simple solution. I had an ulcer and before I went to my doctor I did a little research to try and figure it out on my own. I bought an over the counter ulcer medicine and it worked. So I went to the doctor looking for a cure, why would I want to take medicine every day for the rest of my life? Aren't there any solutions? I was told to take a certain drug and change my diet. The claim was that the drug would last longer than the over the counter medication. It didn't last the 24 hours I was told and I woke up in the middle of the night with the original pain. I told a friend the next day what happened and he said, all you have to do is buy a bottle of aloe vera juice and drink it, it will cure your ulcer and is actually good for your entire digestive system. I thought he had to be kidding. You are telling me there is a simple solution to a huge medical problem and doctors don't even tell you. That can't be true. This must be something new that the doctors don't know about yet.

So I went out to the grocery store and sure enough I found it in the produce section, it was a whopping $8. I took it as soon as I got home and noticed it working almost immediately. I finished the bottle over the next 4 days and all of my symptoms were gone. The following week I went back to my doctor for a follow up. She asked how the new medicine was working for me. I said I only took it once because it didn't last 24 hours. She said it takes time to build up. Then I told her about the aloe vera juice. I asked if she knew about it. She didn't answer. I asked why don't people know about this, why aren't doctors giving this option to their patients? She said, "People would not take the aloe vera juice, they would rather just take the medicine." I didn't reply, but I thought, "How does she know that and who gave her the right to decide what is best for everyone else?" I wonder if people had the choice to take drugs for the rest of their life or fix the problem for $8 in just one week, which one would they choose. I am not sure if it works for everyone, but for $8 it was worth a try for me.

Why doesn't everyone with an ulcer know about this? The reason is because the messaging is so strong that people just accept it as truth and don't feel the need to prove or disprove it. Some of this messaging is actually against "so-called" alternative medicines. The claims include it doesn't work and it is not regulated by the FDA. Doesn't the FDA do studies on medicines all the time? I read about medicines created by traditional pharmaceutical companies that made specific claims and a few years later those claims were proved wrong and the drug was taken off the market. I guess that drug didn't work. Why doesn't the FDA get more involved with alternative medicines or even vitamins, is it because the drug companies don't want people to find out what other options they might have? Remember, the FDA gets their funding from their clients.

In the last ten years the truth about alternative medicine has been exposed more and more. Nowadays you can find a multitude of doctors and hospitals that use traditional and alternative methods to treat patients. Do you understand that some of these alternative methods have been around for hundreds of years, what took so long for the experts to validate them?

How hard is it to find out if something works or doesn't work? I have a simple solution. There are examples of alternative treatments that work. Find out what the claim is and test it in a way that anyone can verify the results. This truth exposing method is discussed more in Chapter 26: Transparent Studies, Inquiries and Research. Prove the claims right or wrong and let's move on.

You may be aware of innovations that are available right now that would make the world a better place, but the information is suppressed by lies, misleading messages, and sometimes government regulations. One of the reasons this happens is because companies do not want to lose their market share and they are willing to suppress solutions to accomplish that. Their main goal is making sure the public doesn't find out there is a better or less expensive way of solving their problems. If they do, then the company will have to adjust to the market or it will no longer exist. This happened throughout history as technology has advanced and most recently claimed Kodak as a victim. Very few people use film anymore, they chose to go digital. Other companies captured that market and Kodak fell behind. There are so many examples of this: iceboxes, typewriters, 8-track tapes, printing, appliances and it will continue to happen as discoveries are made. The public will always choose the better option if they know it exists.

I don't want to waste time or space creating a list to prove my point. Companies spend billions of dollars a year creating messages that assure you there are no better options out there when there are. I need you to understand this happens. So if you need more information, Google suppressed inventions and you find all that you are looking for. Beware of any conspiracy theories, if it can't be proven maybe you shouldn't believe it.

PART 3:

THE SKILLS
YOU WILL NEED

What You Will Learn

In this section you will learn the basics of crafting questions that will expose the truth.

Chapter 12: The Great Equalizer
- Questions are the way we get to the truth and the way we learn.
- Probing questions will get you the information you need to determine if something is true or not, good or bad, right or wrong.
- Ask questions that require short answers, are to the point, and the answer is known by the person you are asking.
- Whether questions are answered or not, you still get information that can be used to expose the truth.

Chapter 13: No Discrimination With This Tool
- You don't have to be part of an organization, have wealth, or be connected to powerful people in order to ask questions when you think something is wrong or you don't understand.
- Sometimes you only get one chance to ask a question and you should do all you can to use that chance wisely.
- Always remember what your goal is: to get to the truth. You want to have people agree that what you are saying is right and if they try to disagree, you want to ask questions to show the audience they may be hiding something.

Chapter 14: Advanced Rules Of Questioning
- Ask the right questions to the right people at the right time, in front of an audience.
- You have to be on the right side of the issue.
- Start with a broad agreement.
- Avoid certain open-ended questions.
- Do not make statements.
- Let them answer.

Chapter 15: Powerful One Word Questions
- There are several words in the English language that can get to the bottom of problems, they are why, what, where, who, when and how.
- Sometimes you will need to ask "Why" 2 or 3 times before you get to the real reason.

- If at any point your mind goes blank during a conversation, you can use one of these words to fill the gap and keep you focused on exposing the truth.

Chapter 16: How To Sequence Questions

- The challenge is to craft questions that logically move in a sequence from beginning to end.
- The areas you need agreement on are: the problem, the solution and their commitment.
- Ask questions so the only logical answer is their statement acknowledging the truth.

Additional Tips For Question Construction:

1. Only one sentence with only one question.
2. Ask questions that have one word answers.
3. Craft questions that everyone in the audience knows the answer to.
4. Add a "tough" element that either engages the audience or tests the person's integrity.

Problem Solving Process - PART: 3

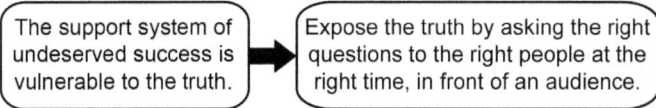

The support system of undeserved success is vulnerable to the truth. ➡ Expose the truth by asking the right questions to the right people at the right time, in front of an audience.

Chapter 12: The Great Equalizer

In a world where some wealthy people have grown accustomed to using their power to take advantage of the system, there is one tool that levels the playing field. It doesn't require money or connections. You didn't have to go to college and it isn't based on your IQ, race or physical abilities. It is an absolute necessity when it comes to fixing anything. As a matter of fact, nothing can be fixed without it. It is the ability to ask questions.

Our daily lives are just a constant stream of questions. We have to constantly ask questions because there is no way you can absolutely know what someone is thinking. I am not a mind reader and you probably aren't either, the way we get information is by asking questions. Questions are the way we get to the truth and the way we learn. Questions can also bind people to their answers, if they are direct. The more direct the question, the quicker the truth can come out or the faster someone can learn something. Whether you want to fix the world or just become more knowledgeable, learning how to ask direct questions is the path you want to be on.

People ask direct questions all the time. Here are direct questions, with specific answers:

1. Where were you? At the mall.
2. Are you ready for lunch? No.
3. Did you get gas? No.
4. Did you pay that bill? No.
5. How does this gadget work? Press the button on top.

The questions above required specific answers and they were designed to get that answer as quickly as possible. If you were to change just a few words in these questions you would no longer be able to get the answer you were looking for.

1. Were you at the mall? No. (Do you know where they are?)
2. What do you want for lunch? Pizza. (You made lunch, were they hungry?)
3. Does the car have gas? No. (Does this mean they are getting gas?)
4. Is that bill due? Yes. (Was the bill paid?)
5. Do you know how that works? Yes. (Do you know what to do now?)

These five questions are similar to the first five questions, but obviously they get different results. The person asking them may have thought they were asking the right question and may have believed they got the answer they were looking for. This is one of the key reasons why there are communication problems between people. Disagreements arise when someone uses the second set of questions when they were looking for first set of answers. They made a "leap" in their minds assuming the answer they got was the entire truth. If this miscommunication leads to an argument, they might use the defense, "Well, you knew there wasn't any gas in the car, why didn't you fill it up?" The reply to that will be, "You didn't ask me to fill it up." Who is wrong? Nobody, they each did what they thought was right based on the question that was asked. This opens up an opportunity to clarify the message so everyone is on the same page, before there is a problem. By asking the right questions, you can direct the other person to only one possible outcome. If there is a discrepancy later on, you can state this outcome is what they agreed upon.

Let's take this a step further and use direct questions to probe deeper. Probing questions will get you the information you need to determine if something is true or not, good or bad, right or wrong. When making decisions, knowing this information will assist people before they decide.

Below are questions that anyone should be able to ask and receive the answers to:

- Who did that study? What do I have to do to get a copy?
- Do you have proof? Where can I get that proof?
- Are there other solutions that we have not discussed? What are they?
- Who is responsible for the final decision?
- Who exactly said that?

Notice how these questions require answers that are short, to the point, and the answer should be known by the person you are asking. These "probing" questions diminish the ability of lies and misleading messages to affect your decisions. They tell the person you are talking with that, "Yes, I hear you, but I just want to find out the facts for myself." Later on you will learn how to add questions such as, "Am I allowed to look at the facts so I can make the best decision possible?" It is extremely tough for anyone to say no to that question, especially in front of an audience.

Asking questions is a way of life. If that is correct, why don't we ask more questions about issues that will affect our lives in adverse ways? People actually are, but they are not getting the answers they want because they are not asking the right questions. Another reason is that people see it clearly in their mind, but when it comes to putting it in words it is easier said than done. They are not able to ask the questions they want to at the right time. I think we have all been there.

Have you ever been in a discussion and you know the other person was wrong, but you just didn't know what to say at the time. Then you walk away and 5 minutes later you rerun the conversation through your mind and come up with several points that you should have said. You may have told a friend about the incident and they gave you several questions you should have asked. This is normal and happens to a lot of people. This is no reason to believe that you will have problems asking important questions. I understand this might slow some people down. Don't worry, besides teaching people how to create their own questions, this book is full of questions that you can read without changing a word and still get tremendous results. Do you know how to read a question? Then you know how to fix the world.

What if you were able to ask the right questions at the right time, would that change the outcome? What if you were prepared to ask a great question that would put that person on the spot? Whether they answered it or not, you and anyone else listening would have more information to make a better decision. Get good at asking great questions and people will stop trying to get over on you. They will realize that a discussion with you better be based on fact and the truth. Wouldn't that be nice?

Asking questions is a win-win scenario. As long as you ask questions, you aren't attacking anyone. You are giving them the opportunity to stand up for themselves and tell the truth. If they are on the right side of an issue they will be more than happen to explain that, especially in front of an audience. It will make them look great and it was all because of you. On the other hand, if they are lying, then they deserve whatever happens, and the audience will be glad you asked the question.

So whether you do it, or someone else does it, it doesn't matter. We have to start asking the right questions in order to get the right answers. Questions are the answer. There have been advancements in questioning techniques, but now it is time to take it to the next level. The end result is being able to ask direct questions that expose the truth, even when the person doesn't want it exposed.

Remember, you have the right to ask questions. If you learn to ask the right questions you will find the right answers. If you find the right answers you will become an informed citizen. If you learn how to expose the truth in front of an audience you will become a hero.

Chapter 13: No Discrimination With This Tool

You don't have to be a genius, have a lot of money or be popular to question someone when you think they are wrong or you don't understand. Well crafted questions will lead to the truth, even when they don't want the truth to come out. If you believe something is wrong and you have the opportunity to speak up, you should do so and asking great questions will expose the truth quickly. We are fortunate enough to live in a country where we have the right to ask questions. There are people around the world who would die for that right and they have.

Asking questions gets to the truth and it doesn't matter who asks the questions. Does the person asking the question have to be part of an organization, group, religion, or have a certain skin color? Does the person asking the question have to have good grammar or be a great speaker? What if the question affects the person personally and they deliver the question in an emotional way, maybe even being irate about it? Just because they are upset should their question be dismissed? Does it mean the person answering the question is off the hook, or that their answer holds no weight? If the question leads to the truth, does it matter how it was presented?

Maybe you are shy or stutter when you feel pressured. Maybe you don't have the most moral lifestyle or cleanest past. Does it matter, especially if you know the truth about something and could change the outcome? The federal government doesn't think so. They give immunity to murderers, drug dealers, and thieves in return for the truth. So obviously the truth can even come from a criminal. That's a big trade off just to get to the truth; let a person who deals drugs to go free. If the truth is that valuable to the government, it must be that valuable to everyone.

What if a mass murderer had verifiable proof that a cure for cancer existed? Does a cure for cancer exist? Don't think too hard, you know the right answer. Does a homeless person have the right to ask a question to a member of Congress and should that question be answered? I know you are saying yes and you are right. So it doesn't matter who asks the questions or what financial state they are in.

Sometimes you only get one chance to ask a question and I believe you should do all you can to use that chance wisely. With that said, if you

58

have the option of asking your question in a calm, respectful manner, that would be more accepted than being loud and aggressive. It shouldn't be mandatory, but why not take the path of least resistance when you can.

It's understandable to attack, yell and scream, especially when you have been wronged. Always remember what your goal is: to get to the truth. You want to have your opponent agree that what you are saying is right and if they try to disagree you want to ask questions to show they are a liar or a hypocrite. Don't let your current situation stop you from getting the truth. Just by learning how to construct probing questions, you will have the power to overcome those situations.

Chapter 14: Advanced Rules Of Questioning

1. The Golden Rule

This is it. If you forget every rule of questioning, don't forget this one. It is the make or break element for exposing the truth. You may not understand the power of this sentence right now, but please do not discount it.

The way to expose the truth and fix the world is to:

Ask the right questions to the right people at the right time, in front of an audience.

If you cannot do all of these at the same time then wait until you can. People use part of this technique all the time and the results are very limited. By employing the full technique the success rate will be exponential.

Let's break it down:

1. **Ask the right questions:** you can be questioning the right person at the right time, in front of an audience and never get to the truth because your questions were not crafted to do so. The better the questions, the more complete the truth will be. The more truth that becomes globalized the more the problem is fixed.
2. **To the right people:** if you are asking an aide, secretary or low level decision maker, it is easy for the top level people to state that those people spoke without knowing all the facts. Now try to get the right person to answer the question, it probably won't happen. The right people aren't your friends or neighbors, although that is a good way to practice.
3. **At the right time:** the right time is when it will have the greatest impact. This is when an issue is adversely or will adversely affect a lot of people and you have a chance to fix it.
4. **In front of an audience:** this is the real key. Hollywood proves this point all of the time in the movies. They show a scene where someone asks the right questions, to the right person at the right time, but no one else is around and even though they admit it, it was a worthless effort. You may be able to get someone to admit to the truth when you are just one on one, but that doesn't help. Later on that person can claim they never even spoke with you. It is easy to deny if you don't have any witnesses or proof. Great questions need to be asked when others can see it and the more people who see it the better.

More About The Audience

I know there are instances where people have spoken up, challenging the status quo, and the wrongdoers were caught and punished or a bad situation was changed. You see this on the news every once in awhile. Therein lies the key, it was on the news. It received national attention and once too many people know the truth, it becomes harder to cover up through misleading messages.

The audience doesn't have to be sympathetic to your side, they just have to be listening. The belief that people don't want to be proven wrong can work to your advantage. Even if someone in the audience originally believed the opposite of you, i.e. "Oil is the best option we have to fuel our economy", as long as they didn't express that belief publicly, they still have the opportunity to change their minds and save their pride. If they are sitting in the audience where well-crafted questions brought out the truth, more than likely they will agree with you, especially if they see other people in the audience start to agree. People want to believe they are on the right side of an issue. This doesn't work if they were attacked earlier for what they believed in. Remember, people have the right to have their own beliefs. You can give them an opportunity to change their beliefs, if the truth is exposed in a common sense way.

So how do you get the right person to acknowledge your questions in front of an audience? We have all had discussions with our friends and possibly have figured out the solutions to some major world problems, obviously nothing happened. I have seen fleeting moments when people did get the opportunity to ask a question to the right person at the right time in front of an audience, but unfortunately the question was crafted in a way that was easily sidestepped. If you get this opportunity and are able to muster the courage necessary to speak up, don't you want your efforts to have results?

Fortunately, there are opportunities where anyone can ask questions to the right people. This is especially true around election time when politicians are campaigning, which seems to be all the time nowadays. There are public forums and town hall meetings happening all over the United States. In these situations you usually get one chance to ask your question, so make it good. Hopefully people read this book and team up to get the right people to answer the right questions. If the first question is side stepped, the next person in the audience asks the same question. This keeps happening until the question is answered. If it keeps getting sidestepped, then someone should say, "It is obvious this audience wants you to answer that question, can you tell me what you are hiding by not answering it directly?" There's a show stopper. It may sound tough to say, but I guarantee you there will be people in the audience who wanted to say the same thing. They just didn't read this book and therefore didn't know how to craft the question.

There is even a greater opportunity for people who have access to the decision makers every day. Their job is to ask the tough questions. These are reporters, interviewers and the people who ask the questions during special inquiries. The decision makers know they are going to be asked tough questions, so why don't these people ask questions that get to the facts and expose the truth the quickest?

If you want to be a famous reporter or talk show host; be the champion of the people. Ask the right questions to the right people at the right time and tell the world about it. And if they don't answer it the first time ask it again. I guarantee you will have at least one huge fan...me.

2. You Have To Be On The Right Side

In order to expose the truth, you have to be right. This book is full of techniques on how to expose the truth. If you are wrong or lying then someone will easily use these techniques against you. If there is an issue where you believe something is wrong, but can't yet prove it, then that is the truth. You come from the side of, "I don't know everything yet, but something doesn't sound right. Wouldn't it make sense to look into this matter further?" Even when you don't know the answers you can still tell the truth.

3. Start With A Broad Agreement

When people feel threatened, because they are on the wrong side of an issue, they will be reluctant to answer your questions. They will disagree with any premise that is made unless they cannot disagree. Whatever the issue is, at some level there is a broad statement that everyone can agree on.

You will need to craft your questions in a way that the person who is objecting has to agree with you, even if it is in the broadest range of the subject. You need to have a starting point where both of you agree. As long as you are you are right, then crafting a broad question is easy.

Broad Question Examples:

- Would you prefer clean drinking water for your family?
- If you have any children, do you want them to be disease free?

It is not easy to say no to either of the questions above. You may have to get them to agree that your broad premise is valid somewhere, at least once. Therefore, if it happened once it can happen again. If they won't agree with a broad premise, then you will have to use the techniques described in PART 4 to expose the truth.

4. Avoid Certain Open-Ended Questions

One of the pitfalls you want to avoid is asking "open-ended" questions. These are questions that don't have a universal answer, which means people will answer them differently. They also allow the person to ramble on and inject their own agenda into the conversation. For this reason, whenever you need specific information, craft the question so you can only get the answer you are looking for.

Don't end a sentence with "What do you think?" Unless you really want to know what they are thinking. For the purposes described in this book, that is not what we want. This book is not about becoming a great conversationalist and learning how to get people to like you. It isn't about asking questions that allow the other person to speak and embellish on themselves. All you want is the truth and the quicker the better.

Just so we are clear, here are "open ended" questions that you should avoid:

- How do you feel?
- What do you think about these candidates?
- What would you like to see accomplished?
- Do you have anything else to add?
- What concerns do you have?

Of course there will be cases where this is unavoidable, that is why I said limit the use of open-ended questions. If you know the answer that will expose the truth, then phrase the question so they can only reply with a yes or a no. Make it so people don't have to hear the answer to know what the truth is. This is one of the keys to problem solving, the ability to expose the truth whether they admit it or not.

Example:

WRONG: What do you think is the cause of the high cost of gas?
RIGHT: Does oil speculation affect the price of gas?

There are two areas of problem solving where you will need to get more than a yes or no answer. The first one is when you need to clarify what the problem is, you may ask how or why. The second occurs after the solution is on the table; you will ask questions to reveal what their objections are right there: "Can you think of any reasons why this solution will not work?" You have to get the "whys" out on the table during the problem solving process. If you wait, they will have time to regroup and create misleading messages to fool the public later on.

5. Do Not Make Statements

Exposing the truth is based on asking questions, not making statements. The reason is, because when you make a statement, those become your words and why should anyone believe you. The person you are talking with hasn't committed to anything and now they can question your statement. So eliminate that opportunity for them. Well crafted questions will cause people to make statements and validate the truth.

Example:

WRONG: People will buy 100,000 cars this year.
RIGHT: Did you make the statement that people would buy 100,000 cars this year?

Of course this is not a game changing question, they will come later on. The idea is to show you how to get the same result, but not give anyone a chance to challenge you, because you didn't make a statement.

I know this will be tough at first. When you find out the truth and you know you are right, it is hard to hold it in. Sometimes it is a good feeling when you prove someone wrong, so you tell them all the reasons how you know they are wrong. As great as this sounds, it will not work as well as asking questions. If all you do is make statements, then there is nothing for the other person to answer to. You must make them acknowledge the facts, even if they appear obvious to everyone.

6. Let Them Answer

One of the most important objectives when questioning is to let them answer. Isn't that your goal? Don't answer for them, because it is obviously your answer. The power comes from being able to get a decision maker to agree with what you are saying. Another problem I see is that the person asking the question asks more than one question at a time. You see this in the Presidential press room. A reporter knows they might only have one shot, so they ask four questions at once. It is now easy for the decision maker to pick and choose what they want to answer and then quickly move on to the next reporter. Don't do this. Ask one question at a time and let the person answer it.

By letting them answer you have changed the whole dynamic of the conversation. The person is now committed to whatever their response is or they risk the chance of going back on their word and becoming a liar or hypocrite, which you can point out later on. You could say, in front of the audience, "Didn't you say that people would buy 100,000 cars this year?"

Ask the question, then listen to the answer. If it is not the answer you are looking for, ask the question again or ask another question that gets to the answer another way. Another reason for letting them answer is so you can write down what they say, especially if it is an open-ended question.

Chapter 15: Powerful One Word Questions

There are several words in the English language that can get to the bottom of problems and most of them start with "W". They are why, what, where, who, when and how. "How" is actually one of my favorites because you hear so many statements about people doing something, but they never tell you how it will get done. It would be nice when someone says, "I can create jobs" and then one person stands up and says, "How?"

These one word questions are easy to use and get a lot of bang for the buck. Don't forget, once you ask the question don't speak, let the person answer.

- When something doesn't sound right and you are not sure, just ask, "Why?"
- When someone quotes an expert, you ask "Who?"
- When someone says it's happening all over, you ask "Where?"
- If they say something has already been done, you ask "When?" Then you ask, "By who?"
- If they say they can fix the world, you ask, "How?"

I know, it sounds too simple. Exactly, that's why we should all be doing it. These words are just that powerful. As usual don't believe me, there is a way you can prove it to yourself. Watch the news and see how many times they make statements as if they are facts, but never say where they came from, who did them or how it was done. They just make a statement and you are supposed to believe them. See how many times a one word question could have been asked.

In my opinion, the best word in the English dictionary is "why". By asking why, you are able to understand where the decisions are coming from. When solving problems you need to know what the problem is. The word "why" can do that for you. If you know something wrong is being done and you find out why, then there is your answer. Fix that and you will have fixed the problem.

Sometimes you will need to ask "Why" 2 or 3 times before you get to the real reason. Here's an example:

1. We have to increase property taxes by 5%. Why?
2. Our budget has shortfalls and we need to close the gap. Why?

3. Because our healthcare costs have risen 100% in 2 years. Why?
4. Because that was when we began providing healthcare to part time government employees.

Now I know why you want to raise people's taxes. The next question would be, "Who approved part time employees receiving health insurance when taxpayers can't afford the health premiums for themselves?"

Use any of these one word questions more often in your life and you will be amazed at all the new information you can find out. The other benefit of a one word question is that you can use it as a safety net. If at any point your mind goes blank during a conversation, there is a good chance that one of these words can fill in the gap and keep you focused on exposing the truth.

Chapter 16: How To Sequence Questions

One word questions are a good way to start, but what if you were able to ask several questions. This brings on a new dynamic. It gives you the opportunity to expose the truth by asking questions in a specific order, in a sequence. This is nothing new. It just hasn't been exploited as a tool, which anyone can use to expose the truth. This technique is used by lawyers and law enforcement all the time. You begin with a simple question that they have to agree with. Then each question after that builds on that basic agreement. In law enforcement, these conversations are videotaped so they can be used as evidence later on and show the world what the truth is. Sounds like a good plan.

The challenge is to craft questions that logically move in a sequence from beginning to end. The areas you need agreement on are the problem, the solution and their commitment. You need to craft questions so the only logical answer is their statement exposing the truth.

1. **PROBLEM:** The first questions you need to ask have to do with getting your subject to acknowledge and agree to the problem at hand. Let the audience know that this person agrees, or make them say they don't agree.
2. **SOLUTION:** The second part is to get them to agree that if there was a solution it would work. Then show them and the audience what the solution is, if you know it.
3. **COMMITMENT:** The last part is to solidify their commitment to action with a final closing question. This can be a tough, in your face add-on, that lets the audience see whether or not this person is on their side, or protecting their corporate supporters.

NOTE: I understand they will have questions of their own, which is why the entire next section details how to handle just about every objection someone can throw at you. For now, I want to keep the focus on crafting sentence sequences.

You are only limited by yourself when it comes to creating questions. The questions that I have used in this book may not fit your situation. That's okay. Just create your own. Ask yourself what needs to be done.

1. How can I write a question that will expose the truth in animal cruelty?
2. How can I make this question better?
3. How can I write a question that will insure that the audience understands the crisis and is exposed to the truth?
4. What questions must I write that will commit the person to fixing the problem?

Remember the key to asking questions, even to yourself, is to wait for their answer.

There was an opportunity where the right questions could have been asked in sequence to get the right person to admit the truth on a daily national television show. It had to do with an issue being researched, discussed and debated about the juice industry. There is concern with arsenic in our food supply, specifically apple juice, which is highly consumed by toddlers and infants. The show was able to get a spokesperson from the juice industry to come on and defend their side of the story. The host did a good job trying to expose the truth, but a few questions were left unanswered, literally.

Here's another approach that could have been taken to expose the truth. The first question to get the broad agreement could have been, "How much arsenic do parents want to feed their babies?" That is a show stopper, especially in front of an audience. Ask it with a serious face and when they look at you just say, "Really, I want to know how much arsenic is good for babies, do you know the answer?" The answer is simple – none. Your toughest adversary has to agree to your most basic premise and hopefully the audience is shaking their heads and thinking, "Yes, that makes sense."

What is the end game here? Why start the questioning if it isn't going to get you anywhere? The fact is that juice companies don't want the arsenic information to be widespread and if it is they want to limit their losses. Do you think they want to maximize profits or maximize the health of our children? They can take measures right now to significantly reduce the amount of arsenic in the juice, but that would cost them money that they don't want to spend. The end game would be to have them admit that arsenic is bad at any level and they will agree to reduce or eliminate the amount in the juices our children drink.

69

Arsenic In Apple Juice Questioning Sequence

You probably wouldn't ask all of these questions, they are just here to show you a variety of ways to get people to admit the truth. These are questions I thought of, there is a good chance you can think of better questions and I hope you do.

Problem Questions:

1. Is there arsenic in the apple juice sold in the United States?
2. What level of arsenic is good for an infant or toddler to consume?
3. If none of it is good, how can any level be safe to ingest?
4. Are you stating that, even at low levels, it has absolutely no effect on the developing brain of a toddler?
5. Is there any monetary value that parents should put on the health of their children?
6. Do I have the right to insist on a higher standard for the food that my children consume?

Solution Questions:

1. Are there companies that have low or no levels of arsenic in their apple juice? (The answer is yes)
2. So you would agree that it is possible right now to deliver apple juice to the U.S. consumer with low levels of arsenic? (the answer is yes)
3. If one company is able to do it, wouldn't basic common sense say that any company could do it also? If for some strange reason they say no or they don't know, take out a pen and paper and ask them why. Write down everything they say and when they are done read it back to them stating that they are the ones who said it.
4. Is it impossible to check a factory to find out why their process is producing more arsenic?
5. Isn't it the function of your agency to protect consumers from elements like arsenic in our food source?
6. Do you think that the people who purchase these products would want to reduce the arsenic levels in them?
7. What would it take to reduce the levels of arsenic?

Commitment Questions:

1. We know there is a problem. You stated how it could be reduced, so my last question is: can you give me any reason why these companies would not start this as soon as possible?
2. Are you the type of government official who acknowledges there is a problem, understands there are solutions, but then goes back to work and does nothing about it?
3. Do you believe you get paid to protect consumers or companies, which one?
4. So now that you see there is a simple solution, everyone in the audience can sleep better because you will take action to correct it, is that right?
5. Can you tell this audience the first phone call you are going to make to get the ball rolling?

There you go. With these questions you have pointed out the problem and brought to light the fact that there is no "good" level of arsenic. Through additional questioning, everyone in the audience sees there is a solution and there is no reason why it shouldn't be fixed now, because you can't put a price on the health of our children.

PART 4:

QUESTIONING TECHNIQUES

What You Will Learn

Let's be realistic, nobody wants to admit they are lying, especially if it is going to affect their professional lives. They are going to put up a fight, which means they are going to object to as much as they can. They will object until they realize you have the skill to take every objection they have and turn it around to show the audience that they are hiding the truth.

Some of the techniques outlined in this section may overlap. That is because they work in several different scenarios, plus repetition is the key to learning. Like everything else in this book, all of these examples are not set in stone. There is more than one way to expose the truth. Use these examples as I have written them or as guidelines to create your own.

The key to overcoming objections is anticipating what the objections will be. When you are finished this section you will know how to overcome objections that might otherwise inhibit your ability to expose the truth.

Chapter 17: They're Not Going To Like It
- Sometimes just asking questions that require a direct answer is not enough.
- Understand there is always a reason (motivation) behind the decisions people make.
- You will notice, as you move through your questioning process, people will become more and more reluctant to answer.

Chapter 18: How To Master The Power of "So"
- The basic construction of the "ownership" question is as follows:
  - So what you are saying is, [clarify and repeat their claim], is that correct?
- Whenever someone has a "real" objection, what they are telling you is they aren't sold yet. They need more information.
- When people are suppressing the solutions, they are objecting because they don't want the truth to be known. This is exactly what you want.

Chapter 19: How To Stop Lies From Spreading
- When trying to prove a lie, people will resort to claiming what are sometimes called "global" truths. This is achieved by using words that assume it happens every time, to everyone, everywhere.

- These so-called "global" truths come in many packages. They use phrases like: Americans say, There are a group of people, It is common belief, A study was done, In a poll taken, An anonymous source, Up to, As much as, It's been said, Possibly, and Countless.

NOTE: The following is a mini Table of Contents to make it easier for future reference. It is not the summary of what is in each chapter.

Problem Solving Process - PART: 4

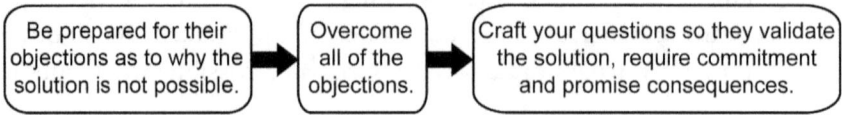

Be prepared for their objections as to why the solution is not possible. → Overcome all of the objections. → Craft your questions so they validate the solution, require commitment and promise consequences.

Chapter 17: They're Not Going To Like It

Sometimes just asking questions that require a direct answer is not enough. It would be nice if everyone just answered the question, but they won't. They will come prepared to prove the solutions do not exist, they will not work, or there is no way to tell if they will work. Their main goal is to make sure the truth doesn't come out, which is the exact opposite of your goal.

The main problem for them is that they will have to find a way to lie in front of an audience and hope that everyone believes it. They will try to divert the conversation, downplay what you are saying, quote some expert or data and even play stupid. None of that will work with the skills you will have.

I have taken an untraditional approach to exposing the truth, it can be brutal and in your face. As you read these techniques two thoughts will probably come to mind. The first will be, "That is right. There is no way they can go against that without lying or looking like a liar in front of an audience." The second thought may be, "I could never do that." The reason is you are probably a good person and you know that these techniques will make the other person look bad and probably prove them to be a liar in front of a large audience. I understand, but if they are part of something bigger and proving them wrong can fix a world problem, isn't that something you could live with.

Think about the people who this person's decisions ruined, think about how they will feel that someone had the guts and the brains to stand up and say the right thing. Someone has to stand up, put people on the spot and tell it like it is. If we don't, we will continue to spiral down a path that doesn't lead to a good place.

There was a time to be nice, that time is over. If someone is lying and adversely affecting your right to the pursuit of happiness, then you have every right to prove those lies. As long as you aren't doing anything illegal, you should be able to use every advantage available to expose the truth.

You will notice as you move through your questioning process, people will become more and more reluctant to answer. If this happens you know you are on the right track, you know you have struck a nerve and so will everyone else. This is when their defense mechanisms will kick in. In their minds they are thinking, "Please don't ask me the hard questions, because I am wrong and I don't want you to figure it out. Worse off I don't want the whole world to know that I am wrong." The last thing anyone wants is to be proven wrong in front of an audience, and they will do anything to avoid that. So be prepared for the objections.

Understand there is always a reason (motivation) behind the decisions people make, even when these decisions are not in the best interest of the people they affect the most. Sometimes the decision makers know it is not the best solution, but they do it anyway and unfortunately the motivation is money.

By asking the right questions at the right time to the right person, in front of an audience, you will have the power to expose the truth. When you do this there will be several options the person answering your questions will have:

1. Prove you are wrong - if that is the case then move on, you have found the truth and hopefully you can now sleep at night knowing it has been solved.
2. Accept that you are right - this is a great victory, but don't gloat. Thank them and find out how this new insight is going to be used to fix the problem.
3. They will lie, cherry pick data, or quote other people to support their stance on the issue. This is where your ability to ask "truth exposing" questions will determine your success.
4. They will walk away and not answer your question. This is a victory, especially if it happens in front of an audience or while being videotaped. Use this to advance your position and if there is another person ask them same question, or say, "Would you agree with the people who believe your colleague walked away because they are hiding something?"
5. They say an answer that goes around the question or isn't even related to the original question. You see this in almost every political debate. It is a clear sign that they know you are on the right track and don't want you to get any closer.
6. Be prepared, they may take the loser option, which is to attack your integrity, intelligence, personality, religious beliefs, etc. All of which should have nothing to do with the questions, but this has become one of the key tools used to divert attention away from their lies.

7. They can act ignorant. They will make claims as if they didn't know what was going on, therefore they are not at fault.

There may be more outcomes then the ones I listed above, but knowing these will be more than enough. Success comes when you are prepared, when you are ready for whatever your opponent may throw at you.

Chapter 18: How To Master The Power of "So"

There is a sales technique used when prospective clients have objections to buying a product. Whenever the person had a reason not to purchase, the salesperson would turn their reason into a question and then ask it back to them using the word "so".

Sales Technique Example:

> **Prospective Buyer:** I am not sure I can afford the payments.
>
> **Salesperson:** So if you could afford the payments, you would like to make this purchase?

At this point the prospective buyer locked themselves in to saying yes; if not then they were lying about their original statement. They said they had a problem and now the salesperson wants to know if they fix that problem will they buy the product. Sometimes the prospective buyer will come up with more objections. These objections are just "unsolved" problems. The salesperson will be successful if they can solve all of the problems.

You are not selling a product, but you are solving problems, so the technique is the same. The only difference is that the objections are against the solution (It won't work, People won't do that, We don't have the technology, etc.). It is likely the audience will have the same objections, especially if the misleading messages were strong enough.

Whenever someone has a "real" objection, what they are telling you is they aren't sold yet. They need more information. This is what you want, an opportunity to show people the truth. On the other hand, if people are suppressing the solutions, they are objecting because they don't want the truth to be known. This is also what you want. They have given you the opportunity to prove to the audience that their objections are invalid and they are only objecting to hide the truth. In order to use this technique you have to be right, it doesn't work if you are on the wrong side of the issue.

Whenever someone has an objection to what you have to say, one of the first things you should do is clarify their statement and make them own it. If they want to claim something is true, then they better be right or else you will show the world they are not.

The basic construction of the "ownership" question is as follows:

So what you are saying is, [clarify and repeat their claim], is that correct?

Example:

- Their Claim: Well, if we had more drilling that would reduce gas prices.
- Ownership Question: So what you are saying is, if there was more oil available, then gas prices would go down, is that correct?

Now you have locked them into their objection. If later on you prove this wrong and they want to change their story, it is too late and you can remind the audience of what they said earlier. Even if you don't point it out, the audience will know something doesn't sound right.

Sometimes their objection to the truth is a statement of hypocrisy. In other words they might say, "That is not how we do it" or "It just can't be done that way." Whatever the issue, there is a good chance they already do it that way and are just hoping you don't figure it out.

"So" questions for exposing the hypocrisy:

- So what you are saying is, if we had done it that way in the past, then we can do it the same way now, is that correct?
- So if there was a similar situation where your company already did it the same way, would that mean someone isn't telling the truth?

Chapter 19: How To Stop Lies From Spreading

When trying to make a lie appear to be the truth, people will resort to claiming what are sometimes called "global" truths. They will use words that assume it happens every time, to everyone, everywhere. They are insinuating there are no exceptions. By using this technique they are able to hide parts of the truth. The strategy is to get people to believe it is happening everywhere to everyone and therefore they should accept it as the truth, because everyone else is. This is used all the time and it works.

The delivery of this message (the half truths), is sometimes reported as a story and the person behind the claim isn't the one reporting it. The reason I mention this is because the misleading information is still getting out and the affects are the same. So if the main culprit isn't the one reporting the message, then you have to hold the person who is accountable. Somewhere in their job description, I have to believe that telling the truth is part of it. If they want to repeat facts or data, then they should make sure they are true. This accountability does happen with rare consequences, that's what "retractions" are for. Reporters aren't the only people who do this, sometimes the "global" truths are being told directly by the source.

These so-called "global" truths come in many packages. They use phrases like: Americans say, There are a group of people, It is common belief, A study was done, In a poll taken, An anonymous source, Up to, As much as, It's been said, Possibly, and Countless. I have taken the time to point out as many as I could think of, gave examples of how they are used, offered questions that you can use to find the truth and added follow up questions to make them think twice before they report false information in the future. A question and follow up from one example may work well in another example, you can mix and match the questions to suit your particular "truth exposing" situation.

EXAMPLE 1: Experts say that the toxic waste in the sand is not harmful.
Questions:
- What experts, can I get their names?
- What qualifies this person as an expert, can I see their resume?

Follow Up Questions:
- So what you are saying is, you reported a statement from a so-called expert, but you don't even know who the expert is?

- So what you are saying is, your company would rely on important information without even checking out the source?

EXAMPLE 2: A study was done that shows vitamin C does not help a cold.
Questions:
- Who exactly did the study, can I get their names?
- Are there any other results that I may need to make an informed decision?
- Who paid to have the study done? Was any of the funding from a company that someone may think had a conflict of interest?
- Can I get the complete details of the study?

Follow Up Questions:
- So what you are saying is, you want to give me advice about my health, but you don't even know all the facts yourself?
- What would happen if I took your advice, would you take responsibility if you were wrong?

EXAMPLE 3: The data shows that kids 9-12 play video games 5 hours per day.
Questions:
- Who exactly collected the data, can I get their names?
- When, how, where was the data collected?
- Did you only use a part of the data in order to prove the point you are trying to make?

Follow Up Questions:
- So what you are saying is, this data is only for a certain cross section of kids, but you made it sound like it was all kids 9-12, is that correct?

EXAMPLE 4: The arsenic in apple juice is within the acceptable limits.
Questions:
- Who exactly approved these acceptable limits, can I get their names?
- So what you are saying is, within these limits, there is no possible way for this to affect anyone?

Follow Up Questions:
- So what you are saying is, there is a way to reduce arsenic in apple juice?
- So I am just wondering, what would happen if you were wrong?

EXAMPLE 5: It has been shown that eating more red meat is healthy.
Questions:
- What exactly has been shown and by who?
- Have other studies shown different results?

Follow Up Questions:
- So if it can be shown that the study didn't document all the facts, would that mean someone is trying to cover up something?
- So if the study was funded by a cattle company, would it make sense for people to second guess those results?

EXAMPLE 6: People were... People have... People are... Sometimes they add a label to this: doctors, lawyers, teachers, mothers or families. Doctors across the country believe we will have a swine flu pandemic.
Questions:
- When you say doctors do you mean every single doctor?
- If it isn't every single doctor, then what percentage of that group are you talking about?

Follow Up Questions:
- Since this is such an important health issue, wouldn't an intelligent person get information from both sides, including doctors who refute the data and refuse vaccination?
- Is there any data that shows people have been harmed by vaccinations? Can we see it?

EXAMPLE 7: Where the $60 billion went could not be determined.
Questions:
- How did they try to determine and fail?
- So what you are saying is, with all of the technology and resources we have today, there is no way to determine that?

Follow Up Questions:
- If there was a way to find what happened to the $60 billion dollars would you want to see that happen?
- If it turned out that part of the money was embezzled or fraudulently distributed, would you agree if we can catch the people they should go to jail?

EXAMPLE 8: Whether or not the oil spill has killed the plant life has not been verified.

Questions:
- Why didn't anyone verify it?
- Can you think of any reasons why a smart company like yours would not take to the time to verify something that seems easy to do?

Follow Up Questions:
- So what you are saying is, we have the technology to verify it, we just haven't done it?
- Now that we know we can verify it, when can I tell the press you will begin the verification process?

EXAMPLE 9: No proof has been found to link fracking to earthquakes.

Questions:
- Is that because nobody took the time to look for any proof?
- Can you tell me the names of who investigated it and where did they look for the information.

Follow Up Questions:
- So what you are saying is, we have had earthquakes that coincide with the fracking process and all of the scientific geniuses can't tell if it is related, is that what you are saying?
- If I can find qualified professionals to see if there is a relationship, will you help them by supplying the necessary data?

There is one last scenario I want to go over. It has to do with news agencies that show images and videos that are outdated and use them to supplement a current story. What happens is the viewer sees the images and doesn't realize they don't depict what is happening right now, but they believe they are. They have no reason to question it.

EXAMPLE 10: The U.S. is contemplating military action due to the violence. The images that are shown with this news story may be weeks, months or even years old.

Questions:
- When was that image/video taken?
- Can I get the name of the person who took it?
- Does that image/video correspond with this story exactly, meaning location, date and time?
- Are there other images or videos that you have, but chose not to show?

Follow Up Questions:

- So what you are saying is, you purposely show outdated images to the public, but you don't believe those images affect what the public believes? Then why don't you put dates on them?

Additional questions to be used in the above scenarios:

- If I can prove that has or has not happened at least one time, doesn't that mean your statement would be false? Or, doesn't that mean that you are currently lying about this?
- Doesn't that mean if it has happened at least one time, it could happen again?
- Are you bringing up objections just because you don't want to see this happen or once the objections are proven unfounded you plan to fix the problem?

Chapter 20: How To Get To The Facts

1. Just Ask Them

Sometimes you will hear negative reports about people doing something that is actually beneficial. The message is crafted to convince you it isn't right and you shouldn't do as they do. The only problem is they don't give any logical reason why, they just say, "Don't do it." One of the best examples has to do with the push to vaccinate the entire U.S. population as much as possible. Unknown to a lot of people, there are Americans who have absolutely refused to vaccinate themselves or their children, this includes doctors and nurses.

Questions I would like to know:

- Can you tell me why doctors and nurses would adamantly refuse to take a vaccination that the CDC says is imperative?
- Why have some doctors and nurses resigned from the hospital they worked at because there was a rule for everyone to be vaccinated?
- Do you find it odd that a doctor would resign over that; is there something that the public needs to know? Maybe we should find out from those doctors directly. Even if they are wrong, at least we have more information to base our decisions on. Would you agree with that?

So when it comes to getting to the truth, why don't we just go to the source? Is it really that tough to ask someone what happened, or why they did or did not do something? What if in the middle of an exchange of words you picked up your cell phone and called someone right there? What if you got the answer right in front of the audience? Isn't the goal to get the truth as quickly as possible?

2. Get The Specifics

When someone can make a statement and doesn't have to give specifics such as who, where, when or how, then there is no way to check out the facts to see whether it is true or false. This is where a lie gets its power. Short one word questions can get the specifics you are looking for (why, who, what, where, when and how). You can also craft probing questions so the person knows exactly what information you are looking for.

STATEMENT: Up to 30,000 people die from complications of the flu each year.

SPECIFIC QUESTIONS:

- What complications are you talking about?
- Were these people already ill?
- What was their physical condition when they got the flu?
- Does this mean that a healthy 30 year old person has a high chance of dying from the flu?
- Has any healthy person ever died from taking the flu vaccine? Then what's the difference?

The point is, statements are made without details so people will not question the true impact. You have the right to ask questions about anything that will affect you or your family. It doesn't necessarily mean they are hiding anything from you, it just means you need more information in order to make an intelligent decision.

3. Don't Let Them Hide The Truth

Some global problems deal with knowledge and data that is not readily available to the general public. If your plan involves this data, I would suggest doing all you can to get it first. If you can't, then there is a way to pressure someone to deliver it to you.

This situation will come up when they have an excuse to hide the truth. Some of those excuses could be:

- That is patented information.
- Those are company secrets.
- I do not know that data off hand.

It will come off as, "I would like to supply that information, but unfortunately I do not have access to it at this time." That sounds fair and the audience will probably agree and accept that excuse. They now believe they are protected behind this veil of secrecy. Remember, they are trying to prove they are doing what is right for the people, so they don't want to upset anyone. This is where you step in.

How to ask for data they don't want to give:

- I understand why you can't produce the information, but I was wondering if you understood how knowing that information might be important to people in the audience?
- So what you are saying is, if you could supply that information to the audience you would, is that correct?
- What exactly is the reason why that data is not available today? Whatever the reason is, you would craft your next question using the "So" technique from Chapter 18.

For patented or company secrets:

- Do you understand why we are requesting that patented or private information?
- The reason you patented something or have company secrets is to protect them from competitors, is that correct?
- Does anyone know the data now?
- How come it is safe with them?
- So what you are saying is, if we took the same precautions, then your company secrets wouldn't be at risk and we can also solve this problem, isn't that correct?

Additional Questions:

- Should criminals be allowed to hide behind the law?
- If the American public suspected wrong doing, what you are saying is there is nothing they can do about it? Are you saying our country was setup so the citizens could not fight government or corporate corruption?
- You understand that by not delivering the information, it is obvious to people in the audience that what I am saying is probably true and now the onus is on you to prove me wrong.

Here are a few more examples with the solutions you can use. Again, these are only what I thought of while writing. You can use this as a template and alter them to work with the situation you will be dealing with.

1. That data is in my office.

    a. You say, "So what you are saying is, you have the information, but cannot produce it now because the data is in your office, is that correct?" They will say yes.

b. Then you say, "Would you agree this is an important issue?" They will say yes.

c. The next question would be, "Are you the type of person that gets things done or do you believe we should put off important issues?"

d. Lastly, you say, "Since this is an important issue and you have the data necessary to complete what we are talking about, can you think of any logical reason why you shouldn't have someone get that data and bring it here now?" Or, "Great, let's get the details now, because it is such an important issue to so many people, do you want to have them wait any longer?"

2. I am not the one to make that decision.

a. You say, "Who is the person that would make that decision?" They will tell you.

b. Then you say, "Would you agree this is an important issue?" They will say yes.

c. Lastly, you say, "Since this is an important issue and you know who the person is that can make this decision, what is stopping us from giving them a call and finalizing this right now?"

3. Those documents are at the bank.

a. You say, "What bank would that be?" They will tell you.

b. Then you say, "Would you agree this is an important issue?" They will say yes.

c. Lastly, you say, "Since this is an important issue and the documents we need are at the bank, can you think of any logical reason why you shouldn't have someone go to the bank and bring them here now?" Or, "I understand the bank is closed now, so is it safe to say you will get those documents to us on Monday when the bank opens?"

Chapter 21: How To Handle The Uncooperative

1. Question Their Intelligence

If you ever had a conversation with anyone who was defending the wrong side of an issue, they may have used arguments that were irrelevant or made no sense. Maybe this caught you off guard and instead of turning it back on them all you could do is say "Huh", because you knew it was just that stupid. The problem is YOU KNEW. You have to make it obvious to the person saying it and anyone else around. Just because you caught it, doesn't mean everyone else did.

There may be other ways, but the one way I have seen this stopped was to consistently prove the same person wrong in front of an audience. The pain of showing other people they are not intelligent is the deterrent and it works. After awhile they changed and made sure they knew what they were talking about whenever we discussed facts. It's not nice, but neither is lying to you. It works on a small scale and I believe it will work better on the world stage. Do it enough times and people will begin to think before they speak. When they have something to say that affects others, it better be right and it better be pertinent to the subject at hand. Wouldn't it be nice to sit back and watch people debate the challenges of our world intelligently?

FOR THE POLITICALLY CORRECT READERS: Yes, I used the word stupid and if you read on I will use the word dumb. Look them up in the dictionary; they are exactly what I meant. Maybe I should use something else that has the same meaning. How about "Mentally Challenged"? I am sure the American public will sleep well tonight knowing the major decisions guiding their lives are being made by the mentally challenged. This is not a book about making friends. Trust me; the people that will catch the brunt of this book are not your friends. Friends don't take advantage of friends. Enough said.

So if you are going to make stupid statements or stupid decisions, be prepared to defend yourself. This is nothing new. Late Night television, comedians and news channels have a field day when people are stupid. The goal is to empower you to combat the stupidity that is ruining the world. Over time, people will think before they speak, for fear of being shown they aren't as intelligent as they want the world to believe.

Acting as if you don't know something about a particular issue, when you really do, is also a tactic used to hide the truth. Their strategy is to not answer the question and therefore people will not be able to prove anything. It may be an issue where they are the only person in the room who knows the truth:

- How many barrels of oil are leaking out of the well by the hour?
- What is the level of radiation that has been released from the reactor's meltdown?
- Does fracking the earth's crust cause adverse affects (earthquakes)?

These are three important questions that were asked early on during a crisis. Does knowing the truth affect others directly or indirectly, either now or in the future? In one case the truth came out later and was a hundred times worse than people were led to believe. If intelligent people are withholding important information that affects your life, you have to attack their intelligence now and use it to stop them in the future.

So let's get to it. The goal here is still the same; you want to expose the truth. I don't think anyone should fault people if they use harsh tactics to expose the truth about world problems. Obviously, this section is not going to be nice. As I said above, my goal is to make people fell so stupid, so many times, that they finally stop doing it or the world knows they need to find someone else to tell them the truth. If that means attacking people's intelligence, their Alma mater or their professional experience, then so be it. They are in a position of making major decisions that affect people's lives; they should know what they are talking about.

There are three possibilities when you can attack their intelligence:

1. You ask a simple question and they don't answer. You assume they don't know the answer and question them as if they are not intelligent.
2. They intentionally make a stupid statement in order to hide the truth. In this case they are "acting" stupid, so if they want to act that way show the audience it might be the truth.
3. They do not know what they are talking about and therefore the assumption is they are not intelligent enough to hold the position they are in.

It comes down to education, perception and reality. The people making decisions usually have a good education. The perception is they are smart. The reality is what you have to show the world.

Instructions – When They Make A Stupid Statement:

1. Verify and clarify the stupid statement.
   a. Make sure they "own" it. Repeat their statement. Clarify anything that can be misconstrued later on, and then say, "Is that what you know to be true?"
2. Add one or more of the following to show the audience that just because their resume says they are intelligent, doesn't mean they are.
   a. Experience: You have also been in your field for 10 years, correct?
   b. Education: Didn't you graduate Magma Cum Laude and have your MBA?
   c. Current Position: You are the Executive Director of XYZ, correct?
3. Expose the truth.
   a. Use the audience: If the stupid statement is about what "Americans want or believe", you can poll the audience on the spot and prove they are wrong.
   b. Reveal the facts: If they just made a false statement, and you are prepared, show the proof to the audience.
4. Take a hard line.
   a. If you are wrong about that premise, then why should people believe you when you try to tell them anything else?
   b. That shows your understanding of this issue is not correct, so why are you in charge of making decisions that affect others?
   c. Shouldn't we have someone else who understands the job better?
   d. Here's the problem. We have someone who is in charge of making life changing decisions for millions of people and they are making false statements thinking they are right.

Instructions – When They Won't Answer A Simple Question:

1. Verify that they heard and understood your question.
   a. You may not have heard me; I will ask the question again. To avoid confusion, I will write the question for you.

93

2. Prove to the audience that they are refusing to answer the question.
   a. Is there any reason why you are not answering that question?
   b. Do you understand the audience probably knows the answer to that question and may make their own assumptions about your intelligence?

Another option would be to have them tell the audience why their decision is intelligent:

1. If there's an important decision, should it be made intelligently?
2. How is this decision intelligent? Then write down their response and question those answers.

Sometimes statements are made so quickly that the audience doesn't have time to digest them and realize they make no sense or are obviously false. This is where you stop them and repeat the statement in a way that everyone realizes how stupid it really is. Here are a few examples:

- So what you are saying is, people don't want a car that gets 80 mpg, because it would hurt gas stations and the profits to oil companies?
- So what you are saying is, people who lost their life's savings in the stock market don't want the perpetrators prosecuted, they just want to make sure it doesn't happen again. Is that what you are saying?
- So we should pay more taxes, because Americans want to support regime change in the Middle East, is that your point?

Obviously they will be interjecting in between the questions you are asking and it may not go as smoothly as it is written here, but that doesn't mean this won't work? This technique is designed to attack their intelligence and display it to the world; it may or may not bring out the facts. It does expose the truth, which is this person is not smart enough to be in a decision making position.

2. If They Like To Use "I Don't Know"

This is used way too often, so they should be put to the test.

- Do you "not know" because you just don't have the intelligence to figure it out?
- Do you "not know" because you just didn't take the time to find out?
- Is it true you actually do know, but you don't want to tell us?

These are harsh, you can soften them up. They don't have to answer. They will be judged in the court of public opinion, so if the question is worded right, the public will convict them. My thoughts are simple, too many people get away with crimes by stating, "I don't know" and nobody questions them in a way that makes them look like the criminals they are.

3. When They Won't Answer Your Question

There will be situations, when it won't matter how many times you ask the question, they will refuse to give an answer. The reason should be obvious; it is not the information they want to admit to, which means you did a good job with your questions.

What you need to do now is formulate the next question in a way that everyone in the audience knows the answer. When they don't answer, you ask them if they agree that the audience would assume the worst case scenario.

Example:

1. Are you willing to state on camera whether or not an outside audit of the DOD would find their financial practices unsound?
2. They will probably give you a roundabout answer instead of yes or no.
3. You say, "Is it possible for you to answer the question Yes or No?" or, "It's a Yes or No question and I would really appreciate a Yes or No answer."
4. Again they give a roundabout answer.
5. You say, "Since you gave no clear answer to that question, is it safe to assume that the American public will believe there are unsound financial practices in the DOD?"

4. If They Can't Recall What Happened

There will be times when they think they can use the old tactics of "I forgot" and "I don't recall", as a way to not answer any questions. Here's how to approach that:

1. What is your position?
2. Does that position carry a lot of responsibility?
3. Do you think that memory is a prerequisite for an executive director, is that something the Board of Directors would expect from you?

4. You went to college right? Do you think that Harvard produces a lot of graduates who are unable to remember and/or answer simple questions?

5. Do the people who rely on you expect an above average performance or a mediocre performance?

6. How would you rate an executive, in your similar position, who was unable to recall information such as discussed here today? They might say, above average.

7. So what you are saying is, in our business culture today, a person who runs a large corporation and forgets several important facts is considered above average, is that correct?

5. When They Claim They Are On Your Side

Once people realize they will have to answer tough questions that will lead to the truth, they will start to tell partial truths. They will figure out ways to make it look like they are doing what is right so the public will see them as a hero. If they are doing what is right, don't stop them. Everyone is not doing the wrong thing. On the other hand, if you know it is just a public relations stunt, then here are some questions to throw a wrench in their scheme.

- You say you have a team working on that. Can you tell me who they are and what exactly they are working on?
- I see you have a solution. My question is whether or not that is the best solution available? Is there a way to get it done for less taxpayer money?
- I know it sounds like you have done the right thing for the people. So I just have one last question. If this doesn't get fixed, would you agree that the voters shouldn't vote for you in the next election?

6. How And Why To Expose A Hypocrite

There are people who want to tell you what to believe and how you should live. What's interesting is these rules are good for you to follow, but not for some of the people who are telling you. They live by the rule, "Do what I say, not as I do." Sometimes these rules aren't easy to live up to and some of them affect your life in negative ways.

If anyone says you should or shouldn't do something and that is the cause of your life being adversely affected in any way, then you have the right to question them and their beliefs. If it is found out that they said one thing and did another, then someone should expose them to the world as a hypocrite. They used a false belief to get other's to believe it is the right way. If they are a hypocrite that didn't affect anyone's life, then I am not worried about that person. There are too many problems in the world to waste your time exposing something that will have no impact.

There are a several definitions on the Internet for the word hypocrite. The most basic definition I could find is: a person who acts in contradiction to his or her stated beliefs or feelings. The global problem with hypocrites is stating one thing and doing another.

What is the reward for people contradicting what they tell everyone else?

- They can get money from people who think they share the same beliefs.
- They can get people to vote them in to office because the voters believe what the candidate told them.
- They can get things they don't deserve by stating certain beliefs that will get others on their side.
- They can make any statement they want about living a certain lifestyle, benefit from that, and then go out and do what they want anyway, as long as nobody finds out.

Examples of people being a hypocrite for personal gain, while adversely affecting the lives of others:

- A person raises money against gay rights using the Bible as a tool and is found to have discrete homosexual encounters.
- A paid expert concludes that "Red Slime" is safe, but isn't feeding it to their family.
- Declaring alternative energy sources aren't efficient, but they use them in their homes.
- The CDC recommends people to get controversial vaccines for their children and don't vaccinate their own children.
- Alternative medical treatments they use personally and then support legislation that blocks those same treatments.
- A political candidate states they are for abortion and then conveniently say they are against it, because it will mean more votes in certain demographics.
- Making statements that they want to stop illegal immigration, while employing illegal aliens as nannies, maids and yard workers.

This is just another form of lying, but it is hard to prove someone believes something or they don't. A person can say, "There are no reports of people getting ill from eating Red Slime and no, my family hasn't eaten it." They may have told the truth, how do you know? All you want to get out of this section is to prove someone is a hypocrite and show the world their words cannot be trusted. They will lose their power to get what they don't deserve, especially in politics. Just because you prove someone is a hypocrite doesn't mean you will fix anything, but it will get the audience on your side and you can use other techniques to expose the truth and fix what is wrong. The power behind this is that nobody wants to be proven a hypocrite in public.

Want to stop a hypocrite? It just takes basic logic. Your goal is to show the audience that what this person is against is something they do themselves or approve of others doing. As with every truth exposing technique, you need them to make statements by using well crafted questions. You can't just say, "See, I told you, I knew you were going to say that even though you did the same thing last year." That becomes your statement and even though it is hard to deny, the audience did not get the benefit of having them acknowledge it.

Whatever the issue is, you have to ask them what the rule is: How does it work? When is this valid? Before you get in to exposing them, add on the consequences: What should happen to anyone who does or doesn't follow this rule? Is this for everyone? You need them to clarify what it is they think everyone should be doing.

Sequenced questions that can be used:

- What is the issue, problem, etc?
- Is this for everyone or just me, you, women, gender-based, etc? (People make up rules for the current situation – being hypocritical). They're going to say yes, you just need to have them say it in front of the audience.
- Then confirm it, "This is where you stand, right?"
- What should we do with people who did this?
- This isn't a temporary belief right, this is how it has always been?
- So, if anyone ever did this in the past, then they are part of the problem and they should pay the consequences also, right?
- So what you are saying is, you would be willing to uphold this, no matter who it is?

98

Next you would point out how somewhere, either now or in the past, there was an exception with them, their family, their co-workers, their religion, etc. Show them (and the audience) the proof of their hypocrisy and ask them if this is the same thing they are against. Give them a chance to answer and bury themselves. If they keep talking, let them. Most hypocrites will never admit they are being a hypocrite. The objective is to prove it to the audience, have it recorded and then show it to the world.

7. Challenge The Obnoxious

If you ask enough people the right questions, inevitably some of them won't handle themselves gracefully when they realize they are about to be proven a fraud. You may have seen people like this before and they can be obnoxious. Their tactics include cutting people off before they have a chance to be heard, verbally attacking them, and storming off. You probably won't get this person to make statements about the truth, but you can use the opportunity to expose them. This is achieved by asking simple questions that the audience knows the answers to and the person does not answer. Just because they don't answer doesn't mean the truth was not exposed. Sometimes not answering gives the audience enough information to see that someone is lying. Remember the goal is to expose the truth. If the person exposes the truth by not answering, then you were successful. If you were to video this incident, it will become proof and the world can see the true colors of this person.

If you know this is the type of person you will be dealing with, start off with a question that will tie their integrity to their actions and make sure the entire audience hears it. Ask, "When two people are trying to solve a problem and one of them starts to verbally attack the other, what would you call that person?" Let them answer and say, "I agree with you. I don't want to be that kind of person and I am sure this audience would lose all respect for me if I was." Now you have set it up so the audience will lose respect for them if they become obnoxious. You can use different words to get different results such as, the audience would think they were not intelligent or capable of doing the job they currently have.

Below are questions you can use to turn their aggression into proof that they are hiding the truth. For constructing these questions you can use the same lead in and then just add whatever is appropriate at the end. See the example below.

LEAD IN:

Do you think it is true that people are hiding something when they…

1. keep talking over you and don't let you say anything?
2. walk away or change the subject when asked a tough question?
3. become mean, loud and aggressive?
4. don't answer a simple question that the entire audience knows the answer to?

Other ways to deal with an obnoxious situation:

- I know exactly what is going to happen. If you are hiding something from the audience, then sometime during this exchange you will stop answering the questions and will probably get up and leave.
- Am I allowed to ask questions or are you just going to talk over me and make this a one-sided conversation?
- So what you are saying is, we have limited time to discuss how to fix a problem and you choose to talk about something that has no relevance. How is that fair to your audience, who watch because they believe your interviewing skills are worthwhile?

You can come up with other ways to disarm someone who chooses to be obnoxious. Use the tools you have already learned. Ask yourself the question, "What can I ask or say to the most obnoxious person that will prove they are wrong to the audience, whether they answer me or not?" Or, "What can I logically say that will put this person in their place and have the entire audience agree with me?"

Chapter 22: How To Give Them Consequences

1. Put It In Writing

How many times have you heard politicians, government officials or corporate spokespeople say they will do something and then never do it? They can actually go back to the video and prove they didn't say they would do "exactly that." They left themselves wiggle room and they wiggled out of it.

If you are going to take the time to expose the truth, why not take the next step and get them to commit in writing. They will probably say no, but it will look great on a video to prove that person has no integrity later on. Even if they seem like a nice person and smile as they agree with you, that doesn't mean they are going to do anything.

If they are so committed to doing what they say, then why don't they sign off on it? That's right; have them sign a mini statement that outlines exactly what they just said they would do. If they don't sign it, you just ask, "So what you are saying is, you are not sure if you are going to do this, you were just agreeing for the cameras and the people standing here, is that correct?"

2. Anchor Them To The Future

It seems like the people behind the problems aren't always the ones who are delivering the messages. They have lower level employees, no name experts or even government officials come out with an official statement validating their claims or exonerating their actions. If that person (the messenger) is benefitting from their actions, then they should be willing to pay the consequences if they are wrong. A deterrent is to attach their career to the validity of the statements that they make. This means there are consequences if someone does not do their job truthfully. Does any company want employees who lie?

It's what every parent and law enforcement agency does when they want to get to the truth. They intimidate with what the consequences will be if the person doesn't come clean.

It is easy for them to brush aside the truth now, because it appears as if they have no consequences. So give them consequences in front of an audience and on camera.

Ask them questions similar to:

- Do you think the taxpayers should have to put up with government employees who lie to them?
- If later on it is proven that you are wrong, will you willingly resign, because you made a mistake with an important decision, which affected people financially?
- Before we start, if it turns out you are not telling the truth, would you agree that would be grounds for dismissal?

Why should people be allowed to make statements that affect millions of people and not be responsible for what they are saying?

3. What If They Are Wrong

"What if they are wrong" is a useful tool to get the conversation going in the right direction, which should be towards the truth. It doesn't matter if the topic is high gas prices, bombing a foreign country, high health care costs, polluting the environment, policing the earth or why people don't make as much as they could in the stock market. Someone needs to get people to think before they act and this is a simple way.

Try it yourself, "What if you are wrong?" When they say, "I am not wrong." You say, "How do you know?" Now you have opened the door so people can find out what is behind their reasoning. What may happen is this person is not used to being challenged and will probably stop in their tracks, but being a professional they will compose themselves and maybe start quoting some study or so-called expert. This is where you write down everything they say and then use the "So" question technique to make them own those statements. From there you use other questioning techniques to expose the truth.

If they say something like, "I can't tell you what will happen if I am wrong." Then you say, "Do you ever make forecasts within your business?" They say yes. You say, "So you are able to take an uncertainty and look ahead to see how it may turn out, so let's do the same thing."

Guidelines for using "What If They Are Wrong":

1. **CONFIRM THE PROBLEM:** You have to know what is wrong and stick to one issue at a time, don't "bundle" issues together. Ask, "What is the problem?", or maybe you heard a speaker exclaim that the problem is, "Gas prices are too high." And then say, "So what you are saying is, if we had more oil, gas prices would go down, is that correct?"

2. **FIND OUT THEIR REASONING:** You need to know what they are basing their statement on. You can't start pointing out facts that you believe are right. You have to combat what their message is to the public. In the past they could say anything, with the right questions they will have to explain themselves. Once they confirm the problem: "Not enough oil", you would ask, "Why?" That's it, don't add anything else and don't give them your answers. Let them answer. They might say something like, "The recovery in the U.S. has created more demand or the industrialization of Asia has spurred a huge need for oil." Whatever it is just listen and write it down.

3. **CONFIRM THEIR MESSAGE:** When they are all done you ask, "In your professional opinion, would you say that the main reason for the high costs of gas is (repeat whatever they said)?" This will catch them off guard. If they want to give a better reason, let them. Once they confirm their message they are locked in. If later on they have to admit they are wrong, they cannot go back and say, "Well, that isn't the main problem." If they do, you just say, "That's odd, I thought you confirmed to this audience that it was the main problem, were you wrong when you said that?"

4. **QUESTION THE VALIDITY:** Once they are done you ask, "What if that is wrong?" You can add to or change this as the situation demands. They won't want to answer this question anyway, so pile on with the next question: "Hasn't oil consumption dropped dramatically since 2007?", or "In 2006 didn't Brazil have the largest oil discovery within the last 30 years? They're pumping oil now, how come oil prices didn't go down?"

Chapter 23: How To Prove The Point

1. Bring Up Past History

You can plan head to use this technique or it can be used spontaneously if you have a smart phone and a data plan. Whenever the person you are talking with resorts to selective memory about what they said or did in the past, you present the past proof to the audience. The goal is to clarify the lie first (make sure there is no misunderstanding) and then have them confirm it.

Instructions:

1. Don't make a statement claiming you know of a time when they said or did something.
2. Clarify every part of the lie so they cannot use a "technicality" to defend themselves later.
3. Ask them a question to confirm, "Are you sure this hasn't happened before?" You can even add a "so" question for more effect. "So what you are saying is, you have never seen anything like this before?"
4. Now, after they have confirmed the lie, this is when you provide the facts (articles, statements, etc.) to them and the audience, proving they did it in the past.

2. Define And Clarify Their Words

Make them give a definition for their point, issue or objection. People string several words together creating messages as if they have some kind of universal meaning. The truth is they have an ambiguous meaning and therefore cannot be tied to any facts. Whenever you hear someone say something that doesn't appear to be defined just ask them, "What exactly do you mean by...?" Let them answer and write it down.

Sometimes the only problem is the wrong definition of a word. This doesn't mean they are lying, they just don't know what the word means. You can say, "Maybe each of our definitions are different, that is why we are not on the same page." On the other hand, it may be beneficial for you to define it for them and point out the facts. If they give a definition that is wrong, then look it up and show them they are wrong. If they try to say that is not what they meant, your reply would be, "So what you are saying is, you have created new definitions for words that everyone else already understands?"

Below are definitions that should be used when dealing with people who have found ways to get things they do not deserve.

Here's the definition of "illegal":

1. Forbidden by law; unlawful; illicit.
2. Unauthorized or prohibited by a code of official or accepted rules.

The definition for "fair" taken from two different sources:

1. Consistent with rules, logic, or ethics: a fair tactic.
2. In a proper or legal manner: playing fair.

1. Marked by impartiality and honesty: free from self-interest, prejudice, or favoritism.
2. Conforming with the established rules: allowed: consonant with merit or importance: due.
3. Open to legitimate pursuit, attack, or ridicule.

You can use these definitions and create questions that will get to the truth and prove that what they have done is unfair and can be construed as illegal.

3. Use Visual Aids

Have you ever watched an interview where the host asks a question and the guest gives an answer that has absolutely nothing to do with the question that was asked? You sit there thinking, "Did that person hear the same question I did?" If you have never noticed this, just watch any political debate on television. It is as if they have one message and they are going to tell that message whether it is relevant or not. Saturday Night Live had a field day spoofing this during the 2008 presidential elections. I have also seen this tactic used during Congressional hearings, when the truth should be absolutely mandatory.

How do they get away without answering the question in a government hearing? This should be a fairly simple fix. When someone asks a specific question, make sure that question is answered. Unfortunately the moderator just moves on and accepts the non-answer. I have an idea on how to fix this and put the person to the test. It is another simple solution. It has to do with visually showing the truth to everyone.

This will be one of the greatest tools you will ever have when exposing the truth. It works for the simple reason there is no way the question, answer, or facts can be misconstrued when they are written out and displayed for everyone to see. You can use a dry erase board, a video display connected to a computer, an overhead projector, large seminar flip pad, poster pad and even notebook paper. It is effective because nobody wants to see their stupidity up in lights. The goal is not to fight with the person, claiming you are right and giving all of your reasons. The goal is to get them to show the world what they are stating. Try this one at home and see how powerful it is to write down exactly what someone claims to be the truth, when you know it isn't. Please read Chapter 61: "Tact: Love, Family and Friends", before attempting this experiment.

When you put something on paper (big) it makes whatever the point is amplified. So if you are right it just increases the belief. If you are wrong, it easier for people to see that it doesn't make sense or it is even a lie. The other bonus is, once their words are on paper, it is hard to take them back.

When someone totally avoids answering a question, you can assume they didn't understand it, that is one option. Write that question down on the top half of the poster board and show it to the person who didn't answer it. Say, "Do you mind if I ask this question again?" They may look at you funny, but they will still need to answer. Underneath the question write the person's name and put the word "says" after that. When that person starts giving their rehearsed answer you write it under the question and start after the words "says". This way it shows that this person said this answer, to this question and now everyone can see it. The next question you ask is, "So what you are saying is, your answer to [REPEAT THE QUESTION] is [REPEAT THEIR ANSWER], is this correct?"

It may take a few times of doing this, but after awhile, people will start answering the questions you ask them. Once someone, who portrays being intelligent, starts seeing their name attached to stupid answers, I am sure the dynamic of this meeting will change. This is more powerful if you have an audience, because everyone else can now verify that this person is sidestepping the issues.

This is a good technique to use when someone thinks you are out of line for asking a certain question. Write the question down and then ask them why. Write their answer down. There is a good chance that their answer is not a valid reason and it can be easily shown to an audience for validation. If you want to add some heat to the fire, turn to the audience, show them the poster and ask, "Are you satisfied with their answer?"

This technique will also help when there are people in the audience who were fooled by previous messages. When they see the person, they used to believe, faltering and it is on paper, it is hard for them to keep believing. There is the possibility that the person decides to change their mind once they see what they really said. Just say, "So what you are saying is, when the truth becomes evident people have the right to change their minds?" By doing this you are really telling the audience it is okay to change your mind now that you see the truth.

Chapter 24: How To Leverage The Audience

1. Enlist The Audience

If you craft your questions in a way that everyone knows the answer, then you can use the audience to assist. There will be times when the person you are asking questions to will not want to answer, even though the answer is obvious. The reason is simple, it will prove they are wrong or at least get the conversation going in that direction. If they don't want to answer, that is fine. There will be plenty of people in the audience who can't wait to speak up. Give the person a chance to answer. If they just sit there quietly or say they can't answer, confirm that with them. "So what you are saying is, you don't know the answer to that question?" Or, you can say, "You realize by not answering, the audience is assuming you don't know the answer?" Then you look to the audience and ask, "Who would like to help this person and answer the question for them?"

Here is something I would like to see done on a televised political roundtable, when they have political candidates as guests. When there are questions that are easy to answer, but are avoided by the guests, the moderator then introduces a few sixth graders who are there to answer these "tough" questions. Every time a guest doesn't want to answer a simple question, call up the sixth grade team and ask them the question. Let the audience see just how simple it is and how ludicrous getting to the truth has become.

2. Use The "Outsider" To Make A Point

This can work for the person you are having the conversation with or an audience member who wants to speak up and is obviously on the wrong side. They are against you for the sake of being against you, similar to what happens in everyday life anyway. The difference is, in your normal life, you usually aren't recording the event in front of an audience, with the plan of putting it on the Internet. It's amazing how people think twice when they know there may be consequences to their actions, even if that consequence is giving everyone access to a video that shows just how dumb they were acting. So when you have someone who is against you for no real reason, point them out.

Example:

You ask a question, "How many people would like to have an extra $300 per month in their pocket?" Either the person you are questioning or an audience member speaks up and says no. Ask them why and let them answer. Even though the answer probably won't make any sense, don't fight them. Instead look at the rest of the audience and say, "What if this was the only person who could make this decision for you? How many of you would give this person that power?"

The answer should be obvious. Why would a large group of people allow one person to make decisions for them, especially when that decision will have an adverse financial effect? In reality, there usually is another element to this scenario. Look at the audience and say, "I forgot one more detail, this person also gets $3000 if he says no to your $300. Now, if you knew all these facts would you want that person in that position?" See what the audience thinks about those questions. You were now able to turn an interruption into an example of how people choose to make bad decisions that affect other people. In other words, how someone found a way to get something they did not deserve, in this case $3000.

3. Reinforce Other People's Questions

You can use the audience even if you are part of the audience. When there is an open forum where people get turns asking questions, each person usually only gets one question. If that is a "truth exposing" question the speaker might brush it off and move on to the next. What if there are others in the audience who are thinking just like you. You have an important universal question that affects everyone there. The next person who gets to ask a question does so as if "they" had asked the first question. If the first question (from the other questioner) wasn't answered, then they will just repeat it adding, "Can you please answer that, because it is important to me." If the first question was answered, then move on to the next question (Problem, Solution or Commitment). This way, even though each person only gets one question at a time, as a group they can sequence questions together to expose the truth.

If the audience can get in sync, it would be an ambush of truth exposing questions. What is the person going to do, not answer anyone's question? Even if that is what they do, the damage will be done. People aren't stupid and they know when someone is hiding the truth. Once the video goes

109

up on social media, the rest of the world can also see how this person is hiding something. That video would also be a great learning tool for others to execute "ambush questioning". If someone is going to speak in public, then they better be ready to tell the truth and this is just another way to make it happen.

Chapter 25: How To Shine When They Attack

1. Refocus The Conversation

Unfortunately, people aren't going to like you for exposing the truth. That's okay, because you probably won't like them. There may be times when you feel out of your league, the person you are up against has money and power. The only attribute they are missing is the truth and that makes them a liar, which means you are much better than they are. Remember why you are there. It is probably because something is wrong and you are trying to expose the truth and have it fixed. Is that a reason for someone to berate you?

So what do you do when someone starts attacking you personally? They belittle your education, financial status, experience, your past, your beliefs, where you live and who you associate with. None of which have anything to do with the issue at hand. You can get in an argument with the person and try to defend yourself or you can refocus the conversation and get the audience on your side.

Use the following technique to refocus someone who is attacking you. It has three parts. The first one declares that you can fix or prove something. The second part involves the audience with the benefits. The third part puts the attacker on the spot, but now they aren't just facing you, they have to explain themselves to the audience.

1. If I can prove (fill in your scenario) and...
2. it is good for the audience (point out how it will help)...
3. then please tell them why you are trying to stop it.

Completed examples:

- If I could prove there is a way to get 80 mpg and everyone could benefit, will you please tell the audience why you are trying to stop that.
- If I could prove there is a university in California that runs its vehicles on hydrogen, that is extracted from water, using solar panels and I had a plan for anyone to get this free fuel source, why would you stop that?

111

Here are other questions you can use:

- Are you upset with me because I want to know the truth?
- Why would you attack me if all I am trying to do is find the truth?
- Is it too much to ask you to do what is right?
- I don't get it. What part of fixing this problem are you against?
- I understand. It is hard to believe something like this is done by people who are supposed to be protecting us, but all I am saying is let me prove it. If you can't give me 5 minutes, then the obvious assumption is you don't want the truth. So please tell this audience why you don't want to solve their problems in the next 5 minutes.
- Yes, you are wrong and you may have the money and the power to quiet a nobody like me, but why are you ruining the lives of people because they ask for the truth?
- If I can prove it to you, will you agree or is your plan to just disagree with whatever I say?
- Why would you want to win an argument, if by winning your family loses?
- Do you think people should be mad at the person who exposes the truth or the person that lied to them?

A 1-2 punch to use at the beginning of the discussion:

- If someone has proof that they were taken advantage of, do they deserve to be personally attacked if they speak up?
- So if I know the truth about something you are not going to attack me, right?

If you are being attacked because you don't know something, but you could quickly verify it on your smart phone, then say, "All I am trying to do is solve a problem. If I can get that information, how does knowing it now or in 5 minutes change anything?"

If they attack you by making a claim that can't be proven, make sure the audience understands they could be lying:

- Has there ever been a time when someone's source said something that wasn't true?
- Has there ever been a time when someone lied under oath?
- So why should you assume this audience will believe you when you say you have a source and you won't tell them who or what it is?

2. What To Do About Being Labeled

Ever find yourself wanting to speak up and don't, because you have seen people say something and then they were labeled un-American, un-patriotic, anti-capitalist, anti-family, unfit parent, or you hear some pundit crying, "Class Warfare". Does it seem ironic how that labeling scheme protects some of the largest industries in the country, which include finance, energy, defense contracting and pharmaceuticals?

It happens when someone tries to expose the truth behind messages that always seem to have a huge price tag on them.

- We have to pay executives multi-million dollar bonuses or they will go somewhere else.
- We have to invade that country or they will kill us here at home.
- We have to bail out Wall Street or the whole financial system will collapse.
- We have to spend billions to export democracy to other countries.
- We have to drill for more oil, America is addicted.
- We have to drill for more oil domestically for our national security.
- We have to keep taxes low for the rich, they create the jobs.

The "labeling" shield has been built and it is designed to divert the public's attention from the real issue. The challenge is to get past the shield so you can get to the truth. If labels work against you, is it possible that they can work for you? On a tough playing field you have to play tough. Use their own playbook against them and go on offense before they put you on defense. The next time you are on a tough playing field, where you know they will use labels, get the jump on them and adapt one of the examples below.

- I am proud of our capitalistic system and it is important to protect it so every citizen has a chance for their American Dream. That is why I need to ask some questions.
- As a patriotic American, if I knew someone was undermining people's pursuit of happiness, should I defend that right?
- If you didn't stand up for your country could you be labeled a traitor, coward or communist?
- Strong families are the core of our society and we need to protect that at all costs. I believe there is a crisis that is attacking American families and I have a few questions.

- If you loved America would you ruin its environment, over medicate its people, embezzle their money, feed their children subpar food and say it's okay to put toxins in their bodies? If someone was doing this wouldn't they be considered a threat to our society?
- This is our country and we should protect it, whether the threats come from outside or from within. Would you agree with that statement?
- Is it un-American to stop those who are truly ruining America?
- I know your company is trying to find oil for our country so we don't have to import it and that is why you will appreciate the questions I will be asking as a patriotic American.
- As a citizen, do I have the right to question my government?

If they already put a label on you, then you will need to prove it is wrong. Below is an example that shows how you can create a few questions that put your opponent to the test.

- So what you are saying is, I want the terrorist to win, is that exactly what you want people to believe? If they said it, they have to answer yes.
- So if I can prove that is wrong, I guess that would make you a liar, right? It doesn't matter if you prove it there or later on. As long as you have the video, you can attach the proof later and show the world they are a liar.

See how easy it easy to turn those labels around? By labeling yourself first it will be hard for someone to re-label you. You can even put the labels back on them. If you are pretty sure they will question your patriotism, then beat them to the punch. What would happen if you brought a short video and affidavit proving that while connected to a polygraph, you have answered the following questions?

1. Do you love your country?
2. Do you hate capitalism?
3. Do you want to see the terrorists win?
4. Do you hate people that are ruining our country?
5. Do you have solutions that can fix our country now if people would listen?

Make it short and sweet. Change the questions to reflect whatever you think their labels of you will be. You want to see a video go viral, pull that one off in front of a Congressional hearing.

3. Bad Lawyers – Good Lawyers

One of the greatest travesties is how lawyers are used to diminish the rights of people to expose the truth by suing them, whether it is warranted or not. This is why you see news reports of obvious crimes and you always here "allegedly". Example, "This clear video of this man shooting this other man point blank and then looking up at the camera is still under investigation. The alleged shooter was captured last night." This has to be done to eliminate the possibility of a lawsuit.

One way to eliminate a lawsuit is to have the other person admit to the truth. If they insist on suing, it may be a frivolous lawsuit and they can be countersued for damages. The other problem, for companies trying to hide the truth through lawsuits, is if all you are doing is asking a question, how can you be at fault? I would love to see the judge who rules on the side of the wrongdoer and states the reason you are at fault was because you asked great questions.

What if a group of lawyers, who are fed up with this system, decided to help out the people who were exposing the truth? What if the people exposing the truth got together with those lawyers and started suing the other lawyers, for their participation in "suppressing the truth"?

Another strategy would be to let the world know that a certain person or company is trying to sue you for telling the truth. Maybe millions of people will stop using their products. I saw this happen on network television not too long ago. It was a doctor show and he told the audience and the world that he had lawsuit issues from a major organization because he was exposing the truth. He also said he was not going to stop exposing the truth. He is a true hero of the people, in my opinion.

4. Admit When You Are Wrong

Being wrong is something I find hard to swallow. Who likes being wrong? Guess what, we are all wrong sometimes during our lives. I would like to meet the person who was never wrong. So this means, sometimes during your questioning, you may find your initial premise was wrong. What do you do?

If you make a false statement or blame someone for something they didn't do, you have to do the right thing. You gather your courage, raise your integrity, lower your pride and admit you were wrong. Once you admit you are wrong the debate is over, now you can move on. One of the golden rules of admitting defeat is to do it quickly. Don't wait one day, because that day turns into a week, which turns into a year, and guess what, you are still wrong a year later.

I have been wrong a lot of times and I don't like it, but wrong is wrong. What can I do, change the laws of nature, go back into the past and change an event? I just look them in the eye and say, "You know what, I was wrong and you were right." That is all you need to say. Don't follow it up with any excuses of how you were almost right. I promise you will gain more respect if you do it this way. You might even be surprised how the other person comes around to your defense, which is human nature.

My suggestion is to avoid this scenario altogether. If you stick with asking questions and not making statements, there's a good chance you won't falsely accuse anyone. All you have to do is take the approach of trying to expose the truth, right or wrong. Don't get over zealous without having all of the facts. You might be feeling bold, you might think you are helping someone else, but make sure you are on the right side.

Don't forget, this works both ways. If the person you are talking with comes around and says, "Hey, you know what, that sounds right. I will fix it." Do not gloat and do not be a good winner. You can soak in the victory later, but for now you have succeeded in fixing a problem because you were able to expose the truth in a logical way. Sometimes all someone needs is to see the situation clearly.

PART 5:

ADDITIONAL AMMUNITION

What You Will Learn

There will be questions that will need to be physically proven. There will be times when someone needs to be shown how, and there will be times when you need to make it personal. If you had other problem solving tools at your disposal why wouldn't you use them?

Our world is full of products, techniques and processes that have advanced over time because someone decided to do it a better way. In some cases, the new ideas were not initially accepted, even though they made sense and no one could prove them wrong. The same scenario is going to happen with problem solving and exposing the truth. At first people will give excuses as to why it cannot be done, but once they are shown the facts, it will make sense. Every technique described in this section is already being employed. There is no need for any new technology.

Chapter 26: Transparent Studies, Inquiries and Research
- When something needs to be tested or verified it should be done so anyone can watch it happening live and verify the results if they want to.
- People want to know truth and have proven they will make the commitment to watch and understand.
- Companies and governments have presented falsified results for the main purpose of suppressing the truth.
- Know the objections and learn how to counteract them.

Chapter 27: Deliver A Plan They Cannot Deny
- When trying to fix a problem, it would be beneficial to have a plan in hand.
- It is hard for anyone to deny a solution, when they were delivered a plan and that delivery was videotaped for the Internet.
- Plans can be in-depth or just a few short lines, adding a note stating there are professional Project Managers who can fill in the details.

Chapter 28: Reward And Replace
- Offer information about multi-million or billion dollar corruption schemes and receive a cash reward.
- Everyone should be held to the standards of their position, whether it is paid from tax dollars or company revenues.
- If people aren't doing the job they are paid for, then they should be replaced.

Chapter 29: A Workforce For Good
- There are intelligent and capable people who would be willing to donate their time to prove, disprove, do research, crunch numbers, etc., if it meant finally getting the truth.
- Lawyers take cases "pro bono", which means "for the public good." What if these lawyers could get together with people who are willing to do what it takes to fix the world?

Chapter 30: Polygraphs – Do They Work
- Law enforcement agencies around the world use polygraph tests.
- If there is any doubt to the validity of polygraph tests, then do a test and let the entire world watch. If they are not reliable then let's stop using them. If they are, it is the ultimate tool for exposing the truth.

Chapter 31: Make It Personal – They Do
- Companies and the government use sweet old grandmothers, disabled veterans, wholesome families, and small children, in order to emotionally sway the public to believe their message.
- Use the techniques in this book and the same "emotional" tactics they use to impact the audience and expose the truth.
- If shaming a person in to doing the right thing works, then what is wrong with that?

Chapter 32: Record It For The History Books
- People act differently when they know they are being recorded.
- Video is the proof that people are able to believe, especially when they have no clue who you are.
- Videotape reporters who are videotaping you, just to keep them honest.

Chapter 33: Globalize The Truth
- Social media is shaping and changing the world by giving a voice to anyone who has access to the Internet.
- Use social media to pressure decision makers to answer the right questions.
- Always upload your video proof to the Internet as soon as possible.

This is the final part of the "Problem Solving Process".

Problem Solving Process - PART: 5

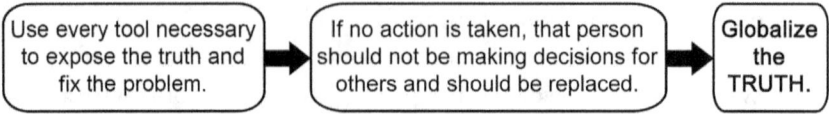

Use every tool necessary to expose the truth and fix the problem. ➡ If no action is taken, that person should not be making decisions for others and should be replaced. ➡ Globalize the TRUTH.

If you believe people will resist you, for suggesting these techniques, you can ask simple questions that will show there aren't any excuses when it comes to fixing the world.

1. If we had a problem that could be solved, would you want to fix it?
2. If this problem drastically affected millions of people would you consider it to be critical?
3. If there was a solution to a critical problem, can you think of any reason why we shouldn't use all the tools at our disposal to solve that problem?

I know people will think these ideas sound nice, but they will never happen. Why not? Is there anything logically incorrect about them? None of them are truly original ideas, they are all being used in some form or fashion right now.

There are problems with solutions that aren't being used, because people have found ways to get things they didn't earn or deserve. How do you fix this? You expose the truth and show it to the world. Why does it matter how you get to the truth, as long as it is legal? You need to use every tool available, because it is just that important.

Chapter 26: Transparent Studies, Inquiries And Research

This has already been done. There is a group of competent people who go out and perform experiments to prove or disprove certain "questionable" theories. The results are then shown on television. It is called "Myth Busters". By the way, go Google the episode about using hydrogen as a fuel for automobiles, even though it is shown on television, people are unaware of this fact. Here's the big question: "Were any taxpayer dollars used to produce the TV show Myth Busters?"

There is another television show that exposes the truth about diabetes, heart disease, the food pyramid and pharmaceutical companies. For years they keep proven conventional wisdom wrong and millions of people get to watch their success from their own living room. It is called "The Biggest Loser". Thankfully the trend is catching on and the truth "flood gates" are starting to open with shows like Dr. Oz and The Doctors, who are courageous enough to tell the truth even in the face of corporate pressures. I personally applaud anyone who will do this. It's an odd state of our country when our new heroes are people who tell the truth. See how powerful the truth can be.

Over the Internet people can watch the Mars Rover Being built by NASA. Universities offer distance learning and there are several medical shows that live stream complete surgeries. There are legal battles in live courtrooms and government inquiries that are broadcasted for days at a time. So it is obviously not that hard. Let's just do it for the big questions, let's answer them once and for all and find out if something is true or false.

People watch reality TV. Let's start a reality show called "Fix The world". If the government spends ANY money (which means taxpayer dollars), on ANY study, it should be streamed over the Internet, so anyone of the financial contributors (taxpayers) can make sure their money is being spent wisely and no results are being falsified. If a research facility refuses, find another one. I understand the government pays well; it shouldn't be too hard to find someone who wants that money.

So if the taxpayers are funding these studies, don't they have the right to see how they are going and what the conclusions are? Why do they have to get the results second hand after the data has been manipulated to prove

121

someone's point? Just give us the facts and most of the time we will be able to make up my own minds. One of the first responses from people will be, "Sounds great, but it will never happen." Okay, that's their belief. But I have a question, "If it doesn't cost a dime would you mind if someone tried?"

Why Is Transparency Necessary

Industries are forever conducting experiments and testing products, doing studies and releasing the results to the public. These results then sway how we feel about products, medicine, health, banking, marriage, and are designed to make us buy, vote, do nothing, etc. The problem is when there is a conflict of interest. Some of these studies are being paid for by the entity that wants a specific result and the company conducting the testing doesn't want to lose a good paying client, so they deliver. People know this is happening.

Here's a great question for the people who don't want transparency, "Has there ever been, even once, a firm that paid an outside testing facility for a study and when it came back negative against the product the company did not use those results?" Sadly, any American reading this statement would say, "Yes, why would they use the results if they were bad, who would buy their product?" EXACTLY! What if test results showed it was a dangerous product that could even cause death, would you like to know that information before you made a purchase?

Do companies and governments manipulate data or not, I think you can answer that question, but I have the solution from here on out. Do the tests so no one can manipulate the results. How do you do that? You put millions of eyes in the labs 24/7, watching every step of the process and the results. If there is a product that does what it claims then this will be a windfall in sales for that company. If they are trying to hide the negative results, then this will be a windfall for consumers who could have wasted their money and maybe even died. So it is a win-win for good companies and the consumers who buy their products.

Why do we need this transparency? Try these questions on for size:

- Has there ever been a study and the true results were never reported to the public?
- Shouldn't the people who are paying have the choice to see what their money is being used for?

122

- This is a simple way to stop the ambiguity and conspiracy theories that go along with official and non-official research, tests and study results. Just show the obtainment of the proof and nobody will dispute it.
- There, a simple way to prove your research and the technology is readily available and extremely inexpensive. The PR Firm savings alone will pay for this one.
- If had a choice, do you think people would prefer to have the option of seeing the tests conducted or just trust the results from the team performing the tests?

How about studies that have ridiculous conclusions, some of which are just common sense:

- Study finds that eating donuts everyday could add to your fat content.
- Study finds that fish caught in polluted waters could result in health hazards to humans who eat it.
- Study finds that dieters who snack in between meals lose less weight than dieters who don't. Really, you had to perform a study for this?

Why do we waste money on these studies when we are in an economic crisis? If you are one of the researchers proving the obvious, have fun, but don't use taxpayer funding to do it. Start using your own money; I am sure that would slow your progress on the next incredible study, "Whether or not lighting yourself on fire can cause severe burns." If you are doing it to cherry pick data and prove that "fried butter" is actually good for me, I have one thing to say... shut up! I am so tired of inept people selling their souls to anyone who wants them to falsify data and sway consumers. Is that the best you can do with your life? You are a cog in the machine that takes advantage of consumers, way to go. I bet your kids are proud of you. Do they say things like, "I love my daddy, he is the man who provided the data that showed cigarette smoking does not cause cancer, he kept people smoking for decades, he's my hero"?

Why don't we find out once and for all the definitive answer to issues that are strangling our economy, damaging our earth and killing its people? There are big consequences at stake. Why wouldn't any sane human being want to save the economy, our planet and its people? Who could say no and why? Actually, thousands of people will say no and they will have their money machines out there explaining all the reasons why. Therefore, I have written the objections they may have, along with questions that can be asked to overcome them.

123

Objection 1: We Won't Be Able To Facilitate It

- There is no way we can do this. So what you are saying is, if there was a way to do this you would be on board?
- Who's going to put those cameras in? If we could find people to install the cameras you would accept this idea? If I could show you a vendor that sells Internet cameras so inexpensively that you could do the entire facility for just a few thousand dollars, would you agree that is a viable solution?
- Who is honest enough to work in a facility where they are on camera every minute? If we could find honest people who are willing to work on camera, then you would agree that would make it possible? Wouldn't you agree that our country already has workers in surveillance positions, such as bankers and casino workers?

Objection 2: It Will Cost Too Much

- The costs to run a facility would be tremendous and we shouldn't burden the taxpayers any more than they already are. So what you are saying is, if we could create a transparent testing facility that had a negligible cost to it then you would be onboard?

Projects cost a lot when the government pays for them, it seems like they never negotiate and get a good deal for the taxpayers. Why is that? Whenever the cost issue comes up the real reason is they just don't want to do it the right way. There is no doubt in my mind if push came to shove and you had to ask qualified people to donate their time to do the research and experiments, they would do it. The motivation would be the "possibility" of the truth coming out. Even if someone wanted to be a capitalist and make money, that is fine with me; as long as it doesn't come from taxpayer dollars. If they want to create a reality show and make money proving right or wrong, why would anyone care.

Objection 3: Will They Agree To Testing Certain Products

1. If I showed you a product people use every day and tell you it has been proven in studies to cause major diseases, would you believe me? Probably not.
2. I agree, how do we know the tests were done right or maybe there is some other pertinent data we weren't told about?

3. What if I told this to families and said it affects small children and could be the cause of major medical challenges. Do you think those parents would want to find out the truth? Yes.

4. So if you were able to give those parents the truth can you think of any reason why you wouldn't?

5. Great, let's just redo the study/experiment using a transparent laboratory so all of those parents can watch the results as they happen. Would you agree that more people will believe the results if they see it happening themselves?

6. Can you think of any reason why someone would want to hide that process from those families?

Objection 4: We Have Patented Processes And Secret Data

If we let this information out to the public it could inhibit our business model. This is one of the arguments used during a Congressional hearing following the downturn of the mortgage and banking industry.

Investigators and the world wanted to find out what really happened. One of first steps of an investigation is to get all of the facts: data, testimony, processes, etc. In this case the companies didn't have to comply completely because of patented or secret information. While I am watching the hearing, I think to myself, "What a ridiculous argument, there are literally thousands of trade secrets; someone had to learn about them in order to validate them as a trade secret." As I am waiting to hear the questioner pounce on this ludicrous premise, all of a sudden they are on to the next question and I could feel my stomach getting queasy thinking, "Wow, that's it?"

So I thought about it. Is this such a tough dilemma that even a Congressional hearing is legally blocked from getting to the truth? Probably not, but that is how it played it out. Then I came up with some simple, common sense questions that would have produced the truth. If they claim patents or proprietary information as a reason why they cannot present it for evidence, then here is what the following dialogue should be:

- So you have information that you do not want anyone to see, correct? YES

- Because you don't want to adversely affect your business/profits, correct? YES

- Has anyone ever seen this information? YES - Company officials and the U.S. Patent Office.

- How do you protect your company from them? THEY SIGN CONFIDENTIALITY AGREEMENTS.
- Okay, so what you are saying is, if we have a few outside investigators sign confidentiality agreements, then you would be protected – as you are now. Isn't that correct?

This is where the whole room gasps and then holds their breath waiting for the answer. The answer is obvious and when they try to wiggle out of it, pile on a few more questions:

- How about I personally sign a confidentiality agreement also, I understand how important business secrets are and you don't have a problem trusting me... do you?
- You understand we are having this Congressional hearing because the public is outraged, wouldn't it be better to show them you have nothing to hide and no wrong doing took place?
- If you were guaranteed the same protections you have now, even in a transparent study, then wouldn't you agree that objection would be eliminated?

If it is easy to facilitate, why shouldn't it be transparent? Is someone trying to hide something? If the public wants this to happen, then they might slow down the process by trying to form a commission and get to it later, why? Make a phone call and talk to the person in charge now. We stream everything else across the Internet, why don't we stream the truth and give citizens the opportunity to make their own informed decisions.

Chapter 27: Deliver A Plan They Cannot Deny

I believe there is one missing element that reduces the success rate for people who try to fix a major problem. Most people get caught up with what the problem is. Rarely do you see people offer a solution. Better yet, they should make someone admit there is a problem, ask them if a solution could solve it and then offer them the solution. That solution should be in the form of a step-by-step plan on how that particular problem can be fixed. Presenting a plan is not mandatory to be successful in fixing major problems, but I would highly recommend having one if you can.

If you don't have a plan, an official can use that as a reason to not do anything. They can say they are putting together a plan now, which may never get done. If you were able to give them a plan, that excuse is eliminated. The advantage is that everyone now knows you gave them the plan, so make sure everyone else can get a copy of that plan. Now everyone knows there is a solution, everyone knows that the person who makes decisions now has that solution in their possession and everyone can see that the plan makes total sense. Next, the people will want to know when that plan is going into action.

The same way people have researched and written about the problems of the world, some people have also created plans to fix those problems. All it would take is a little Internet research to see if a viable plan is available. You might find a plan that needs reworking, don't discount anything. Sometimes you might have to put the plans together yourself. This is where understanding the problem and being able to do your homework will pay off.

Obviously, the more detailed the plans the better, but that doesn't mean simple plans cannot work. You could present a simple plan and then add the following sentence to it: "I know this plan doesn't have all of the details, but those details are just logistics and if your team can't figure them out, I know we can find someone who can." You could also find people, like yourself, who could assist you. There are people who plan, organize, secure and manage resources to achieve specific goals, they are called Project Managers.

Project Management is defined as a temporary endeavor with a defined beginning and end. The project normally has time and funding constraints to meet unique goals and objectives. The project manager's objective is to complete these goals within the scope, time and budget, while aspiring to optimize the use of resources. There are project managers who can take on many of the issues talked about in this book and be more efficient than most government agencies. For any of the Project Managers reading this and anyone else who believes they can put together a common sense step-by-step plan, I challenge you to go through the issues in this book, or choose your own, create a plan that solves the problem and then deliver it to the right person at the right time, in front of an audience.

TIP FOR OCCUPIERS: Create a plan to fix whatever it is you are protesting and get it into the hands of everyone that is there. There has to be at least one project manager in the crowd willing to offer their services. Make it viable and don't forget, you have to be right.

*Details on creating and delivering plans are discussed in Chapter 37.

Chapter 28: Reward And Replace

Why do they offer cash rewards to find people who are accused of murder, bank robbery and other crimes, but don't offer cash rewards for people who commit fraud, are involved in corruption or commit other government and corporate crimes? Rewards can be offered to people who supply information that leads to the arrest and conviction of people who have found ways to get things they don't deserve criminally. You could also offer cash rewards to people who are willing to leak information, proving that someone is doing something wrong that needs to be stopped.

Think about all of the industries you could offer these rewards to:

- Insurance
- Energy
- Banking
- Investments
- Government
- Defense Contracting
- Pharmaceutical Companies

Of course this list would encompass much more. It would be like having people on the inside, policing for the protection of the general public. You may say, "Why do we have to do that, we already have protection agencies?" I would say you are absolutely right, we need to offer these cash rewards to people who work in all of those protection agencies also, because something just isn't right.

People offer information when they witness criminal activities happening in their company. I am wondering if they would be more motivated if there was a cash reward. What if they could offer information about multi-million or billion dollar corruption schemes? Could we offer cash rewards on a sliding scale? Maybe they get a percentage of what was recovered. That way no one has to put up the cash and the money they received is "found money" anyway, since we wouldn't have it if that person didn't come forward with the information.

Questions for the naysayers:

- If we could stop a small portion of the corruption in our country would that be worth it?

- If we could have people more conscientious about being caught for fraud would that limit the criminal activity?
- If we could add another layer of surveillance to combat fraud and corruption would that be good?
- If we could do all this without hiring one new person or costing the taxpayer's one extra dollar, can you give me any reason why it shouldn't be done?

Examples of when this could have paid off for the general public:

- Mortgage companies using criminal practices.
- Investment brokers taking unnecessary risks.
- Federal and local governments engaging in "Pay to Play".
- The United States government spying on its own citizens.
- Wall Street insider trading.

All of the problems above are policed by U.S. Protection agencies. So why aren't these problems being stopped before they happen? I am not sure exactly how the details would work or maybe it is already being done in some cases. Either way, I don't see any harm in having more people motivated to look after the best interests of all citizens. When the people are caught, then they should be replaced and face criminal prosecution if the situation warrants it.

We need to get protection agencies back to doing the jobs they are paid for. These positions are paid fairly well through taxpayer dollars. I think we could find plenty of qualified applicants, especially with the current job market, who would want those jobs. Who wants to be part of running a country honestly and by the law, without being influenced by outside sources?

- If anyone has a job in a U.S. Protection Agency, is it too much to expect them to do the job they are getting paid for?
- If there is anyone in these agencies who is not doing their job, is it too much to expect them to get retrained or be replaced?
- Is it too much to ask for honesty and integrity from the people who are entrusted with protecting you and your family?

How do you question someone's job performance if you don't know what it is they are supposed to be doing? That information has to be available somewhere, just find the job title and search for the job description. As a public agency, that information should be readily available to anyone. I said it earlier in this book and I will say it again, these statements do not pertain to all the agency employees who do their job with integrity and respect. All I am saying is, we need more people like that if we want to fix the world.

I wonder what will happen when regulators realize their livelihoods are on the line if they decide to be on the wrong side of an issue. Let's not forget about the officials whose job it is to watch these regulatory agencies or to investigate them. Maybe a slap on the wrist will no longer be acceptable for wrongdoers. Maybe a campaign contribution and a look the other way won't be worth the risk.

This also goes for members of government committees, whose job is to make important decisions for the public. If this small group makes a decision that is deemed wrong by a major majority of the public, then they are not doing what the public wants. Who gives them the power to go against the major majority? When that happens, you need to ask the question, "How can we have these people removed so they don't make other bad decisions for us in the future?"

If someone is in a position of benefitting by delivering and endorsing the message, then they must pay the consequences when they get caught, they are an accessory to the crime. They chose to benefit while a few people unfairly gained and the masses lost. Therefore they deserve to lose, which means lose their job and preferably pay restitution.

Isn't this how a job works in the normal world anyway? You do the work and you get paid. You don't do the work and you don't get paid. This is a basic employment agreement. That is why everyone should be held to the standards of their position, whether it is paid from tax dollars or company revenues, it still comes from the same place.

Chapter 29: A Workforce For Good

Have you heard this one before, "The reason we cannot catch all of the problems in this particular field is because we do not have the resources"? It is one of the reasons used by nearly every government protection agency in existence when something goes wrong and their department is scrambling to play the blame game. Just Google, "don't have resources" along with any of our agencies: SEC, FDA, CDC, USDA, etc. Maybe they could use more resources, maybe they could manage the money they have a little better or maybe a combination of both those solutions would help. Unfortunately, that is the recipe for a Washington DC budget fight, which means nothing will come of it and sometime in the future, when the American people get defrauded again, they will use the same old excuse, "We don't have enough resources."

I believe there are intelligent and capable people, who are so fed up with what goes on in Washington, DC, that would be willing to donate their time (work for free) to prove, disprove, do research, crunch numbers, etc., if it meant finally getting the truth. Think about it, would you? This idea of giving your time for a cause is nothing new. Our country has an entire industry devoted to it. It is called volunteering and it is done by people from all walks of life. Doctors, lawyers, business people, church groups, students, teachers, etc., volunteer their time to a cause because they believe they can affect positive change.

So when a government official says, "Yes, we want to crackdown on Medicare fraud, we just don't have the personnel or resources to do so", you can say yes we do. As a matter of fact, they will work for free, because it means catching the people who are stealing their money. I could understand having a tough time getting doctors, accountants, scientists, etc. 20, 30, or 40 years ago, but nowadays there are thousands of highly skilled professionals who donate their time. So tell me again why you don't want to solve this billion dollar dilemma with quality people for free.

I wonder how many volunteers you can get if you made one request on national television looking for people who want to go over financial records of companies suspected of fraudulent activities during the recent stock market crash? I am willing to bet we can get competent people, to donate their time, to do ANY government oversight and best of all, they probably wouldn't mind doing it under the watching eye of the American public. That would be the number one reality show of all time and the government could sell advertising and actually "earn" some money.

I can hear it now from the people who don't want this, because it would put them in a big predicament. They'll say, "No way, we can't do that, how do we know we are hiring competent people?" You ask that person, "How do we know you hire competent people now? Your past record of hiring doesn't look too good." Obviously they didn't read this book. The answer to their question is, "So, if I could guarantee you top notch people with experience in their respective fields and it would cost the government ZERO dollars, could you think of any reason why you would deny taxpayers the chance to get their money back?" Wait for the answer, write it down and show the world how stupid they are.

How about this one: Has any government office ever hired someone who was incompetent for the position they were hired for? Do elected officials give jobs to their friends and supporters, at the taxpayers' expense, and these people are highly unqualified? Has that ever happened?

One of the reasons government agencies don't have the resources is because they spend so much to get their current results. Why do we have to pay $300, $400, $600 per hour for someone to access information, when there are people willing to do it for a fraction of the cost? Those figures are consultant and lawyers fees.

I believe there are great lawyers, who chose law to do what is right and for the right cause they would work for free. It is done all the time. Lawyers take cases "pro bono", which means "for the public good". I believe our country's future is the right cause. What if these lawyers could help out the people who are willing to do what it takes to fix the world? Having a good lawyer on your side could be the difference in situations where they try to hide their lies behind the law.

Chapter 30: Polygraphs – Do They Work

It is a shame there isn't some type of device being used to detect if a person is telling the truth or not, an electronic machine that could be used by thousands of government agencies, something our national security agencies could use to protect us from possible threats. A device that could be used as a deterrent to child sex offenders to make sure they don't do any harm to our children. If only someone could invent such a device. It would have to work, because we know the government wouldn't use something if they knew it had flaws and it was affecting the lives of so many people. Is there anyway an industry could earn 100s of millions of dollars, selling a device to government agencies, if that device didn't work?

Oh wait, news flash. There is such a device and it is being used every day in all of the above scenarios and it gets better. Researchers claim that the human brain processes memories in a different location from where it creates a thought. When you map the brain during a question and answer session, it will reveal whether or not the thought you just had was created in your mind or you accessed it from a memory that you experienced. Wouldn't you think it is pretty hard to beat that one?

If we are searching for the truth, shouldn't we do everything possible to get it? This may or may not ever happen, but if you want to put someone on the spot, just tell them you would like to make sure they are telling the truth and that you are willing to pay for the polygraph test. You may see an abrupt change in their current state.

I am not 100% sure that lie-detectors work, but I have never seen a scenario live or recorded where a criminal beat the polygraph, actually I have never seen anyone beat a polygraph. There are several videos on the Internet that claim they did, but they are very suspect. There are also several videos that show people not being able to beat a polygraph. If we have this tool, which has been updated and perfected over time, wouldn't it be great if we knew whether it worked or not. I know law enforcement agencies in the U.S. believe it works, they use it every day.

Flawed or not, why don't we just do a test and find out if it works, once and for all? If it doesn't, fine, take it out of service. Why not find 200 people, put them on a polygraph (without them knowing the questions prior to the test), and broadcast it live on TV so the whole country can verify it. Yes, it would take a little time, but once it is done we will either have a powerful tool to fix the world or we can move on.

What if out of the 200 people 10 of them were able to beat it? That is 5%. There are 100s of people who make questionable decisions that could be tested. If 5% can pass it while lying, then the end result is, we got the truth 95% of the time. This means that 5% of the time, whatever that situation was, the end result will be what it was anyway. So they were not caught and their lies lived on, but what about the other 95%? That would be more than enough to affect major change in our world today. So what exactly is the reason why this cannot be used to question anyone?

The person in question has an amazing opportunity to prove they are telling the truth. Since they have nothing to hide, I am sure they will have no problem going though the polygraph session. You have seen this in the news when someone willingly takes a polygraph to show they are not lying and prove their innocence.

You can also use this in reverse. Some people have easy access to polygraph machines. During a questioning session the audience may not get the truth, but what if they see you prove the truth. Let's assume you have specific information about a company that caused toxic dumping and nobody is doing anything about it. They finally put together an open forum for the town's people to ask questions. Before the forum, you videotape yourself answering questions about what you know, while attached to the polygraph. Make 20 DVD copies and give them to someone else, who doesn't stand next to you.

Here's what you say:

- YOU: If someone knew the absolute truth about what happened would you want them to prove it?
- THEM: Yes, that's why we are here.
- YOU: Would you offer people the opportunity to prove their point or would you stop them?
- THEM: We're not here to stop anyone.
- YOU: Great, I have XYZ Polygraph Company with me and I am going to take the polygraph test and answer questions about the truth because I know it. I am the local foreman who worked on that project and I saw your company dumping the toxic waste. Now I want these people to know the truth.

135

At this point you may be ushered out or something else, but I doubt they will let you go on the polygraph. After they clear that up, they will probably take some more questions. Have the other person with the DVDs ask, "If we could have got that polygraph testimony, do you think the audience would have wanted that information?" They probably won't respond. That person then raises the DVDs in the air and states, "The polygraph was done prior to this meeting. Take a copy and make the decision for yourself."

I know most people won't be able to do this, but if it is your daughter who has leukemia and is dying, there is a good chance you would have no problem exposing the truth this way. As always, have a third person there videotaping the entire event. It is your proof to the world. If this company has committed toxic dumping crimes in your community, where else have they done it? The video will show other people how to expose the truth in similar cases.

Chapter 31: Make It Personal – They Do

It is known that companies and the government collectively spend billions of dollars per year creating messages to convince you of something. They use every tool available, which includes tugging at your heart strings. They use the sweet old grandmother, the disabled veteran, the wholesome family and a small child just to give a few examples. Are they exploiting those people?

Here are a few definitions of "exploit":

- Make full use of and derive benefit from (a resource).
- To employ to the greatest possible advantage.
- To make use of selfishly or unethically.
- To advertise.

The only words I see that won't sit right with people are "selfishly" and "unethically". Nobody wants to think of themselves that way, but isn't that how companies use certain people and situations when delivering a message to us? As a whole, these definitions state, if you have something that can give you an advantage and you make use of that advantage you are exploiting it, not necessarily doing it selfishly or unethically.

The questions you need to ask yourself are:

- If I exploited a situation with the intention of fixing something that was wrong, isn't that the correct use of my resources?
- Why wouldn't I use everything at my disposal to fix the world's problems?
- If the person being exploited had a problem that was then fixed, isn't that the point?
- Should I be more concerned with the definition of exploit or should I just go fix the world?

Their goal is to tie an issue to something personal so it has more meaning to us, most of the time it is our religion. Other options include patriotism, security, our children and freedom, don't be afraid to use the same techniques right back on them.

So there, I have made my case and therefore grandparents, disabled, vets, single mothers, religious leaders, their children and spouses should all be used when it comes to righting the wrongs of others.

The Application

What if you are one of the people listed above and you wanted to exploit yourself. The ideal situation is to question someone coming from the point of view of being the victim, because you probably are. Ask questions as if they make total sense and you can't understand how your country let you down. Do it in a way so the audience can empathize with you. I am not saying you should deceive people. I am saying this will produce faster results, because it is hard for the person being questioned to go against you when the audience empathizes with your situation.

Have you ever seen a grandmother, disabled person, war veteran or single mother who hasn't gotten sympathy from the audience, just because who they are? Could you imagine the impact of the questioning techniques in this book, if they were used by someone who had the empathy of the audience? It would be pretty hard for someone to dismiss them, the public could get outraged. What if it was a high profile sports star, actor or TV celebrity, even if the person shuts them out, the rest of the world will take notice.

Shame Them

That's right, shame them. If they are willing to ruin your life and the lives of others by finding ways to get things they don't deserve, then letting their wives, husbands, parents and children know the exact details of how they became "so successful" is definitely an option. The risk of this happening can be a great deterrent. This is one of those techniques that would probably have to happen a few times before the next person realizes their loved ones might find out the real truth.

Another reason why this could work so well is, there are only a few truly bad people doing bad things. The rest of the people are caught up in it and don't always feel good about what they are doing. They live their lives with the skeletons in the closet, but I doubt their family knows all the facts. What would happen if they started finding out? Could you see that topic at breakfast?

- So dad, you are the one who approved the toxic dumping near the playground, which gave those kids cancer?
- Your joking, right mom? You were on the committee that actually lost $100 million dollars and nobody knows where it is?

138

- Son, you knew about this technology that could save Americans billions of dollars and fix our economy and you did nothing about it? I thought I raised you better than that.
- Honey, I just got a package in the mail showing emails from you telling people to forge signatures on legal documents, is this true?

The game changer will finally come when the daughter looks up at her father, with her debilitating disease, as she realizes he had the chance to stop what happened to her, but chose the big fat payoff instead.

Chapter 32: Record It For The History Books

It is amazing how differently people will act when they know they are being recorded, they are somehow aware of what they say. They know they have to put on their ambiguous hat and try not to make any definitive statements. Unfortunately for them, you now know how to get around whatever they throw at you and make them answer your "truth exposing" questions.

With the ability to have a video recorder in just about everyone's cell phone, there is no reason why you cannot record what is happening. One of the benefits is, if in the same conversation someone is denying they said something a few minutes ago, you can easily play it back and prove they were lying. For reasons that almost everyone can understand, you need to videotape ever question exchange you have. It is the proof that people are able to believe, especially when they have no clue who you are.

Use It Against Them

Use videotaping as a way to combat false stories getting out about good people. This won't happen all of the time, but if the opportunity arises you should exploit it. One scenario would be if you see a news crew at a protest and you know why you are there, use what you have learned in this book and have them interview you. If you are good, they will probably just erase the tape because you gave them logical facts, but what if you had someone else videotape you being interviewed? That's right, they're taping you and you're taping them. It is the perfect way to combat misleading messages that are created in the editing room to sway a television audience.

This is an opportunity, especially if the video goes viral. Add a little more heat to it and expose the news company and the reporter who was doing the interviewing. There is a good chance they did find the "clueless" person and put that on the news. Your video could counteract that effect. This is a perfect example of knowing the truth and how powerful it can be. What if thousands of people were creating videos of news teams creating videos, it just might get to the point where they would think twice about their integrity as a news reporter before they go out looking to disprove the "real" story. Again, there are "high integrity" news reporters, but even they know there is bias news designed to cloud the truth.

An Uncut Version

Sometimes, even when something is videotaped, it is then edited to turn the truth into a lie. Try to stop that before it happens. Before the questions even begin, make a statement such as, "Just in case this conversation is not agreeable by both sides, I want to make sure the audience gets to review the entire discussion. Therefore my team is also videotaping and it will be on the Internet in its entirety." You can also use the full version of that video to prove which news agencies cherry pick clips to prove a point.

There are a number of different types of video recording devices for sale all over the Internet. For less than $20 you can get a mini digital video recorder that is hidden in a pen. I am not saying you need to be secretive about it, but I have seen instances on television where someone was recorded without their knowledge, and that recording was then used against them to prove they were lying. If you are going to question someone and you do not have an audience, then maybe using a hidden camera is the approach to take. Once you have the conversation on video, use Social Media to expose the truth to the world.

Inhibit Future Injustice

Incidents happen every day that are recorded on government video cameras. Officials decide when and what to release from the video that was recorded. Sometimes the people get to see the truth and sometimes they don't. When the complete video is not released, there is always a reason why they don't show the proof to the public. I am willing to bet that 99.9999% of those reasons aren't valid, especially if someone asked the right questions about them. In the US, people have seen just about everything and therefore there isn't much that can shock them.

From here on out, people should create their own proof and not rely on someone else who may have "shady" motives. Whenever an incident happens, people should use their smart phones to video as much as possible. That would include surrounding shots, panning the entire scene, capture license plates, official vehicles, check for aircraft, etc. It may not seem important, but you never know. If later on the news states a completely different story, your video will prove there's a problem.

There are literally thousands of cases of injustice that may have gone unprosecuted if it wasn't for a bystander videotaping the incident. Knowing

141

that people are going to video every incident will be a deterrent to those who will lie about what truly happens. In a time when news agencies are being used as corporate and government sounding boards, this will be a way to keep people honest.

Chapter 33: Globalize The Truth

There have been changes happening in the United States and throughout the world due to information being globalized. Whether you use it or not, one of the reasons is a phenomenon called Social Media, which has started shaping and changing the world by giving a voice to everyone. It facilitates the mobilization of millions of voices and can focus that on one particular issue. It proves that good can still win out over bad, by exposing the truth and people taking a stand, which changes the future.

Social Media has become so powerful that dictators have been toppled, companies have pulled back from price hikes and lawmakers have reversed their votes based on what people rallied behind through Social Media. These are just a few examples. It has proven to be a viable vehicle for change and it will be used even more in the future.

Although it is a great tool, someone still has to get face to face with the decision maker and ask them the right questions. Social Media can be used to pressure the decision makers and get the issue to the front of the line. This is done by showing people there is a problem that has a solution. Make a "Call To Action" to get people behind having the right person answer the right questions. Social Media can be the vehicle that gets that meeting setup.

Combine Techniques For Effect

The goal is to fix problems. Social Media is a way to get the truth globalized. Social Media works best when an issue goes viral. Issues go viral when they make a universal impact. One idea to make an impact can come from filmmakers who put out commercials through Social Media, using ideas from Chapter 31: "Make It Personal – They Do". It is being done, but let's do it some more. The idea is to use EVERY tool available to fix the world's problems.

PART 6:

APPLYING PROBLEM SOLVING

Chapter 34: You Are Ready

At this point you now have all the tools you need to fix the world. It doesn't matter who you are or where you came from, you can do it. This section is going to teach you how you use what you have learned and put it all together.

Below summarizes what you have learned and should understand about solving problems:

1. The problem with the world is people making decisions that adversely affect others directly or in directly, either now or in the future.
2. These people are motivated by the rewards they don't deserve and could not attain on their own merits.
3. These rewards can be diminished by someone asking the right questions to the right people at the right time, in front of the right audience.
4. The right questions will expose the truth, even when they don't want the truth to be known, and anyone can ask them.
5. You have the right to use whatever tools are available when exposing the truth.
6. When the truth is known, people will act and fix what is wrong.

In order to solve problems discussed in this book, you need to know what the causes are. On the next page is a visual representation of what empowers the people who cause the problems. On the left side are areas that have problems with solutions. On the right side will be the benefits when those problems are solved. In the middle is undeserved success, supported by the five building blocks (discussed in PART 2) used to suppress the truth. These building blocks act as a barrier, able to repel solutions that can fix many of the world's problems.

Supports of Undeserved Success:
1. Lies - Call Them What They Are (Chapter 7)
2. Messages - A lie Appearing True (Chapter 8)
3. Limited Consequences For Bad Behavior (Chapter 9)
4. Protection Agencies Not Protecting (Chapter 10)
5. Real Solutions Being Suppressed (Chapter 11)

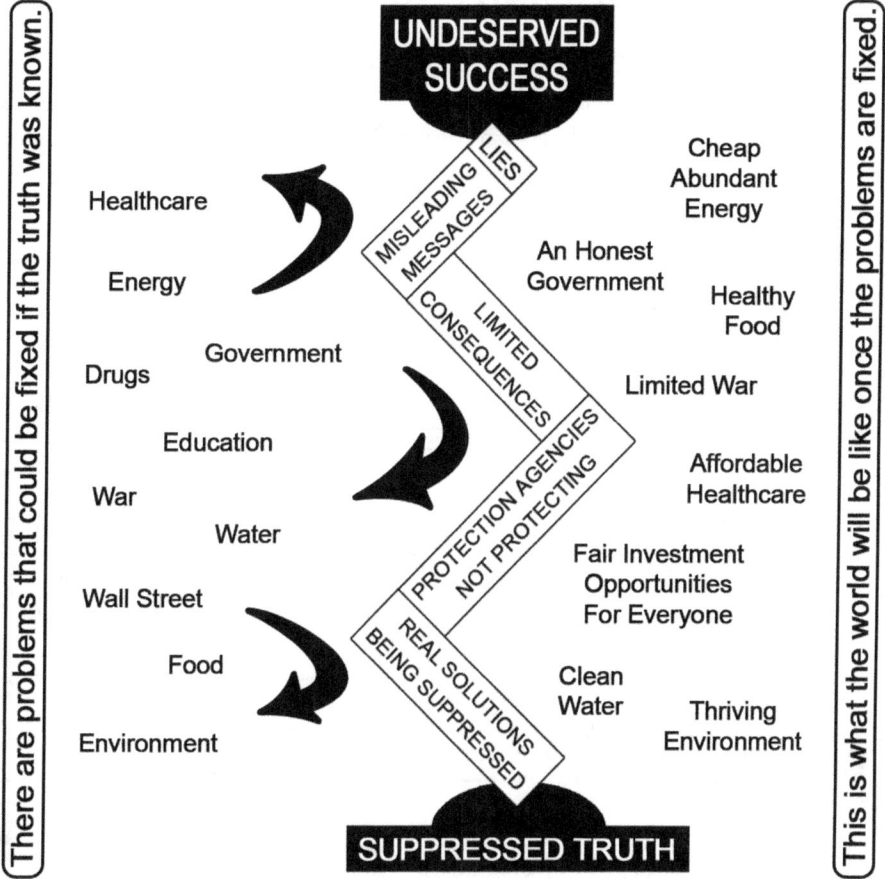

If you want to fix the problems that already have solutions, you need to breakdown the support system that sustains the undeserved success. These building blocks cannot withstand the truth. Even though they stand together, knocking out just one has the ability of bringing down the entire structure.

Chapter 35: The Entire Problem Solving Process

In each "What You Will Learn" section of Parts 1 through 5 there are "mini" flowcharts, which represent key elements to the Problem Solving Process. These five flowcharts go together to create a logical, step-by-step process that can be used to fix problems. The rest of this book is focused on applying this process.

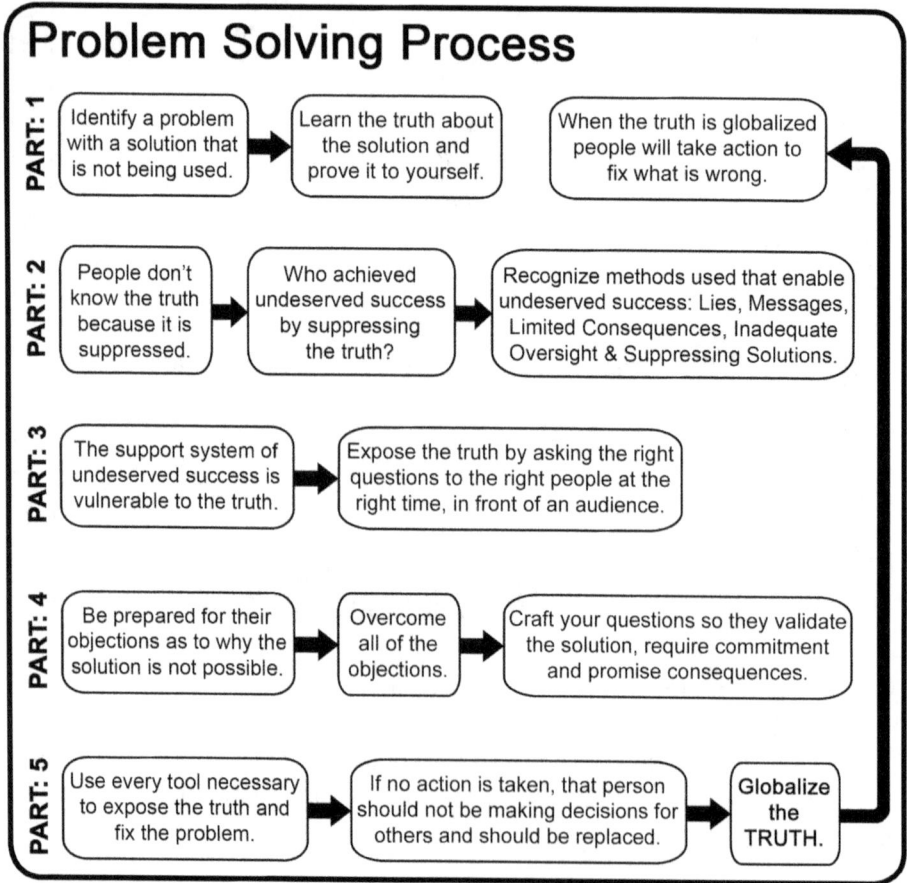

Problem Solving Process

PART: 1
- Identify a problem with a solution that is not being used. → Learn the truth about the solution and prove it to yourself.
- When the truth is globalized people will take action to fix what is wrong.

PART: 2
- People don't know the truth because it is suppressed. → Who achieved undeserved success by suppressing the truth? → Recognize methods used that enable undeserved success: Lies, Messages, Limited Consequences, Inadequate Oversight & Suppressing Solutions.

PART: 3
- The support system of undeserved success is vulnerable to the truth. → Expose the truth by asking the right questions to the right people at the right time, in front of an audience.

PART: 4
- Be prepared for their objections as to why the solution is not possible. → Overcome all of the objections. → Craft your questions so they validate the solution, require commitment and promise consequences.

PART: 5
- Use every tool necessary to expose the truth and fix the problem. → If no action is taken, that person should not be making decisions for others and should be replaced. → Globalize the TRUTH.

You may not have to go through the complete process to fix a problem. Problems can be solved anywhere from PART 3 to PART 5. When this happens, you are done. If someone says they will fix it and they take action right there, don't keep questioning them to prove how wrong they were. Always remember what your goal is. You want to fix a problem, not make a person look bad in front of an audience, which is just a side effect of the Problem Solving Process.

148

Where Do You Fit In?

Not everyone is going to take the "Problem Solving Process" and start fixing what is wrong. People are different. We all have different circumstances, but we do have one thing in common. We agree there are problems we would like to see fixed. I know that people will use this process differently, which is fine. There are many levels of participation when it comes to fixing the world. You just need to decide where you fit in. Maybe you are at one level today and a different level next month. It doesn't matter. We need to fix some major problems right now and it has to be done by us.

One person can make the difference, but 1 million would be so much better. Even if that 1 million consists of 999,999 people who are supporting the one person who is making it happen. Be part of it, they will need that support. You may never say a word or you may lead a million people to fix the world, everyone can do something. You have to figure out what your role will be and do what works for you.

LEVEL 1

Maybe you are not the type of person who speaks up in a crowd or just don't believe you can "rock" the boat, but you know something is wrong and you don't want to be the victim bystander anymore. You read this book, you understand it and it makes sense. Here are your options:

- Take the time to understand the problems and find the truth. If you happen to be questioned, at least you can give them the right answer, instead of being the person who sabotages someone else's plan for fixing a problem.
- If someone else begins to fix a problem, it will probably be written about on the Internet. Find out what they are doing and support their quest, even if you do it quietly. People respond to numbers. When an issue catches fire, people want to see how many other people have signed on. Don't wait for anyone else, they are waiting for you.
- You can write the right questions that should be asked and get them to other people who have the access to ask those questions.
- You can enhance the effect of a rally just by being another body in the crowd.
- You can skip PART 7 and go right to PART 8 of this book.

LEVEL 2

Maybe you have a need to do more and you have the time and energy to make it happen. You have never done anything like this before, but you are ready to try. You know people need to be questioned and you have no problem being the one asking the questions.

- Sometimes problem solving begins with just one question. You get a chance to ask a decision maker one question in front of an audience and the truth is exposed. It gets put on the local news and then gains national attention. People get behind it and a groundswell happens.
- If you can get more than one question in, then prepare a sequence of questions that go through Problem, Solution and Commitment.
- You can create a plan that shows how to solve a major problem and deliver that to the right person at the right time.
- You video everything you do and Globalize it through Social Media.
- You have the ability to create question sequences and plans that will solve problems, but you don't have access to the right people. You can get those plans to someone else who can ask the questions: reporter, government inquiry panelist, etc.
- PART 7 of this book is the next step for people at this level.

LEVEL 3

Lastly, you can be the person who makes it happen all the way. You either have access or know how to get access to the right people. You have no problem speaking up. You understand the problem and what is sustaining the undeserved success. You will take the time to create the right questioning sequences and add plans if necessary. You may be part of an organization with a mission of righting what is wrong in the world. You may have already done something to fix the world. You have spoken up before and got the world to listen. For this group of people, PART 7 will give you the additional tools you will need.

If you are a reporter, interviewer, talk show host, Congressperson, U.S. Protection Agency Investigator, etc., you already have an advantage over everyone else. You have an audience and access to the right people who need to be asked the right questions. If you are too busy to do the legwork, I am sure you can find volunteers willing to do that for you. Find them.

Chapter 36: Instructions For Starting Now

This technique does not utilize the complete Problem Solving Process. It does use the skills you have learned. Below are simple instructions on how to expose the truth with 1-2 questions.

Expose The Truth In Six Steps

1. **Know The Problem:**
    a. It can be something that affected you personally: predatory mortgages, toxic food and water sources, or it can be part of a bigger picture: oil prices, government spending, heath care costs, Wall Street corruption. Just pick one.
    b. Find The Truth. You don't have to figure it out, other people have already done this and it is all over the Internet. Just do a little research for yourself.
2. **Find What Supports and Sustains The Problem.** At this level, this information is optional. All you need to know is #1 above, in order to ask truth exposing questions. Although, knowing this information will help you craft questions that have more substance and impact.
    a. Why do they want to suppress the truth?
    b. Who is benefitting from this problem not being solved?
    c. Why doesn't the public know there is a problem that can be solved?
3. **Craft The Right Questions** (or use the ones in this book).
    a. You can read the questions I have written right from this book if they work for your situation.
    b. Use what you have learned to create "the" truth exposing question they don't want to be asked.
4. **Find The Right Person:**
    a. Who is the person who makes the decisions, made the statement, is misleading the public through messages, or is telling you there are no other options?
    b. It may also be their messenger, someone who is paid to repeat the message.
5. **Have The Question(s) Asked To Them At The Right Time:**
    a. There are Town Hall Meetings and Public Forums that give a voice to the citizens. Make sure you have your question and their answer videotaped.

151

      b. You don't have to ask your questions, have someone else do it. There are people who want to fix the world's problems, but don't always get to the truth because they don't ask the right questions. Find those people and get them your questions.

6. Globalize The Truth:

      a. Take the video of the encounter and upload it to the Internet or find someone who will do that for you..

Examples:

- For the $2-$4 billion investment loss, can you tell me exactly how I can find out who the person or company is that has that money now?
- Can you tell us why we can't use forensic accountants to find out if there was foul play in the stock market?
- Can you tell us why some doctors refuse to vaccinate themselves or their family, is there something else we should know?
- Can you explain why all Americans don't have access to the vehicles that run on hydrogen extracted from water using solar power?
- Can you tell us specifically how you will create jobs, because most politicians look like a fraud when they speak vaguely about it; do you actually know the details?

Chapter 37: Create Plans That Fix The World

Exposing the truth and fixing problems are a little different. There are people who know what is wrong and have exposed the truth in detail, but that didn't always fix the problem. I believe there is one key element missing. When it comes to fixing problems you need to have a plan. A plan lets the world know that there is a way to fix a problem and that puts pressure on the people who are in charge.

Plans are the missing key to why people have failed when trying to fix problems. That is not saying they are absolutely necessary, but if a plan can add so much power to the cause, why wouldn't you use it? Yes, it takes more effort, but so does working until you are 75, because your retirement fund was lost in a stock market scam.

This chapter supplements Chapter 27: Deliver A Plan They Cannot Deny.

Three Possible Truth Exposing Scenarios

There are 3 different scenarios that cover most of the problems you will be dealing with. The difference has to do with whether or not the truth is easily accessible.

1. The truth is readily available if you just looked for it.
2. The truth could easily be proven through an experiment or research.
3. The truth is being suppressed with barriers that don't allow people access.

The Problem Solving Process works the same for all of three scenarios. The only difference will be the plans (if you have one) and the questions you use to deliver those plans. You also have to know which scenario you are dealing with. It wouldn't help the issue if you had a plan to get access to certain information and they explain that information is already available. Do your homework and make sure they are telling the truth.

Once you have the plans, you have to deliver them to the right people. You can't just hand it to them or mail it to an office, there is no proof they received it. You have to deliver it in front of an audience and have the audience know what you are doing. This is done by stating the problem with the solution (if the solution existed) and a commitment.

In PART 10 of this book there is a more detailed plan using each element of the Problem Solving Process, but for now I want to show you how a simple plan can be used. These plans have five key elements: Problem, Solution, How To, Benefits and Objections. Once a plan gets into the headlines then you or someone else can elaborate on it and fill in the details.

Examples using the three different scenarios:

I. TRUTH IS AVAILABLE: PLAN TO USE THE SOLUTION

This is for problems that have solutions available right now that aren't being used.

1. **PROBLEM:** U.S. Postal Service has a current business model that is not sustainable.

2. **SOLUTION:** There is a technology called Hydraulic Launch Assist. It dramatically increases gas mileage. It is successfully being used on garbage trucks and other vehicles and can cut a fuel budget in half. Part of that savings would be used to fund the vehicle modifications and the other part will keep the postal service solvent.

3. **HOW TO:** Build the equipment in the U.S. and create more jobs. Do not overcharge for the technology. Roll it out across the country.

4. **BENEFITS:** Save thousands of postal service jobs. Create manufacturing and installment jobs. Use less gas and oil.

5. **OBJECTIONS:**

    a. The technology is not ready: So if the technology was ready you would be on board.
    b. It will cost too much to convert the postal vehicles: So if we could cut the "fat" out of the technology costs and make it affordable, would you agree we should do it?
    c. Both a & b are possible and the facts are available on the Internet.

    DELIVERY QUESTION: If there was a way to save U.S. Postal Service jobs without any tax breaks or government stimulus, would you want to do that? When they say yes, you deliver the plan.

II. TRUTH CAN BE PROVEN: MAKE A PLAN TO PROVE IT

This is when you are told something may or may not be good for you, or they just don't have the data to say it is right or wrong. We have so much technology, just figure it out and tell me the truth. You can find examples of this with the FDA and CDC. They may say, "It is not proven", or "No tests have been done." I have an idea, you have millions of dollars, just go prove it. The downfall is when the truth is not what you wanted, but at least you can move on. When you don't know the truth, but you know it exists, then exposing it becomes the question or the plan.

1. **PROBLEM:** People have to pay for solar energy, when it would be more cost effective to have their own solar panels.

2. **SOLUTION:** Do a study that measures the amount of electricity received at a business or household from solar panels in 2 different locations.

3. **HOW TO:** The first location is a solar farm 50-200 miles away. The second location is on the roof of the building being used. Do the measurements over a one month period and present the data.

4. **BENEFITS:** Save billions of dollars to American families. Create installation jobs. Eliminate U.S. power plants as terrorist targets, because taking them out will have a minimal effect on the population. When storms take down power grids, people can still survive and heat/cool their homes, keep their food refrigerated, run medical equipment and cook their food.

5. **OBJECTIONS:**

    a. It is too costly: Why is the technology too costly for individual households, yet solar farms are being built all over the country? Are you saying those businesses are making bad investments?

    b. People don't want solar panels on their homes: How do you know people don't want free electricity, did you ask them? If people did want solar panels then you would agree we should do it? What about businesses, their roofs are flat and no one would even see the panels?

    DELIVERY QUESTION: If there was a way to prove that solar panels were an efficient option for homeowners, would you agree that we should at least redo any studies or tests to see if it was true? When they say yes, you deliver the plan.

NOTE: Once the truth is known and it turns out it can solve a problem, that doesn't mean they will use it. All you did was bring the truth to light. They will have plenty of reasons why in cannot be done: laws, money, need more technology; someone owns a patent, etc. You might have to create a new plan and apply scenario **#1**: "Truth Is Available".

155

III. TRUTH IS BEING SUPPRESSED: PLAN TO EXPOSE IT

This is when the truth can be easily exposed and understood, but for reasons that protect undeserved success the necessary information is suppressed. This is basically corruption. It happens in government when they claim national security as the reason why you can't know the truth. It also happens in the financial sector where large trades are made under the radar and billions of dollars transfer to people who are hidden from the public. In this case, government protection agencies aren't doing their jobs, so they need to be questioned and handed the plan.

1. **PROBLEM:** Can't prove whether or not oil prices are being manipulated by speculators.

2. **SOLUTION:** Have forensic accountants investigate ALL oil based trades for the last 10 years.

3. **HOW TO:** Every transaction, in every stock or commodity market is recorded. Those records consist of who bought or sold and how much money was made or lost. Research the connections to who would really benefit for the high price of oil. Conduct this research transparently so the world can watch and question.

4. **BENEFITS:** We will be able to find if someone hates America so much that they would be willing to destroy families economically through high gas prices. When the truth comes out, the price of oil will adjust to where it should be and the perpetrators should be prosecuted.

5. **OBJECTIONS:**

   a. The anonymity of those traders is protected by law: Who made that law and how does that make sense? If someone was manipulating commodity prices how could we find out? So what you are saying is, people can commit billion dollar crimes and our laws are setup to protect them? Can you tell me what would REALLY happen if the traders were not anonymous?

   b. What if the American people wanted to change that law? Aren't laws created to benefit society as a whole? Maybe we need to enact new laws.

   c. We do not have the resources to do a 10 year study: So what you are saying is, if we did have the resources and it didn't cost the taxpayers any money you would agree we should do it? Then use Chapter 29: A Workforce For Good.

DELIVERY QUESTION: If there was a way to find out if oil prices were being manipulated, would you agree that is something the taxpayers would like to know? When they say yes, you deliver the plan.

At the end of every plan add, "This plan might not go into all the details, but I am sure we can find someone who is more knowledgeable than me to complete that." Plans don't have to be involved. They need to be logical so others can look at them and say, "Yes. That makes sense. Why aren't we doing that?"

You could add more to these questions to make them hit home and commit the person you are questioning. Test their integrity with, "Are you the type of person who takes a plan that works and buries it because it is not good for your campaign donors?" Or, before you give them the plan say, "Can you look these people in the eye and tell them why you won't fix the problem, even though you have a legitimate plan to do so?" They say they don't have a plan. You say, "Are you saying if you did have such a plan you would put it into action as soon as possible?" Now they have to say yes, as long as you are in front of a discerning audience. Once they say yes, you say, "I thought you were a person of integrity and am happy to hear you will do the right thing, here is the plan, copies of which will be blogged later today." Then hand them your plan.

The Steps To Deliver Plans are:

1. Understand the problem.
2. Know the truth or create a plan that will expose the truth.
3. Craft the delivery question (or use the ones in this book).
4. Find the right person.
5. Deliver the plan at the right time, which is always in front of an audience.

Engage The Media To Ask The Right Questions

Problem fixing plans can create an opportunity to expose the truth in the media. Every week there are a multitude of television news shows, round tables and forums. These shows frequently have official decision makers who go on to "push" their message to the American public.

- **STEP 1:** Use the techniques described in this section to create and deliver a plan to an official who has a say in whether or not to move forward on the issue. Have someone videotape this encounter.

- **STEP 2:** Contact one of the many news programs that have public officials on as guests and deliver them the plan and the video tape.
- **STEP 3:** The news program invites the public official on to discuss the matter.

QUESTIONS THEY CAN ASK:

- Did you receive a plan that outlined how to…?
- Is there any reason why that plan would not work?
- So what you are saying is…
- If this plan needed adjusting, don't we have intelligent people in this country who can figure out the details?

Not that I am pushing to sell books, but sending the interviewer a copy of this book, along with the plan and videotape, may give the them the tools they need to expose the truth. Also, this technique will show whether or not the interviewer is a puppet to the guests that come on their show. If so, you have the proof of that fact also. Take that information and send it to a competing news organization and put it into the Social Media circles. Keep sending it out until someone addresses the problem correctly.

A Challenge For Authors

If you are an author who writes books, essays or editorials about what is wrong with the world, wouldn't you like the problems you wrote about to be fixed? Your readers are interested in what you have to say, but they may also be interested in doing something about it. Your research and conclusions could be the missing information they were looking for. I challenge all authors to add a section at the end of their work that offers a plan on how to fix what they discovered to be wrong. Take the time to craft the right questions and supply a list of people who should be asked those questions. Go over possible objections and give the facts to overcome them. You never know who is reading your book and you don't know what they are capable of.

If PART 7 Is For You

Problem Solving On Steroids is exactly what it sounds like. It is your ability and skills to verbally expose the truth and fix problems, even in the harshest environments. You will learn how to put together a plan of attack that will literally squeeze the truth out of any situation. You will sequence questions that will put people's integrity to the test. You will be prepared for objections. You will present the proof, demand commitment, and follow through with consequences.

PART 7:

PROBLEM SOLVING ON STEROIDS

Chapter 38: Fedison's Problem Solving Method

I have created a method for solving problems that is based on the Problem Solving Process you already know. It is not as complicated as it looks.

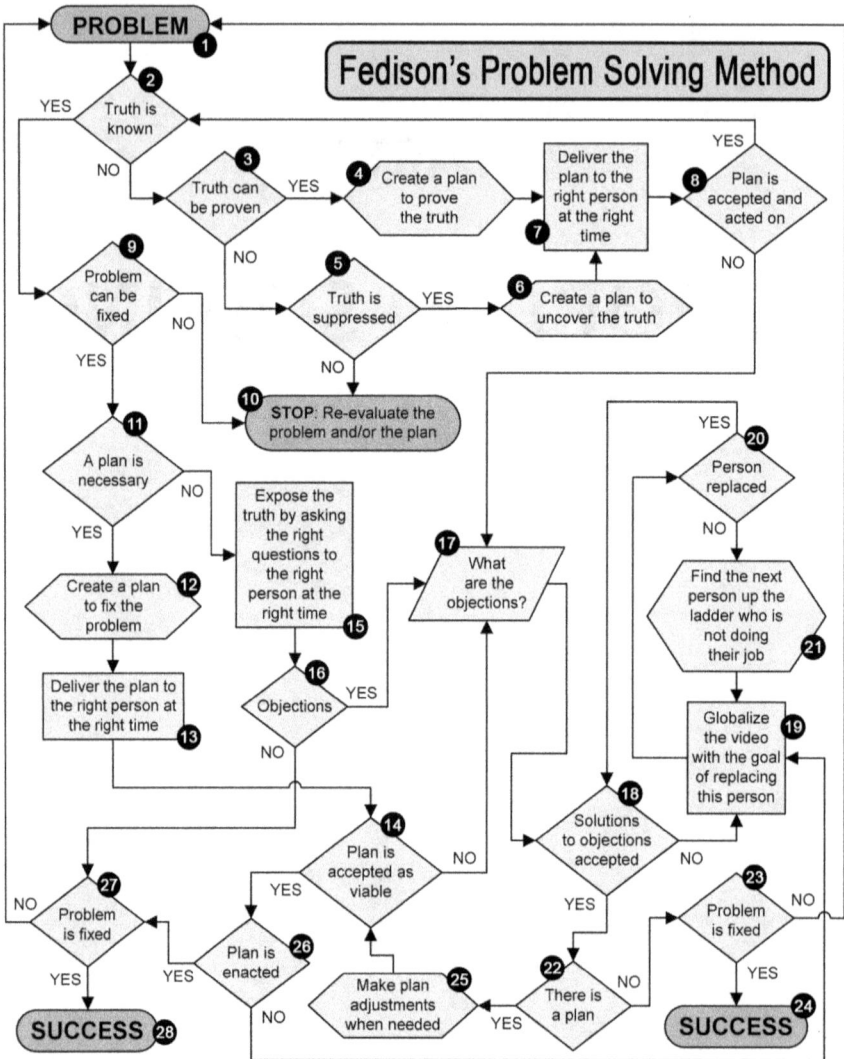

Each function (shape) in Fedison's Problem Solving Method has a number inside a circle; this is not the order by which the method is used. These numbers are there to refer back to the diagram when reading the instructions that follow.

INSTRUCTIONS:

1. It has to be a problem that can be solved.

2. Is this a problem where the truth is known (you can find the truth by just looking), but because of misleading messages the world doesn't know a solution exists? Example: Vehicles run on hydrogen that is extracted from water using solar panels.

3. Is this a problem that can be proven by an experiment or study or needs to be re-proven, because the initial results are not what certain people wanted to hear so they suppressed the benefits through misleading messages? Example: There are studies that claim babies drinking cow's milk is one of the causes of diabetes. Redo the study to find the truth.

4. Create a plan that shows how to do the experiment or research and include transparency.

5. Is this a problem where the information needed to expose the truth is not easily accessible? Examples: Oil prices are manipulated by speculators, but we cannot look at the daily trades to prove or disprove any theories. The DOD cannot account for billions of dollars that was spent during the Iraq war and no outside agency is able to legitimately investigate the DOD.

6. Create a plan that shows how to get the information needed; it may include using forensic accountants and volunteers willing to work to expose the truth. Include transparency.

7. Deliver the plan to the right person at the right time using "Plan Delivery Questions" (Chapter 37).

8. Did the person accept the plan and is the research or experiment being facilitated? If so, then the truth should have been exposed. Now the truth is known, move on to number 9.

9. Is this a problem that can be fixed?

10. If the truth cannot be found or it is a problem without a solution then stop working on it.

11. If it is a problem that needs to be fixed, then a plan should be used. If the problem is about someone lying or not doing their job, then a plan is optional.

12. Create a plan that will fix the problem. Use the tools you have learned in this book.

161

13. Deliver the plan to the right person at the right time using "Plan Delivery Questions" (Chapter 37).

14. Did the person accept the plan as a way to solve the problem?

15. If there is no plan, use the questioning techniques you learned in this book to expose the truth.

16. Does the person have any objections to what you are questioning?

17. Find out what the objections are and write them down.

18. Use the techniques in PART 4 of this book to answer ALL of the objections. If there are reasonable objections then use the "So" technique to overcome them. This may mean you need to get additional proof or you have to adjust your plan, but that doesn't mean the problem can't be fixed. Did they accept the solutions you offered to their objections?

19. If you present a problem, offer a solution, overcome all of the objections, and the person still does not agree with the facts or refuses to do anything about it, then that person should not be in a position of making decisions for everyone else. Use the videotape from this encounter and globalize it through Social Media and the news. Expose the truth so people can see they need to have this person replaced.

20. Was the person replaced? If they were, find out if the new person objects to your solutions.

21. If the person was not replaced, find the person who should have taken action. If this person is not able to make the right decisions then they should be replaced also. Keep going up the ladder until the issue is resolved.

22. Was there a plan used for fixing this problem?

23. If there was no plan, you exposed the truth and overcame their objections; did the problem get fixed? If not, what was the problem for it not being fixed?

24. This success is for fixing a problem that did not involve a plan.

25. If the person agreed your plan is viable, but you used stipulation questions, then you need to fulfill what you said you would do. Example: You asked, "So what you are saying is, if I can find forensic accountants to investigate at no cost to the government you would be onboard?" If they agree to this, then you need to find people who will do this. See Chapter 29.

26. If there is a plan that can fix a major problem and the people who can do the fixing accept the plan, but then do nothing about it, then those people need to be replaced.

27. After the plan was facilitated did the problem get fixed? If not, what was the problem?

28. This success is for fixing a problem that had a plan.

Fedison's Problem Solving Method Rules:

1. It must be a problem that can be solved.
2. You have to know the truth or know how to get the truth.
3. You have to be right.
4. If you are using a plan it has to make sense and be viable.
5. You have to be willing to take it to the end if necessary.

This method will not get completed in one encounter. Therefore the same person does not have to complete every task, as long as people follow the Problem Solving Process that was learned in PARTS 1 through 5. The first task is to find out the truth. The second task is to present the findings to someone who can do something about them. The third task is to overcome any objections they may have. The fourth task is to have the problem fixed. The fifth task happens when all the proof is on the table and nothing gets done. At this point the only option left is to remove the obstacle, which would be the person who is suppressing the solution.

Example:

One person finds the truth, makes a plan and gives that plan to someone who has access to the right people. This person then asks the right questions and delivers the plan (while be videotaped for proof). The person who received the plan does nothing, but is scheduled to be on a talk show. Someone crafts the questions that should be asked and sends them, along with a copy of the plan and the videotape of the plan delivery, to the host of the talk show. The host asks the right questions to the right person at the right time. If the problem isn't fixed, take the videos and globalize them with the goal of replacing the person with someone who will fix the problem. This is an option for many participants, but it can also be completed by one person.

Chapter 39: How To Prepare To Win

Please don't overlook the power of being prepared and having a plan of action. I am sure there are people who don't think they need to be prepared, but it can be the difference between success and failure. There is no doubt that the better the preparation, the better the outcome. Below is an outline you can use as a checklist to make sure you have everything you need to succeed.

1. **Understand The Problem You Are Trying Fix**

   There is a good chance you already understand the problem, because it affects you personally. If not, do your research. Get a basic knowledge of what is going on.

   There are issues that need to be fixed; the Problem Solving Method will not work unless you can prove something. If you try to fix a problem, that is hard to prove or doesn't affect a majority of people, you may find it back-firing. My suggestion is to focus on global problems with solutions that can be fixed now. For a list just Google: global issues or world problems.

2. **Plan On Having It Documented**

   This means videotape the entire interaction. The event may already have media attention, but I recommend you have someone video record it for you.

3. **You Have To Know The Truth**

   If you don't know what the truth is, how are you supposed to convince anyone else this is actually a problem and not just "the way the world is"? If you don't know the truth, but you know it exists and the facts can be proven with a study or a test, then that becomes the truth.

4. **Find The Solution**

   Either it is something you have specific knowledge about or you need to confirm the knowledge. At the least, you have to know that something is wrong and can be fixed. You might not know exactly how to fix it, but it is something that well crafted questions will get to the bottom of. If any of these are the case then proceed. If not, then maybe you need to rethink what it is you are trying to fix. Your job is to find the solution and get a basic knowledge of how and why it is the solution.

5. Write A Plan

This can be 2-3 sentences or a full blown plan that was created by a volunteer project manager. It needs to make sense and be viable. It must benefit the masses and not just a select few.

6. Add The Proof

Print out photos. Make copies of newspapers or magazine articles. Find reports, studies or data that will prove the truth. Whatever you think is necessary and you can find, then do it. You can never have too much proof. Bring that proof with you.

7. Write Truth Exposing Questions

This is what everything else is designed to assist. The entire goal is to ask the right questions to the right people at the right time, in front of an audience. Write all of these questions down and bring a copy with you.

8. Pre-answer All Objections

Figure out what the objections will be before you get there. You can probably find them on the Internet. Once you have them, use what you learned in PART 4 and write down all the questions you will use to eliminate their objections. Bring the proof you will need also.

You can stop the objections before they start, by displaying them along with the answer as to why the objection is not valid. Write this on a poster board so the entire audience can see it. You could also display objections as they become relevant during the debate. Either way, just make sure you are ready for whatever they throw at you.

9. The Right People

Find out who is in charge. Who are you going to ask these questions to? Is this person someone who carries a lot of weight when it comes to this particular problem? Are they the person who claims it can never happen or their company is doing the best for the public? Is it the director of a government protection agency? Make sure all of your work doesn't fall on deaf ears.

10. Have An Audience

I can't stress this enough. Make sure there are plenty of people to witness the event, even if it is being taped. Make a few calls to local news stations and let them know you plan on fixing a problem and they won't want to miss it.

11. Other Notes

- Enlist the help of others who feel like you do and want to right the wrongs.
- Bring extra copies of your plan and proof to give to news agencies and the audience.
- Create note cards with key points.
- Bring any accessories you may need to expose the truth: poster board, markers, etc.
- Write down the problem and display it so everyone knows what the subject is about. Every time they get off course you point at the sign and say, "I know that is important to you, but don't you think we should find a solution to this problem?"

12. Practice and Practice Again

Go through your plan with a friend. Practice all of your questions and have your friends try and stump you. Do as much as you can to be prepared. The best reason for practicing is that in stressful situations your brain can go blank. If you practiced it enough times you may still be able to perform because it was drilled into your head.

Chapter 40: Question Sequences With A Purpose

Using question sequences to expose the truth and fix problems is like putting a puzzle together. You can write several questions in a certain order, but when you read them you decide to move them around to get the desired result. Don't get stuck on any particular sequence. The goal is to expose the truth and fix problems. Sequencing questions will allow you to tell the story to the audience and simultaneously have the other person verify it through their statements. The story line is as follows:

1. There is a problem that has a solution.
2. This person has the power to fix this problem.
3. I might have to set the stage so they listen to what I have to say and don't attack me while I am asking questions (This is pre-questioning).
4. I will have them agree they would act if there was a viable solution to the problem. Have this done BEFORE you show them the solution.
5. I will get them the solution and overcome their objections.
6. I will have them commit to fixing the problem, in front of an audience.
7. If they deny the solution, then the audience (the world) will take over because when people learn the truth they will fix what is wrong.

Below are questions in several different categories that can be used to tell your story to the world. They do not have to be used in any certain order and you don't have to use questions from each category. You need to know what truth you want to expose and craft the question sequence to accomplish that goal. It may take 2-3 questions or it may take 10. Your goal might be to expose several truths at one meeting, do these one at a time. Know what you want to expose before you question anyone.

Pre-Questions

These are used to set the stage when you think they might do something during your conversation that could inhibit the questioning process. You would ask these questions first and then you can refer to them later if they change their mind (lie).

167

- Do I have a right to my own thoughts? Do I have to believe what you believe?
- If I thought that something isn't right am I allowed to question it?
- Don't people have the right to know the truth when it comes to events that affect them?
- Is it possible that someone of authority can make decisions that have an adverse effect on people? Is it possible that person's decisions can be wrong?
- If someone could prove there were no logical, rational or moral reasons for a certain decision, would it be worth it to your audience to get the truth?
- Based on information that shows the U.S. government hasn't always told the truth, do we, as U.S. citizens, have the right to question the government when something doesn't sound right?
- As a citizen of the United Sates, who pays taxes, which pay government salaries and projects, if I know something is wrong, even if there are current laws/regulations in place supporting it - should I speak up or just let the injustice go on? Remember, there was a time in this country when slavery was legal and woman could not vote and a large part of the U.S. population agreed with these laws. Just because they were laws and people believed in them, did that make them right?
- Has there ever been a government official who lied about an issue that adversely affected U.S. citizens financially?
- I apologize before hand, I am a little nervous and I might stutter or even sound abrupt. Please don't take this personal, it is not directed towards you, I am not used to speaking in public. Get this out first and the audience will see your honesty and won't focus on any missteps you may make.

Problem Questions

Understand that people will know what you are trying to do, especially after this book comes out. They will be prepared with ways to divert the question or craft their own answers that sidestep the truth. This is why you start with a broad question that everyone knows the answer to. It will be a well crafted question that forces them to agree with your most basic premise and will have the audience agreeing also.

Important guidelines for the first "broad" question:

1. Make sure it benefits the largest group, which will be the general public most of the time.
2. Make sure it covers a broad range at the simplest level.
3. Make sure it is a YES or NO question.
4. Make sure it is crafted so they cannot disagree on any level.

I don't care if you are at the NRA talking about how to stop gun violence. You can always craft a question that everyone would have to agree on. In this instance it would be: "Do you think we should get as many guns as possible into the hands of teenage gangs?" Let me see anyone of importance answer yes to that question on national television.

Some other examples of starter questions are:

1. Do you think parents want to feed their children toxic chemicals?
2. Would Americans like to get more return on their investments?
3. Do people want their government to tell them the truth?
4. Would people like to spend less for gas?

Don't skip this step. It is what sets the stage for the next questions, because whenever they want to disagree you can refer back to this and say, "I thought you told this audience that Americans would like to get a higher return on their investments, are you now saying that's not true?" What if that broad question was printed on a poster board and placed on an easel so everyone could see it?

Solution Questions

The main objective at this point is to state you have a plan and you want them to agree (in public) that if it worked they would use it. Assuming you have come prepared, the next step is to get the solution on the table. Again, the NRA is not the place to talk about the reduction of guns in this country. So let's say someone has a plan to teach responsible gun ownership in inner cities and it included indoor gun ranges. I am sure there are other solutions; this just came off the top of my head. Knowing this truth, you craft a question that states if there was a solution, then they would be onboard. In this instance it would be: "If there was a way to significantly reduce the amount of inner city gun violence, without affecting gun laws or the number of gun sales every year, would that be a viable plan?" If they want to disagree you can refer back to the PART 4: Questioning

Techniques, and use the "So" option or ask them why, write it down, and overcome the objections from there.

If you are right and you have a solution, it doesn't matter who you are presenting it to. By using logic and well crafted questions they have two choices, agree with you or lie. If they agree you can move forward and fix the world. If they lie you can move forward and have the world fix them.

Commitment Questions

After they have acknowledged there is a problem and they could not deny that you have a solution, the last part is to commit them to action. The final questions should be constructed in a way that makes the person acknowledge they must act or the audience will see they are a hypocrite or they are not doing the job they are paid for. This can be harsh, but so are disease, starvation and poverty.

The goal is to ask questions that are simple to answer, make total sense, and put people on the spot if they try not to answer.

- So what you are saying is, if there was a straight forward solution to fix our economy you would be on board?
- So what you are saying is, if [then fill in their objection here] was not a problem, you would be fully behind this, is that correct, or are you just against U.S. citizens benefiting from a technology that was developed using their tax dollars?
- So if we could solve this now, you will not only support it, you will do it. Is that correct?
- If _____ wasn't an issue, we could do it now, right?

When It Is Over

- Review your results.
- Could you have asked better questions?
- Take the video and globalize it through Social Media. If it is really good, send it to local or national news agencies.

There are unlimited ways to pose questions. There are unlimited ways to expose the truth. Therefore, you could never put all the different variations in one book. This book provides a foundation and examples. From there you will be able to create any logical questioning sequence necessary to expose the truth in any situation. Whenever you are stumped, just ask yourself, "What questions can I ask that will expose the truth quickly?"

170

Below is a questioning flowchart that can give you a visual idea of how the sequencing process works. This is just an example and doesn't mean you will follow it when exposing the truth. It is based on the truth not being known and offering a logical way to expose it before a bad decision is made.

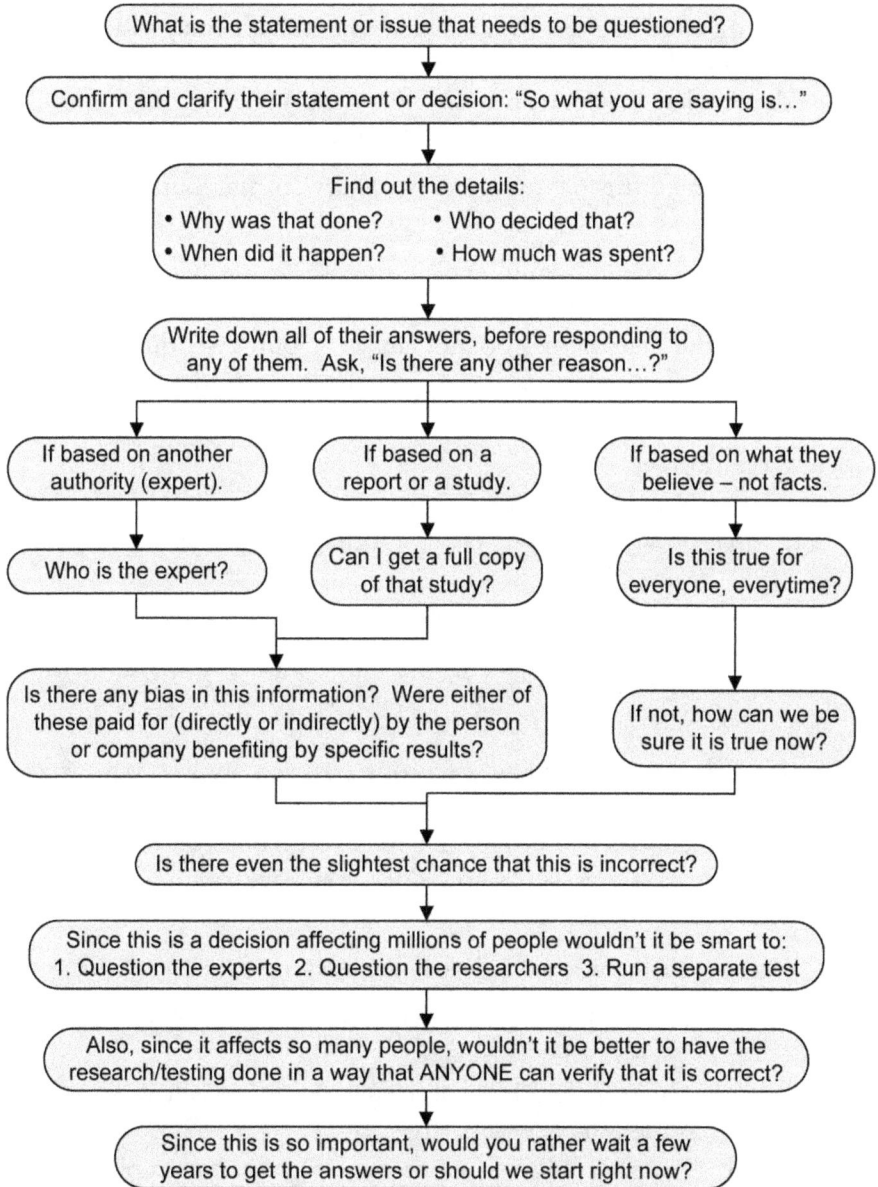

What is the statement or issue that needs to be questioned?

Confirm and clarify their statement or decision: "So what you are saying is..."

Find out the details:
- Why was that done?
- Who decided that?
- When did it happen?
- How much was spent?

Write down all of their answers, before responding to any of them. Ask, "Is there any other reason...?"

If based on another authority (expert).

If based on a report or a study.

If based on what they believe – not facts.

Who is the expert?

Can I get a full copy of that study?

Is this true for everyone, everytime?

Is there any bias in this information? Were either of these paid for (directly or indirectly) by the person or company benefiting by specific results?

If not, how can we be sure it is true now?

Is there even the slightest chance that this is incorrect?

Since this is a decision affecting millions of people wouldn't it be smart to:
1. Question the experts 2. Question the researchers 3. Run a separate test

Also, since it affects so many people, wouldn't it be better to have the research/testing done in a way that ANYONE can verify that it is correct?

Since this is so important, would you rather wait a few years to get the answers or should we start right now?

Chapter 41: Review And Final Tips

1. Make sure you are in front of an audience or at the least it is being recorded. **DON'T ATTEMPT PROBLEM SOLVING ONE ON ONE, WITH NO WAY OF DOCUMENTING OR PROVING WHAT ACTUALLY HAPPENED.**

2. Be prepared to show the audience what is happening visually. Use a dry-erase board or overhead projector. You need to be able to write down what that person is saying so everyone can see it and then there is no way to go back on what they said.

3. Make any diffusing questions necessary so they cannot attack you later on.

4. You have to get them to explain themselves or their organization's position, beliefs, motivation and then write them down. Let them make the statements; do not answer your own questions. This clarification process eliminates any misunderstandings later on. Use the following questions:

   a. Why?
   b. How do you know?
   c. So what do you want (...to happen, people to believe, for our country)?
   d. Tell me why this is good?
   e. What are people getting for that?
   f. Can I see the proof?
   g. What if that is wrong?

5. If they give you any kind of proof (articles, studies, experts, etc.), scrutinize all of it. Ask when it was done, who did the tests, why did you choose that group, give me exact names, let me see the full report and if necessary how does that have anything to do with what we are talking about?

6. Know which truth scenario you are dealing with:

   a. The truth is available. Are they lying or don't know and you can prove it is wrong?
   b. The truth can be proven. Are there factually ways to prove something is true or not?
   c. The truth is being suppressed. Do you have a plan that can unsuppress the truth?

7. Use the questioning skills you have learned in this book to squeeze the truth out of them. Get every objection they have out on the table before you overcome any of them. Use the audience when necessary. Use any other tools you have learned to show there is something wrong here, someone is lying, and you just proved it.

8. Be prepared with the proof. Either bring it with you or produce it on the fly. Have your cell phone, laptop or tablet preloaded with the facts you will need. You can also have a partner who will look up information on the fly via the Internet or you can do it yourself if need be. Have a tablet with you and have someone else send the information necessary to your screen as you need it. This could be facts, quotes, past articles even the questions needed to expose the truth.

9. If they do agree and claim they will fix it, then get a solid commitment. Put it in writing and get them to promise on camera. Ask, "What recourse does the audience have if you don't follow through?"

PART 8:

PROBLEM SOLVING TEMPLATES

Chapter 42: Fix It If It Is Broken

This section has several questioning flowcharts and sequencing templates that can be used in real situations. They are all designed to get to the truth and then fix whatever is wrong. If you are using one and it doesn't work well in your situation, then change it. Use these questions to help:

1. Where does this questioning sequence not work?
2. Do I have to add or take away questions to make it work better?
3. What else can I do to make sure this questioning sequence exposes the truth and fixes the problem?

I believe you can solve most of the world's problems if you can just understand why the people in charge aren't solving them. This can be accomplished through well crafted questions. Below is a step-by-step guideline for using the Problem Solving Process. The questions used in this outline can be changed and adapted for any particular situation. Treat this as a guideline that you can use to make your own templates.

1. CONFIRM THE PROBLEM AND THEIR POSITION
   a. What is the issue, statement, argument, etc.?
2. CLARIFY THE FACTS
   a. Who, what, where, when, why and how.
   b. Use "So what you are saying…" to bind them to their answers.
3. ASK TRUTH EXPOSING QUESTIONS
   a. Pre-Questions
      i. Confirm you have the right to know the truth.
      ii. Prevent anyone from labeling you later on.
      iii. Put their integrity on the line.
   b. Agreement Questions
      i. Have them agree to the most basic premise.
      ii. Bind them to the solution, "If there was a solution…?"
      iii. Have them forecast how good a solution could be.
   c. Action Questions
      i. "If you had a plan…?"
      ii. "If the truth could be found…?"
      iii. "If someone wasn't doing their job…?"
      iv. "If someone was lying…?"

4. OVERCOME THEIR OBJECTIONS

    a. "So what you are saying…?"

    b. "What if that is wrong?"

    c. "Why?" or "Why not?"

    d. "If I could show you the proof…?"

    e. "If there was a way to do that without any cost…?"

5. GET COMMITMENT AND ACTION

    a. If they are onboard, get a hard commitment to do something now.

    b. If they still refuse after seeing all the proof, then show the world there is someone in a position of authority who is obviously not doing the job they are being paid for.

Each template in this section has instructions, including an example of how the conversation may go. At the end of each template is "SUPPORTING TEMPLATES", which lists other templates that can be used to support the one you are currently working with. There may be times when you have exposed the truth, but they refuse to acknowledge it and therefore nothing gets fixed. That's when you use TEMPLATE 6 - How To Replace People, where you take the video of the conversation and globalize it. If this person is a government employee, then they are paid by the taxpayers. If they aren't doing what is right for the taxpayers then they shouldn't be in that position.

Be prepared to answer any objection and have the proof available to show the audience. You may also need to use other "Additional Ammunition" to expose the truth. This person may not want to cooperate at all. That is why it needs to be videotaped, so they can be judged in the court of public opinion. Remember, the truth can still be exposed even if they don't admit it.

TEMPLATE 1: How To Fix Problems – Truth Is Known

This is the main template because the goal is to fix problems that already have solutions (Truth Is Known). The first step is to get the "right person" to admit there is a problem. Then have them agree if there was a solution it should be used. You have to get these verified first so they aren't able to backpedal later on. Next, you deliver the plan and overcome objections. Lastly, you would have them commit to applying the solution to fix the problem.

ASSUMPTIONS:

1. You already know the truth about the solution and are able to produce the proof.
2. You have a plan ready to deliver to the "right person".

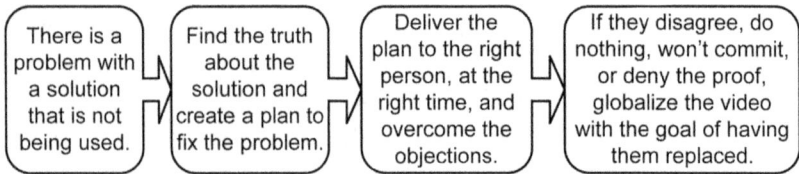

There is a problem with a solution that is not being used.	Find the truth about the solution and create a plan to fix the problem.	Deliver the plan to the right person, at the right time, and overcome the objections.	If they disagree, do nothing, won't commit, or deny the proof, globalize the video with the goal of having them replaced.

The conversation or interview might go like this:

- THEM: We need to create more jobs and the energy industry is where it can be done.
- YOU: What type of jobs are you talking about?
- THEM: We need people to build the pipeline and there are other opportunities. If the government would deregulate, so more drilling can be done, that would create more jobs.
- YOU: So what you are saying is, our country needs jobs and the natural gas and oil industries can provide jobs if the government would stop holding them back, is that correct?
- THEM: Yes, that is right.
- YOU: Let me ask you a question. If there was a way to quadruple the number of jobs created and produce ten times the amount of domestic energy would that be better?
- THEM: That would be great.
- YOU: [HAND THEM THE PLAN] Here is a plan on how that can be done right now. Are you familiar with vehicles that run on hydrogen fuel?

178

- THEM: I have heard of them, but they are too dangerous.
- YOU: So if there were bus companies and government agencies involved and there have been no explosions, would that prove it was safe?
- THEM: Well I would have to see the data to make sure everything was workable.
- YOU: So what you are saying is, if you saw the data and everything was workable then you would be on board.
- THEM: [THEY MAY OR MAY NOT ANSWER HERE] If they do, hand them the data.
- YOU: Can you think of any reason why you wouldn't want to use a plan that puts hundreds of thousands of people back to work and reduces our dependency on oil?
- THEM: One problem is that the oil industry already employs a lot of Americans and I wouldn't want to lose jobs to add jobs.
- YOU: So what you are saying is, if this plan didn't affect any domestic jobs dealing with the oil industry then you wouldn't be concerned about that point?
- THEM: As long as no domestic jobs are lost, that is my concern.
- YOU: Great, our country imports more oil than we produce, therefore this plan will stop the flow of billions of dollars overseas and preserve domestic jobs, is that something you think Americans would want to see happen?
- THEM: Yes, I believe they would agree that is good for the US.
- YOU: So now you have a plan to put in action. I also put that plan on the Internet. Do you think you would be able to look over that plan by next week?
- THEM: I believe so.
- YOU: Are you a Congressperson who does what is good for our country or will you put this aside because it may affect some of your political donors?

HOW TO FIX PROBLEMS - TRUTH IS KNOWN

1. Get their side, what is their point? Either ask them or you say it and ask them to confirm it.

_____

2. Clarify (who said that, what actually happened, why do we need that, where was that done, when did it happen, how did they do it or how many do they mean exactly):

_____

3. So what you are saying is: _____

_____, is that correct? _____

4. If there was...
      A. a way to fix that...
      B. a better way to accomplish the same goal...
and you were able to take what was wrong and make it right, would you do it? _____

5. Are you familiar with [solution]? _____ Hand them the information, make the claims on why others say it will work and unveil your proof to the audience.

6. Can you give me any reasons why we cannot start working on this plan to fix this problem?

List all of their reasons (objections): _____

_____

7. So, if none of those reasons were a problem, then you would agree that we should move forward on this, is that correct? _____ Overcome all objections.

8. Would you agree, if this did work, it would positively impact people's lives? _____

9. Since there is a solution that we know will work, are you willing to do something about it? _____

SUPPORTING TEMPLATES: 3, 4, 5, & 6.

180

TEMPLATE 2: How To Fix Problems – Truth Is Unknown

There are situations where it is accepted that the truth is not available, even though it could be easily proven. The misleading messages assume nobody knows how to get the definitive proof, but the real reason is because they don't want the definitive proof. These are problems reported as: "No studies have been done", "There is no proof", "There is no way to verify", and "The source is unknown."

If you are creating a plan for this template, it would include a research or experiment component that would be able to prove something works or doesn't work, is true or not. Don't forget to add transparency in the plan. See Chapter 26.

You cannot begin to fix a problem if you do not know the truth about a solution. Therefore, not knowing the truth creates two problems.

1. You have to find what the truth is. This may or may not require a plan.
2. Once you know the truth you can now fix the problem, which means taking the information revealed here and applying it to TEMPLATE 1.

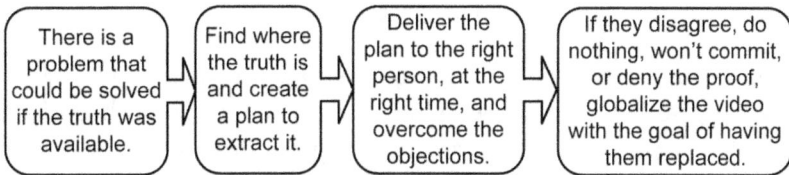

The conversation or interview might go like this:

- YOU: Are you aware that people claim fracking is polluting their drinking water?
- THEM: Yes, I have heard about it, but have yet to see the definitive proof.
- YOU: If it was destroying their water source do you think something should be done about it?
- THEM: Yes, but as I said, there is no proof that it is happening.
- YOU: So what you are saying is, you would be interested in getting to the truth about this situation, is that correct?

- THEM: Yes, I think everyone would be interested in the truth.
- YOU: So I guess if there was a plan to get to the truth you would want to see it, right?
- THEM: I would look it over.
- YOU: Great, [HAND THEM THE PLAN] this is a simple plan that would take only 3 days to prove whether or not the fracking chemicals are polluting the water sources. Since this is such a critical issue for the residents and the drillers, would you agree that the sooner the truth is known the better?
- THEM: Yes, but I will have to get this plan to the right people.
- YOU: Who are the right people?
- THEM: I am not sure at this point who could do that.
- YOU: So what you are saying is, you are the Governor and you don't know which agency is charged with the duties of making sure corporations don't pollute the water supply?
- THEM: That's not what I am saying.
- YOU: Did the state even look ahead to see if this could be a possible problem?
- THEM: Yes, there was a full study done.
- YOU: Who did the study?
- THEM: [THERE ANSWER TELLS YOU THE AGENCY]
- YOU: So what you are saying is, you do know who can use this plan to verify the truth, is that correct?

You can figure the rest out from here. I know, it sounds harsh. How do you think the young mother feels when she finds out she has been feeding her baby using polluted water from fracking? Which one do you think is harsher? This line of questioning could lead to proving that a government agency did not do their job, maybe someone is in a job where they do not belong.

HOW TO FIX PROBLEMS - TRUTH IS UNKNOWN

1. Get their side - what is their point? Either ask them or you say it and ask them to confirm.

_____

_____

2. If _____
is happening, what do think should be done to the people doing that?

_____

_____

3. Do people have the right to know the truth about issues that directly or indirectly affect them? _____

4. If there was to find the truth about this and you had the power to do it, would you? _____

5. Hand them the plan to find the truth, make the claims on how it will get to the truth in a common sense way. Have a way for the audience to see the same plan.

6. Can you give me any reasons why we cannot start working on this plan to find the truth?

List all of their reasons (objections): _____

_____

_____

7. So, if none of those reasons were a problem then you would agree that we should move forward on this, is that correct? _____ Overcome all objections.

SUPPORTING TEMPLATES: 3, 4, 5, & 6.

TEMPLATE 3: How To Expose A Liar

This can also be used to confirm that someone is telling the truth. Sometimes there are statements made that just don't sound right. In this case, you are not claiming they are a liar, all you want is some clarification. The techniques are the same. The bottom line is you just want to know the truth.

If they aren't telling the truth, then the goal is to prove they are a liar to the audience, whether or not they admit it. You cannot say, "You are lying." That is the big mistake that most people make. If you are right, then it is easy to use truth exposing questions to prove it. In this case you may have to use a little finesse in your questioning sequence, because no one wants to admit they were lying, especially when they know the world is watching.

Guidelines:

1. Have them confirm the statement that they made.
2. Clarify any points that could be misconstrued or are vague.
3. Use a visual when possible, write the above information on a dry erase board so the audience (and camera) can see and read it.

Now, as long as you are right, there is no way they can back out when you present the proof later on. The best result will be the person knows they are caught and in order to save their position they admit fault. At that point you ask, "What do you intend to do to remedy what this lie has caused?" Write it down and have them commit to a timeline.

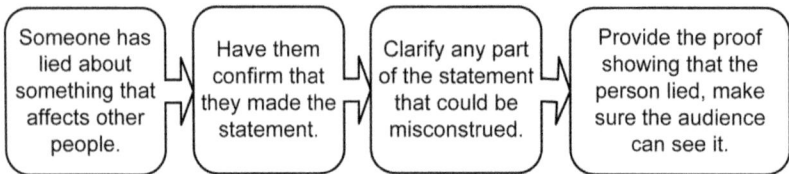

Someone has lied about something that affects other people.	Have them confirm that they made the statement.	Clarify any part of the statement that could be misconstrued.	Provide the proof showing that the person lied, make sure the audience can see it.

The conversation below is based on industrial chemical dumping into our water systems and people believing officials when they say there is no danger:

- YOU: Are you aware that many children are now ill and doctors don't know what to do?
- THEM: This is a tragedy and we will get to the bottom of it.

184

- YOU: Are you aware that scientists have shown that it was caused by specific chemicals, which came from XYZ industrial plant upstream?
- THEM: I haven't seen that data.
- YOU: If you saw that data would you believe it; it was conducted by the EPA.
- THEM: Yes. If they say no or seem hesitant, then you say, "Are you saying that the American public cannot trust data that comes from the EPA?" Then you ask if they would like to retract that answer and say "yes."
- YOU: [HAND THEM THE DATA] Here is the proof. Do you recall telling the public that this lake was safe to swim in?
- THEM: No, I do not recall making those statements.
- YOU: That's okay, here is the article [HAND THEM A COPY], do you remember now?
- THEM: That is incorrect, I was under the belief that they were asking me about a different lake.
- YOU: So what you were saying is that you made a mistake with that original statement?
- THEM: Yes I did.
- YOU: So that means that the people pay a government official to protect them and you were unable to decipher the difference between two lakes, is that what you are saying?
- THEM: [THEY PROBABLY WON'T ANSWER]
- YOU: Can you tell me how that mistake had nothing to do with these people's children getting sick in this lake?
- THEM: [THEY PROBABLY WON'T ANSWER]
- YOU: Why are you not responsible and why should people trust anything you tell them in the future?

For other direct lies, after they make a statement the question could be, "What makes you believe that is true?" Write everything down so they cannot make the excuse later on that they were misinformed about the details involving their statement.

HOW TO EXPOSE A LIAR

1. You have stated that _____

_____

_____, is that correct? _____

2. When you said _____,
what exactly did you mean?

_____

_____

3. So what you are saying is: _____

_____

_____, is that correct? _____

4. Did you know that (proof) _____? _____

5. Now that you know the truth, are you willing to retract your statement and make a new statement based on this information? _____

SUPPORTING TEMPLATE: 6.

TEMPLATE 4: How To Challenge If They Are Wrong

The basis behind this section is: Just because someone with an official title makes a decision, that doesn't mean it is the best choice. So if you know it isn't right, collect your research and create your questions. It will also help to prepare by finding previous bad decisions made by the same person or organization. You may have to overcome misleading information, data, studies, etc., and maybe some people will become obnoxious. That's what happens when someone challenges their ideas. If this happens, use the skills you learned in PART 4.

The example here deals with money being spent. Officials could make better choices and save taxpayers money. There is government corruption in contracts, earmarks, compensation, and foreign aid that could easily be secured for less money. This is no secret.

The goal is to have the person admit they should be good stewards of the taxpayer's money. Then they need to agree that if the taxpayer's could get the same products and services for less money that would be better.

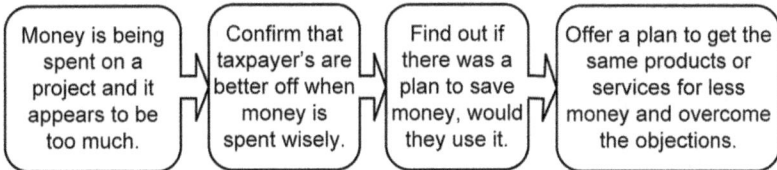

Money is being spent on a project and it appears to be too much.	Confirm that taxpayer's are better off when money is spent wisely.	Find out if there was a plan to save money, would they use it.	Offer a plan to get the same products or services for less money and overcome the objections.

I have written three possible conversations for this template.

CONVERSATION 1:

- THEM: FEMA is going to purchase 224.3 million pounds of ice from the U.S. Army Corps of Engineers for 28 cents a pound.
- YOU: Can you explain what you are going to do with that ice?
- THEM: We are going to truck it down to New Orleans so the people can use it to keep their food fresh.
- YOU: Is that because they will not have electricity for their refrigerators?
- THEM: Yes.
- YOU: So, are they going to use all 224.3 million pounds at once?
- THEM: Of course not.
- YOU: So what are they going to do with the rest?
- THEM: We will store it for them until they need it.

187

- YOU: If there was a better way to do this that could save the taxpayers millions would you do it?
- THEM: Yes. [HAND THEM YOUR PLAN]

This really happened. Over 100 million pounds of ice was stored for years after, costing taxpayers millions more. Someone should go find out who the political donor was.

CONVERSATION 2 (another true scenario):

- YOU: Are you aware that the city left a toxic dirt mound and children play on it?
- THEM: Yes, I am aware of the dirt mound, but experts say there is no danger to the kids.
- YOU: Did you know that lead was found in a study done on that dirt mound?
- THEM: Yes, but like I said the amounts are negligible and the children are not at risk.
- YOU: So what you are saying is, you have proof there is no danger to these children? What if you are wrong?
- THEM: [THEY MAY NOT ANSWER]
- YOU: Can you tell me where I can get the data that shows that proof. If you are wrong and children get ill, will you take complete responsibility for that?

CONVERSATION 3:

- THEM: We are going to update our school system for $15 million.
- YOU: Can you explain what that $15 million will pay for?
- THEM: Upgrades to furniture, books and windows.
- YOU: Would you agree that the taxpayers would want to get the best deal possible when it comes to spending their money?
- THEM: Yes.
- YOU: I haven't seen the contracts, but are you absolutely sure the taxpayer's couldn't get a better deal?
- THEM: Yes.
- YOU: If someone could get the same products and services for less money, do you think the taxpayers would like that and could you give me any reason why you wouldn't support it?

Obviously, this is not how those conversations went, but you see how easy a few questions could have changed the course of these bad decisions.

188

HOW TO CHALLENGE IF THEY ARE WRONG (SPENDING)

1. Are you aware that _____ is costing (or getting paid) _____ for_____?

2. What do we get for that? Is it the right amount, should it be more or less? Why?

_____

3. So what you are saying is: _____

_____, is that correct? _____

4. Where does that money come from?_____

5. If we asked those people if they want to over pay or get a good price for their money, what do you think they would choose (for the same products and or services)? _____

6. If there was a way to get exactly the same _____ [issue in #1 above] for less money, do you think _____ [people from #3 above] would like to have that option? _____

7. If you knew how to get the same services or products for less money would you do it? _____

8. Here is a plan to accomplish that. [Hand them the plan and explain how it will save taxpayers money and get the same results.] If, after reading this plan, you agree it is viable, will you enact it to save taxpayer's $_____? [State the amount that will be saved.]

9. Can you give me any reasons why the people should not get more value for their dollars?

List all of their reasons (objections): _____

_____

10. So if none of those reasons were a problem, then you would agree we should move forward with this plan, is that correct? _____ Overcome all objections.

SUPPORTING TEMPLATES: 3, 5, & 6.

HOW TO CHALLENGE IF THEY ARE WRONG (TEST IT FIRST)

1. If I don't understand why you made this decision, do I have the right to ask questions? _____

2. You have stated that _____

_____, is that correct? _____

3. [OPTIONAL TO STOP SOMEONE FROM LABELING YOU] If a U.S. citizen, whose tax dollars are paying for this, tries to find the truth by asking questions, should people get mad at them and label them unpatriotic, a socialist, a person who wants the terrorists to win or someone who doesn't believe in capitalism? _____ (Shorten for the issue at hand.)

4. Why does this have to be done? _____

_____

5. Who exactly made this decision? _____

6. Can you tell me how it is planned to work? _____

_____

7. What would happen if we didn't do it? _____

_____ How do you know? _____

_____

8. Is there any chance at all you are wrong? _____

9. Can we test it first before we commit all of those resources? _____

10. Why not?_____

11. So what you are saying is, you want people to _____, but there is no way for us to test the idea first just in case something isn't right? _____

12. Will you accept complete responsibility if it is found out this is wrong? _____

SUPPORTING TEMPLATES: 3, 5, & 6.

I have added a second scenario (previous page) for this section. Sometimes you will challenge their decisions and it is not about the money being spent. You will use this template before they make the wrong decision. The opportunity for this is when the government is planning something and has an open forum for the public to ask questions.

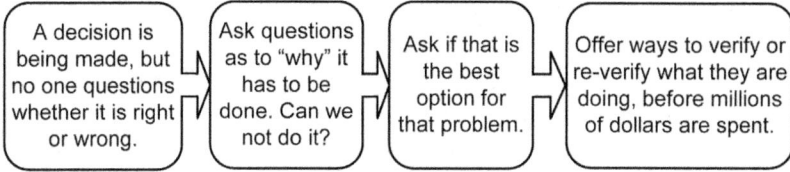

| A decision is being made, but no one questions whether it is right or wrong. | Ask questions as to "why" it has to be done. Can we not do it? | Ask if that is the best option for that problem. | Offer ways to verify or re-verify what they are doing, before millions of dollars are spent. |

TEMPLATE 5: How To Get It Done Now

After all of your work of exposing the truth and presenting plans on how to fix the problem, there is still one more hurdle. When will it get done? People of undeserved success have mastered the art of procrastination. The government does this by enacting laws and stipulating they will take effect in 2-10 years, by that time they are out of office.

The goal is to get the strongest commitment possible from the person who has the power and authority to make the plan happen. Then someone needs to follow up on that commitment. It is called being accountable; every business, school, and organization does it. It comes down to one statement, "If you say you are going to do something, then do it." If they don't do what they committed to, you have the video for proof to take the next step and replace them.

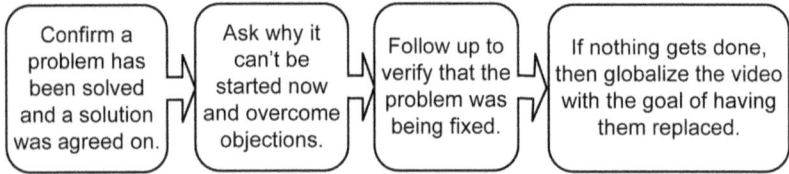

Confirm a problem has been solved and a solution was agreed on.	Ask why it can't be started now and overcome objections.	Follow up to verify that the problem was being fixed.	If nothing gets done, then globalize the video with the goal of having them replaced.

The conversation or interview might go like this:

- YOU: Would you agree we have the solution that it is good for the American public?
- THEM: Yes, I think this is a great day to be an American.
- YOU: Can you give me any reasons why we can't start this plan this week, even if starting meant making phone calls to get other commitments?
- THEM: I have to make sure we have all the people in place and there are no other logistical challenges.
- YOU: So what you are saying is, if there are no other logistical challenges and everyone is in place you will start on this immediately?
- THEM: Yes.
- YOU: Who are the people you need in place?
- THEM: [LET THEM ANSWER SO YOU HAVE IT ON VIDEO]
- YOU: What logistical challenges do you think there might be?
- THEM: [LET THEM ANSWER SO YOU HAVE IT ON VIDEO]
- YOU: Thank you Mrs. Congresswoman, may I contact you next week to see how the progress is moving forward and report that to this audience?

HOW TO GET IT DONE NOW

1. There was a problem, _____ that was solved by

_____, is that correct?

2. Can you give me any reason why this cannot be started within the next week?

_____

_____

3. Overcome every objection and write it so everyone can see.

_____

_____

4. Who is the person responsible for getting this started? _____

5. This is such an important issue that affects people's lives; don't you think we should get in touch with them right now? _____ Yes, right now, call them on the phone. Why not?

6. So what you are saying is, they don't take important phone calls during their actual working hours? _____ Then when do they take them? _____

7. Is there any chance you are coming up with these objections because you don't want to see this get started and obviously get completed?_____

8. Is there anyone in this department that has the authority to get this done? If so, give us their name and let's call them right now.

_____

9. What exactly is the reason why we cannot do this right now?

_____

SUPPORTING TEMPLATE: 6.

TEMPLATE 6: How To Replace People

It is obvious that trying to elect the right people to do the right thing in government just isn't working. So how can you get around this? How can you stop enabling government officials and corporate executives from finding ways to get things they don't deserve? The mechanisms are already in place, they just aren't working at peak performance right now. They are the protection agencies that were created to protect us against ourselves, which include the SEC, FDA, CDC, USDA, FTC and so on.

I believe most of the people in those agencies try to do what is right, unfortunately there are a few who make conscious choices and do what is wrong. So let's just get rid of those wrongdoers. This is the "backdoor" way of cleaning up government. Reclaim the "policing" system for the people and they will in turn watch over the government correctly. Why take this approach? Simple, it is easier to fire an agency official or employee than it is to get rid of an elected official. Plus the elected official is nothing without their friends in the agencies, but they won't risk re-election to save their friends' agency jobs. This applies to the private sector also.

The way it works is you have to know the truth and pinpoint who was at fault. Once the truth is out people will demand something gets fixed. Here are some examples, government and private: SEC dropping the ball with Maddof, FEMA debacle with Hurricane Katrina, FDA approving drugs that later are pulled from the shelves, Susan G. Komen holding back funding, EPA claiming the air was safe to breathe at ground zero, etc.

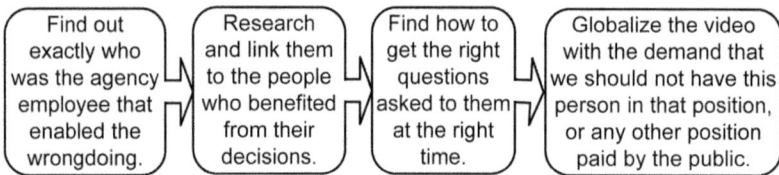

Find out exactly who was the agency employee that enabled the wrongdoing.	Research and link them to the people who benefited from their decisions.	Find how to get the right questions asked to them at the right time.	Globalize the video with the demand that we should not have this person in that position, or any other position paid by the public.

The conversation or interview might go like this:

- YOU: Are you aware of the drug PQR that you approved has caused multiple deaths in the people who have taken it?
- THEM: Yes, I am.
- YOU: Did you know that the data from the company was falsified?
- THEM: No, I did not have the resources to look into that.

- YOU: What do think should happen to FDA employees who knowingly approve drugs that had falsified data?
- THEM: They should be fired.
- YOU: What if that FDA decision killed people, would that be considered involuntary manslaughter?
- THEM: I don't think so.
- YOU: If the person approving it knew it could kill people and they approved it anyway, doesn't that prove gross negligence?
- THEM: Maybe.
- YOU: If I could prove you did know about the falsified data before you approved that drug, would you agree that being fired would be the minimum penalty?
- THEM: [THEY MIGHT NOT ANSWER] [HAND THEM THE PROOF] These are emails showing that you were well aware of the problems with this drug, can you tell me who else knew about this?

This sequence is for the non-oversight of government contracts:

- YOU: Isn't it your job to oversee all of the contracts for XYZ Company?
- THEM: Yes, me and my team.
- YOU: Are you aware that the government paid $20 billion dollars for planes when the original invoice was only for $5 billion?
- THEM: No, I was not aware of that.
- YOU: What you are saying is, your office approved payment of $20 billion in taxpayer dollars and nobody matched up the original contract to the final invoice, and you knew nothing about it?
- THEM: I am saying that our office deals with a lot of contracts and sometimes mistakes happen.
- YOU: So you believe this is a mistake? A $15 billion mistake.
- THEM: Yes, that is what happened.
- YOU: When people make multi-billion dollar mistakes, should they be fired or should we just accept that as business as usual and assume all government contracts can work that way?
- THEM: They should be reprimanded, but not fired.
- YOU: So what you are saying is, there are minimal consequences for misappropriating $15 billion dollars?
- THEM: I am not saying that.
- YOU: What amount of money has to be misappropriated before someone gets fired, $50 billion, $100 billion?

- THEM: [PROBABLY WON'T ANSWER]
- YOU: Would you agree that if this happened once, it is possible that it has happened before and may happen in the future?
- THEM: It is possible.
- YOU: If we could find where it happened in the past and were able to get that money back for the American people would they like that?
- THEM: Yes
- YOU: If we could put together a team that didn't cost the taxpayers one dime to audit your books, can you give me any reason why the taxpayers wouldn't want that to happen?
- THEM: [PROBABLY WON'T ANSWER]
- YOU: If it turns out there are more mistakes, do you agree you should resign and never be in another position that handles taxpayer money?

If after the truth is exposed and that person is not let go, then repeat the same process and use it to have their superior let go. The argument for that would be their incompetence, which is keeping a team of people on staff that is obviously not doing what is right for the American public. When someone claims this can't be done ask them, "Are you saying they are untouchable, that government officials who do not do their job cannot even be questioned? Is that what you are trying to tell the American public?"

HOW TO REPLACE PEOPLE

1. The reason we are here today is because it is believed that a certain problem didn't have to happen, is that correct? _____

2. Specifically, when _____
happened, then _____ agency should have
_____, is that correct? _____

3. Are you at fault? _____ Why or Why Not?

_____

4. So what you are saying is: _____

_____

5. If the same exact situation happened again, would you do the same exact thing? _____

6a. THEY ANSWER YES: So what you are saying is, if you stay in this position and this comes up again, there is a good chance we will be faced with the same problem again, is that correct? _____

6b. THEY ANSWER NO: So what you are saying is, the decisions you made will not be repeated again, why?
_____

7. So based on your answer (to 6b), would you agree the job was not done correctly? _____

8. Is someone is incapable or unwilling to perform the job they are paid for, what should the employer do? _____

9. Should you be fired? _____

10. Why not? _____

11. So what you are saying is, you want the taxpayers to pay you even though you are not doing the job of protecting their best interests, is that right? _____

12. Would you resign your position if this happens again? _____

SUPPORTING TEMPLATE: 3.

197

Chapter 43: How To Use Additional Ammunition

Additional Ammunition is used to supplement these truth exposing templates. All of the techniques learned in PART 5 are not used when actually asking questions. For the chapters that can be used, I have written several questions that can be incorporated into any of the templates.

Chapter 26: Transparent Studies, Inquiries and Research

This goes hand-in-hand with TEMPLATE 2. It can be written in a plan, used to overcome an objection or show the audience there is a solution.

- So what you are saying is, if we could do a transparent experiment your office would accept the results?
- Wouldn't you agree if we _____ with transparency the people would believe the results more than if it was a private study?

Chapter 27: Deliver A Plan They Cannot Deny

If you do not have a plan to deliver, then this can be used as a question to an objection.

- So what you are saying is, if we had a viable plan to produce these results, you would agree to move forward on this? If they say yes, then you have to get a plan to them later on.

Chapter 28: Reward & Replace

- Rewards would be questioned as a problem and implemented with TEMPLATE 1.
- Replacing someone who is not doing their job is TEMPLATE 6

Chapter 29: A Workforce For Good

This option will be valuable when the person objecting claims that the costs are too prohibitive to use the plan.

- So what you are saying is, if we could get this accomplished at no cost, then you would be onboard?

198

Chapter 30: Polygraphs – Do They Work

This is something that should be used sparingly, because they may call you out on it and then you will have to find a way to have a polygraph administered. If you are right and this will expose the truth, then it will probably be worth it.

- If you are completely sure about _____, would you be willing to take a polygraph to quiet the disbelievers?

Chapter 31: Make It Personal – They Do

There are no questions, but these people could be the questioners.

Chapter 32: Record It For The History Books

There are no questions, but everything should be video recorded.

Chapter 33: Globalize The Truth

There are no questions; this is the final action with all encounters.

Chapter 44: Take It To The Next Level

You can use these templates directly, or as a guide for when you are putting together a questioning sequence designed to expose the truth. They may or may not fit into the same situation you will be dealing with. That's okay, just adapt them to what your needs are.

If you are having difficulty crafting questions, just use questions on yourself. I always used dry erase boards, but a pen and paper works fine. Write down the problem or issue at the top and then write your questions to yourself underneath that.

Ask yourself the following questions:

- How can I find the truth about this problem?
- Who is keeping this solution suppressed and why?
- How can I expose the truth to the world?
- What are the questions I have to write that will expose the truth quickly?
- How can I get the right questions asked to the right people?
- How can I find other people who want to fix the world like I do?

There is no limit to what questions you can ask yourself. You may think this won't work, but you don't know what your brain is capable of. Maybe you are a problem solving genius. The bottom line is that the answer will always be no until you try.

PART 9:

FIX THIS FIRST - FIX THE WORLD

Chapter 45: The Underlying Problem

One of the ways a country measures the wealth of its people is to evaluate the disposable income of its largest financial group. In this case "largest" means the greatest number of people, not the greatest amount of money. Therefore you would exclude the extremely wealthy and extremely poor. Disposable income is how much money people have after they have paid their taxes (Disposable Income = Personal Income − Personal Income Taxes and Government Fees). This is not to be confused with discretionary income, which is the amount of income a consumer has available after purchasing essentials such as food and shelter.

The United States has become a nation of monthly bills: mortgage, utilities, food, gas, cable TV, Internet, cell phone, health insurance, life insurance, retirement, maintenance drugs, credit cards, car loans, car insurance, online subscriptions, student loans, etc. The U.S. consumer is literally choking on personal debt. Add to that the cost to raise children today compared to 20 or 30 years ago. Kids used to go outside and play ball. Now your children probably have anywhere from $1000-$5000 of electronic equipment in their bedroom alone.

It is amazing how a complete financial meltdown in the world's largest economy can happen and financial experts claim nobody saw it coming. Now, entrenched in an economic quagmire, nobody seems to be addressing the underlying problem. A basic fundamental to economic growth in a consumer driven economy is people need money to spend. I know what you are thinking, "Wow, this guy is a genius." When you base your economy on consumption and you continually decrease the amount of purchasing power your consumers have, you will eventually cannibalize the very system you rely upon.

Isn't this what financial forecasters and economists are supposed to be looking out for? Did anyone of them say, "Hold on, this doesn't look good. All we need is one disruption in our financial model and this house of cards is coming down." If they did, it obviously wasn't loud enough. Once consumers were tapped out, the dominos started to fall, one sector and then another sector and so on and so on. It became an economic death spiral, leaving numerous casualties in its path.

I know you want to hear about how Wall Street played a part and I will get to that later. For now, I want to point out the underlying problem: too many people in the United States have an income to debt ratio that is upside down or unsustainable. There are many causes, but this is the problem. This is what has to be fixed.

Chapter 46: Economics For The Rest Of Us

There is a basic model used by economists called the Economic Circular Flow. It displays the economic relationships between households, businesses and the government. Each component relies on the other two for its existence. A change in one directly affects the other two, either positively or negatively. In theory, a healthy economy would not waiver too far out of equilibrium; each component is not rising or dropping far below the other two. If there is growth in one component the others would adjust to balance it and vice versa. Unfortunately, the United Sates economy is extremely out of balance.

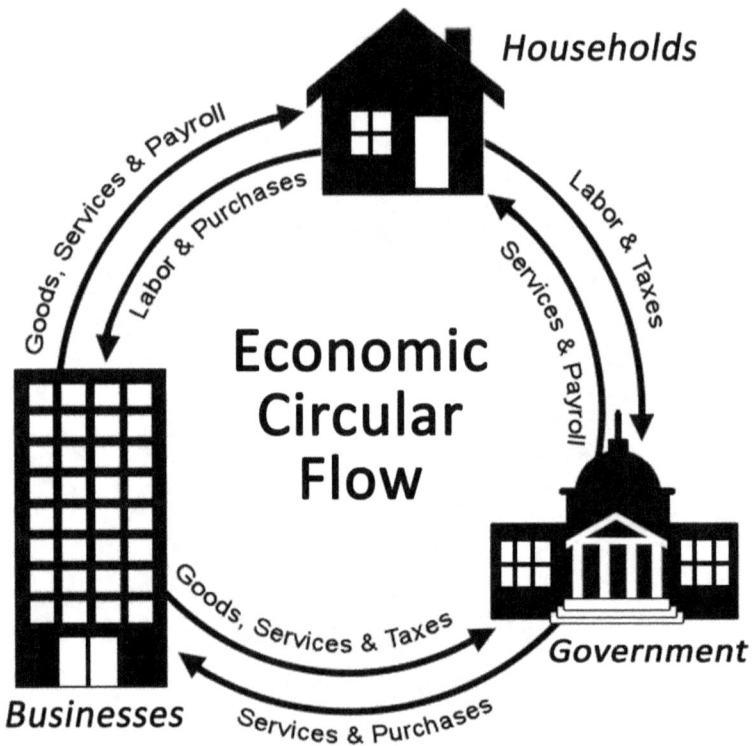

Real world "balancing" examples:

1. There was a real estate boom and people were buying homes. Businesses needed to build more homes, which made them hire more people, which produced larger tax revenues for the government. All three components grew.

2. In 2007 several large companies collapsed. In order to return to equilibrium, households had to lose their jobs, which meant government received fewer taxes and therefore should have reduced their size. All three components shrank.

3. Households began to go completely underwater. The government over-compensated to move toward equilibrium; they created a stimulus program, extended unemployment benefits and social services. This allowed households to pay some bills which added to businesses revenues. One component overcompensated.

The belief was if government over-compensated, it would kick start the U.S. economy, which everyone realizes didn't happen. There is a simple reason for that; they did not address the underlying problem, household disposable incomes. When household disposable incomes are reduced they spend less on non-necessities and even cancel planned purchases. This affects small businesses in their local communities, which includes: restaurants, car dealers, florists, entertainment, etc. These are the businesses that create the jobs within those communities.

As these businesses lose income they cut back and let go of employees, thus reducing the household disposable incomes even more. This begins to effect more purchasing decisions and people decide to hold off on: car repairs, home repairs, dental visits, entertainment, nail salons, etc. The revenues for these businesses are decreased and more employees are let go, reducing household disposable incomes even more. The downward spiral has started and the next businesses to hit the "bill paying chopping block" are the essentials: mortgages, credit cards, insurances and utilities. If there is no safety net, then these households are no longer solvent. There are more homeless people than you probably realize in the US, the news just doesn't report it. These were Middle Class families just a few years ago, who became a victim of exactly what I just laid out. Some of these travesties weren't even caused by job loss; their financial devastation was due to medical bills.

Households have taken a hit financially. Therefore, one of the other components needed to over compensate in order to keep the Economic Circular Flow in balance. The government is over-compensating, but ironically it is with future tax dollars to be paid by future households and it is unsustainable. Businesses decided not to over-compensate. Why should they, it doesn't make good business sense. They are not creating jobs and the reason is because they are not sure people will have the money to buy their products. So the end result is an economic model that is completely out of balance. I am not the first person to realize or write about the effects of diminishing disposable and discretionary incomes. Just Google either one of these and you can read the research and the current impact it has on our economy.

If you fix the largest component (households) then the other two (government and business) will be fixed automatically. Once households are stabilized financially, people will pay their bills and spend their discretionary incomes. This will produce demand for businesses and tax revenues will be produced for the government. It will also relieve the government of its social services burden.

Chapter 47: This Time It Is Different

The United States has had a multitude of recessions in the past and even though the National Bureau of Economic Research claimed the last one ended in June of 2009, there are tens of millions of people who are still being affected. Unemployment is still high, companies are still laying off people, and real estate prices are still falling.

I believe in studying the past so you can learn for the future, but the financial past is quite different from the current financial landscape. This is especially true for households who are taking the brunt of the financial meltdown. The financial makeup of the average household in no way resembles the financial makeup of households in the 1970s, 1980s or 1990s. That's obvious, or is it? To put this in perspective, there was a time when a blue collar worker, with a single household income, was able to send 2 kids to college and not have to mortgage their home to do it. That was only 20-30 years ago. This is probably impossible nowadays.

If you study a problem that was solved in the past, but there is a new dynamic, would you expect the same solutions that worked then to work now? It appears the general wisdom is to do what was done in the past and that will cure our current problems. Is it possible someone needs to look at the current financial pieces and create a new solution to the puzzle? There are many pieces to this puzzle that need to be considered, I will briefly discuss several here. You can easily research any one of these on the Internet to get complete facts and analyze the overall impact.

1. Real Estate

Yes, real estate took a beating in past recessions and there was the Savings and Loan bailout, which the Resolution Trust Corporation estimated the total cost for resolving the crisis to be $87.9 billion. It was bad, but it affected a much smaller percentage of people. There were far less people "upside down" on their mortgages, home prices didn't spike the same way before the crisis, there wasn't as much speculation and there were less exotic mortgage plans.

You want to hear something really scary in real estate? Start probing around commercial property. Asks questions like: "Are there commercial mortgages that are upside down?" "How come you see

207

a lot of empty buildings, strip malls and manufacturing facilities, but you don't hear anything about the mortgage defaults?", or "What happened to all the devaluation of that property?"

One of the biggest problems this time was people pulling the equity out of their homes. Equity, in some cases, that was built up over decades. If this didn't happen, it could have saved us from this financial debacle. One reason would have been when real estate prices dropped, the amount owed would still be less than the value of the home and therefore people would not be upside down on their mortgage. Another reason would be that once the problems hit, people could have borrowed against their house to weather the financial storm. There would not be the gluten of foreclosures that are choking the real estate market today.

2. 401Ks and the Stock Market

During past recessions company pension plans were still intact; 401Ks were just beginning in 1978. Therefore retiree's monthly pension income wasn't affected; they were still able to pay their bills. Compare that to today, where some people's nest egg was devalued by 70%. With people turning to mutual funds in the 90s as an alternative to CDs and savings accounts, they also experienced the same losses. It made it tough to use the emergency fund that wasn't worth much anymore. Even though there was Wall Street corruption in past recessions, it pales to what happened this time. Billions of dollars turned up missing from millions of accounts and oddly only a fraction of the people responsible were convicted this time as compared to previous scandals.

3. Household Income to Debt Ratio

I have already gone over this challenge in a previous chapter. Just to reiterate the problem: when you go from a handful of monthly bills (mortgage, utilities, car payment, car insurance, food, gas, etc.), to a plethora of monthly bills (mortgage, utilities, food, gas, cable TV, Internet, cell phone, health insurance, life insurance, retirement, maintenance drugs, credit cards, car loans, car insurance, online subscriptions, student loans, etc.), it is obviously going to be harder to weather a financial downturn when you are choking on that much debt.

4. Health Insurance and Medical Costs

In the past, it was fairly unheard of to have a household go bankrupt due to medical bills. In 2009 there was a study that suggested that more than 60 percent of bankruptcies that year were due to medical bills. This was not a problem in previous recessions for several reasons. One, the cost for health care has skyrocketed out of control in the last 15 years. Two, there was a time when employers actually provided health insurance to their employees. Three, there weren't many exclusions by the health insurance industry and four, we weren't a maintenance drug society as prescribed by the pharmaceutical companies.

5. Baby Boomers

Starting on January 1, 2011, it is estimated that 10,000 baby boomers will reach age 65 every day for the next 19 years. That is every day! For a tax strapped government, this is a burden that has huge consequences on how to divvy up the money. Adding insult to injury, it is believed that this group lost the most money in the Stock Market. Do you know what they are doing now? They are looking for work to survive their "Golden Years".

How does this affect an economic recovery? For the most part, when people retire they are bringing in less money. In retirement you rarely get raises and you aren't looking to produce more income, that is why it is called retirement. Sadly, more and more retirees are forced to produce more income, because for some of them their retirement funds are not what they thought they would be. Working against them is inflation, rising taxes, higher energy costs, etc. This increasingly cuts into the amount of money left over at the end of the month. That is tens of millions of people who have less money to spend every month, which means less money to spend in their local economies. Which means less demand and negative growth.

6. US Manufacturing

Over the last 20 years the U.S. has dramatically reduced its manufacturing capabilities. The days of one manufacturer being the main employer of thousands of Middle American cities and towns are gone. Those manufacturing jobs have been shipped overseas and do not appear to be coming back. There have been a few towns and cities revitalized by a new automobile manufacturing facility and the same has happened in select areas where oil and natural gas are being exploited. Compared to what has been lost in the last 10 years, it is only a drop in the bucket, and in no way is fixing our economic challenges of today.

7. Second Incomes Are Harder To Come By

The way Americans used to compensate for the decrease in disposable income was to work more by taking on second jobs and having both spouses employed. This used to be the way to get ahead, but now it is the norm just to survive and that's if they are lucky enough to find work. There are many studies that believe this is one of the main causes to the breakdown of the family structure, both spouses working and children raising themselves.

8. Family Consolidation

Families have learned how to consolidate. This is detrimental to the current real estate market and the home builders who rely on it. Thirty year old children living with their parents is becoming the norm. It actually makes a lot of sense. No rent or mortgage, shared utility costs, taxes, etc. Somewhere down the road the parents will pass on and the home will just transfer names, this will not create a new real estate sale. Consolidation can also increase household disposable incomes; that is if the children are actually working. In some cases the children aren't working, so the result is decreased household discretionary income.

As you can see, the options that people had in the past are no longer available and they are not just on the edge, a lot of them have fallen over it. There are people who are thankful the government is going into huge debt paying extended unemployment benefits, but it is my belief a lot of them would rather be working and contributing. Plus, how long do you think the government can keep throwing money at the symptoms without addressing the cause? Sounds like a play from the pharmaceutical industry's playbook.

Back in the day when people lost their jobs and inflation spiked, there was still a cushion to fall back on, people survived without a government safety net. Even if it meant borrowing money from their parents, at least it was an option then. It was still painful, but people made it through. Now the dynamic has changed and it is time to fix the cause.

Undoubtedly, there will be some economic wizards who will make all sorts of claims as to why this isn't the problem or that there were other factors. Yes, there were other factors and they all affected the average American's disposable income, which affected their ability to keep consuming locally, which affected the local economies and so on. If you don't fix this, you will never truly fix the economy.

Chapter 48: Their Theory Is Wrong

Due to the large disparity of personal incomes in the United States, you cannot consider "across the board" data as an average, it doesn't make sense. To clarify, let's take one person who has $99,000 of discretionary income and another one who has $1,000. That is a total of $100,000 in discretionary incomes, which averages out to be $50,000 each. Does this mean they can both go out and spend $50,000 without affecting their current financial status? Yes, a ludicrous question, but there are income statistics that are based on similar assumptions, so you can't always trust them. If you are researching financial statistics for the United States find out how the data was collected and calculated.

I find it hard to believe that when most of the money is in a few centralized locations, people claim that will spur economic growth across the country. Here's a study someone should complete: find out the net worth of everyone in the U.S. prior to 2007 and compare that to the net worth of everyone now. I wonder if it would reveal there is a trillion dollar difference in real estate alone. Then you can just look at the transfer of money from pensions and retirement plans. Where do you think all the money came from that is now funding hedge funds. Do you really believe that money was earned by a company or person who provided a service or product to people who willingly paid for it?

I am not going to delve too deeply into the reasons. Again, there are studies and data on the Internet. The point is, there has been an incredible shift of money from Middle America to a few locations, which include Chicago, New York City and Washington, D.C. Knowing this, didn't anyone look down the road to see what the repercussions would be? What did they think? Somehow the small towns and cities would figure out a way to make more money. And do what with it? Donate it to Wall Street in the form of a retirement plan or maybe invest it in an overpriced piece of real estate, using an exotic mortgage, which they would default on in 5 years anyway.

Someone please explain to me how billions of payroll dollars in Chicago, New York City and Washington, D.C. are going to affect any of the thousands of small town economies across the United States. Let me guess. There is going to be a mass demand of wealthy people road-tripping around the country for the next 5 years, spending their money in Small

Town, USA. That will create the local demand needed in all of those micro-economies, which will spur growth and create new jobs. Brilliant, I knew they had an answer.

The reality is, those large payrolls have spurred growth in their local economies. The local businesses in Chicago, New York City and Washington, D.C. are not feeling financial hardships the same way local businesses in most small to medium cities are. It's simple, people in those demographics are working and spending money. Spending money creates demand. Demand creates job growth. Job growth gives more people more money to spend. How hard is this to understand? If you centralize most of a country's wealth into several key areas, those locations will do fine and all the others will deteriorate. This is why New York City can get away with selling a hotdog for $100. Anyone see a lopsided economy here? Money needs to be spent locally for every town and city, not just a few. It is impossible for a city or town to thrive if consumers don't support the businesses within that city. How can they support the businesses in that city when there are depressed wages, high unemployment and low discretionary incomes?

There is another problem with centralized wealth. The affects of wealthy people spending the same amount of money that the Middle Class would spend is like night and day. This is the true dilemma of a lopsided consumer driven economy, which is what many people believe we are in.

Let's take the effects of $30 billion per month spent in U.S. businesses. On the next page is a side-by-side comparison chart to show the effects. The right side displays money being spent by 100 million people across the country (average income America). On the left side is 10 million people spending the same total amount of money, they will be in centralized areas (wealthy demographic America). The total amount spent is the same on each side. The purchases are for similar items, but the price that each side is willing (able) to pay is much different. So where would the country get more bang for the buck? In other words, if you had to make the intelligent decision, wouldn't you want to use your resources to create the greatest economic impact?

Where does $30,000,000,000/mth being spent affect an economy the most?

WEALTHY: You give 10,000,000 people $3,000/mth to spend. That is a total of $30 billion/mth.		Assume each group spends the money on similar items:	MIDDLE CLASS: You give 100,000,000 people $300/mth to spend. That is a total of $30 billion/mth.	
MONEY SPENT	**RETAIL SALES MADE**	**RETAIL Purchases**	**RETAIL SALES MADE**	**MONEY SPENT**
$700	1	2 Pairs of Pants 1 Shirt	1	$90
$500	1	1 Pair of Shoes	1	$50
MONEY SPENT	**RESTAURANT SALES MADE**	**DINING OUT Purchases**	**RESTAURANT SALES MADE**	**MONEY SPENT**
$1000	10	Dinners	4	$80
MONEY SPENT	**ENTERTAINMENT SALES MADE**	**ENTERTAINMENT Purchases**	**ENTERTAINMENT SALES MADE**	**MONEY SPENT**
$300	2	Broadway Theater Vs. Movie Theater	2	$30
$500	2	Sports Tickets Vs. Video Game Buy	1	$50
MONEY SPENT	**# OF SALES AT BUSINESSES**	**RESULTS**	**# OF SALES AT BUSINESSES**	**MONEY SPENT**
$3,000	16	PER PERSON	9	$300
10,000,000	10,000,000	# OF PEOPLE	100,000,000	100,000,000
$30,000,000,000	**160,000,000**	TOTALS	**900,000,000**	$30,000,000,000

DO YOU SEE THE DIFFERENCE!

Which spurs more economic growth, businesses that get 160 million customers per month or businesses that get 900 million customers per month? Which side do you think would need more employees to service them? HINT: Pick the big number. When you have 900 million additional business purchases a month, there are jobs either preserved or created. Those employees support the same spending cycle and they preserve or create more jobs, thus producing economic growth. Does this happen quicker when 10 million people are purchasing or when 100 million people are purchasing?

You can play with these numbers all you want, but the end result will always be the same. If you need proof, pull up retail data across the country, or just go to Middle America and see how many stores are selling jeans for

214

$300 a pair. The greatest demand comes from the masses, one person can only eat so many dinners, go to so many movies, or buy so many TVs, there is a limit. One of the most profitable companies right now is McDonalds, I doubt most of their sales are coming from wealthy people spending thousands of dollars a day eating burgers.

Referring to the wealthy side of the chart, how much of that money spent affected the small Midwestern city financially. Unless any of the products purchased were manufactured or grown there, the answer would be none. What about the opposite. How much did NYC or DC benefit from money spent in small town America? The products or services they bought probably benefitted the bottom line of a company that is traded on Wall Street. Therefore there is an impact and DC also gets taxes from both sides. It is a Win-Win-Win scenario.

Another benefit of Middle America working and making a decent wage, is that some of them will choose NYC and DC when they travel. You know the opposite rarely happens. NYC and DC will benefit from the economic impact of rural America spending money in those cities, which is a win for everyone. Whereas centralizing wealth, is a win for a few. That is what lopsided means.

Yes, the profits may be less in small town America, but so is the cost of living. There is no rule that says your executive team must make $500 million collectively in order to live their American dream. Remember, it is the same amount of money; it just doesn't produce the same value for the country as a whole. Also, wealthy people will spend more money overseas through travel, that is a lose-lose for the American economy. And don't forget that wealthy households have savvy accountants to reduce their taxes; for the most part, Middle America doesn't do this.

So the net benefit to the economy, for the same amount of money spent, is less when it is spent by the wealthy. I like to see an economist prove that one wrong. Especially if they think that getting more income to the wealthy will cure the economic woes of our country. This is so easy to prove. Take a million dollars to a small Midwestern town and divide it up between 1000 people and have them go spend it. Follow the money and calculate the impact. Then take a million dollars and give it to 100 affluent people in NYC and have them go spend the money. Follow that trail and calculate the results. There's your proof.

This section is not saying wealthy people should not go out and buy extravagant items with their money. It is their money and quite honestly nobody cares how they spend it, they just care how they got it. The point is, if you are going to create laws and tax policies that benefit the wealthy, believing that is the way to grow an economy, you are kidding yourself and everyone else.

Chapter 49: How To Fix The Economy For Everyone

It should be obvious. Household discretionary incomes have to increase. This is not rocket science. If people had more money, could they do more with it? Sorry, just another stupid question. There are only two ways to increase household discretionary incomes. The first way is to increase household incomes. Does anyone see this happening? Incomes have barely increased in a decade and there is no evidence it is going to begin now or any time in the next few years. So that option is probably off the table.

The second option is to decrease household cash expenditures. I know this is already happening, because families are either cutting back or not paying their bills, therefore they have decreased their monthly expenditures. I am pretty sure that everyone will agree this solution doesn't spur economic growth and prosperity. What if you could significantly decrease household cash expenditures without cutting back on anything? I don't want to debate this right now. I am just saying, "What if?"

What if it was enough so families were no longer upside down on their monthly expenses, what would that mean? For some people it would mean they would be able to pay their bills and feed their family. What if this was across the board? What if everyone saw a significant bump in the money they had after paying their monthly debts? This includes: upper-class, middle-class and lower-class. What would they do? Probably what they always do, they would go spend some of it. Remember, I am not talking about increasing household incomes, families cutting back, lowering their current standard of living or enacting a government stimulus.

Increased discretionary incomes will cause more money to be pumped into the U.S. economy at local levels, causing demand across the country. Thus reversing the current economic death spiral we are on and turning it into a growth spiral. If this is possible, show me the person who doesn't want it? I know you are thinking there aren't any, but unfortunately that is not true. The proof is in the fact that solutions have been around for years.

Let's get back to the benefits. If people are able to pay less bills for the same exact services or products, that means they could have more discretionary income, without affecting their quality of life. Some of these people might be able to start paying their mortgages. What does that do?

217

Effects of mortgages being paid:

1. Slows the foreclosures.
2. Slows family homelessness.
3. Stabilizes the Real Estate market, which in-turn will stabilize the (much depended on) property tax revenues.
4. When people realize prices are no longer dropping they may begin to buy homes again.

You want to hear a doomsday scenario? If household discretionary incomes do not increase, home prices will continue to drop past the current amount they are taxed on and then every homeowner will demand a reset on their property taxes to match the true value of their home. You think the government is broke now, what would they do then? Hopefully our leaders will not let their greed get in the way of their common sense.

So what else could happen if you were able to increase the discretionary incomes of nearly every American?

What do you think they might do with it?

1. Buy a new car.
2. Go clothes shopping.
3. Go out to eat.
4. Take a vacation.
5. Pay for an education.
6. Take in local entertainment.
7. Fix up the house.
8. Buy new furniture.
9. Pay down their debt.
10. Save some money.
11. Give to their church or charities.
12. Support the politicians that had the courage to make this happen.

What about the savings from people getting off unemployment, Medicare, and other social programs? That reduces the tax burden on the government, which should reduce the tax burden on citizens, thus giving them even more discretionary income. Some people believe it would only take an increase of $300 per month, per household to create a turnaround of the U.S. economy. If you think $300 is negligible, just multiply that out by 100,000,000 households. That is $30 billion per month, which is $360 billion per year, spent locally across the country.

218

PART 10:

A GUARANTEED SOLUTION

Chapter 50: This Will Fix The World

From Part 9 you learned the way to fix the economy is to put money back into everyone's pocket. The goal is $300 per month, per household. The challenge is to achieve the goal without new taxes, a government stimulus, working more or reducing the standard of living. One way to accomplish this is to reduce household cash outlay for essential living expenditures, without changing the quantity or quality of those purchases. In order to save $300 per month they obviously have to be spending more than that. What essentials do most households spend more than $300 a month for?

The answer is:

- Insurance (car, health, life, homeowners, etc.)
- Food (breakfast, lunch, dinner, snacks, coffee, bottled drinks, etc.)
- Finance (mortgages, 401Ks, car loans, student loans, etc.)
- Government (taxes, taxes, taxes)
- Energy (gas, electric, heating, etc.)

You can use the Problem Solving Method in any of the industries above. I have chosen energy because there are added benefits besides just saving money. The goal is to find a problem that already has a solution and can put at least $300 per month back into American Households. This will be done step-by-step using the Problem Solving Process.

PART: 1

| Identify a problem with a solution that is not being used. | ➡ | Learn the truth about the solution and prove it to yourself. | When the truth is globalized people will take action to fix what is wrong. |

- **Problem:** High gas prices adversely affect people's lives and diminish the opportunity of an economic recovery for everyone.
- **Truth:** There are technologies designed, tested, proven and currently being used in a limited number of vehicles that have produced incredible fuel savings.

PROVE IT TO YOURSELF

You would normally research this information for yourself. Even though I will present the facts, you should still verify them, so when someone tries to tell you something different you have no doubts about the truth.

220

There is a technology called Hydraulic Launch Assist. It is a simple concept. The system regenerates the wasted energy of traditional braking to "launch" the vehicle from a stopped position. A working model was designed over a decade ago in the United States and since then the technology has been deployed successfully in commercial vehicles. A brochure put out by the EPA (PDF #: EPA420-F-04-024), was available to the public at www.epa. gov, as of the writing of this book. In March 2004 the EPA website made the following statements:

EPA's multi-year research program to develop hydraulic hybrid technology has produced a proof-of-concept test chassis that:

- Triples the fuel economy of conventional vehicles (80 miles per gallon for a midsize family sedan that also incorporates improved tires and aerodynamics).
- Saves the consumer money (consumer payback [i.e., recouping the higher vehicle cost] within 1 to 3 years through fuel savings and less brake wear).
- Accelerates from 0 to 60 miles per hour (mph) in approximately 8 seconds.
- Attains higher fuel efficiency without using expensive lightweight materials (test weight of chassis is 3800 lb) to facilitate commercialization.

In the same brochure there was a picture of a Ford Expedition that was modified to demonstrate how this technology could be used on SUVs. On the Official EPA website there is a webpage entitled: "Hydraulic Hybrid Research". It states:

The bottom line is that hydraulic hybrid technology is simple, clean, efficient and cost effective.

- **Simple:** The technology does not require breakthroughs to be cost effective or to be manufactured, and can be produced with the skills and manufacturing base already available in the U.S.
- **Clean**: It has proven to reduce emissions by up to 40 percent.
- **Efficient:** Series HHVs dramatically increase fuel efficiency from 60 percent to over 100 percent.
- **Cost-effective**: The low cost to manufacture combined with reduced brake maintenance and dramatically increased fuel efficiency results in thousands of dollars saved over the lifetime of the vehicle. This makes HHVs one of the best green technologies to invest in.

Data on tests conducted with Hydraulic Launch Assist:

- There was a study done using a shuttle bus with a bus body supplied by Glaval Bus. It had a 14,000 lb. GVW Ford E-450 Cutaway chassis and was powered by a 6.0 L Ford Power Stroke V8 diesel engine. The Hydraulic Launch Assist supplied by Eaton boosted the drive train to approximately 300 hp and 1000 lb.ft. of torque. They combined this with a reduced axle ratio and the shuttle bus was able to get an increase of 26% in fuel economy, and the vehicle noise during acceleration was also reduced. This information was taken right from the Internet. This proves the technology can be used on buses. What would a 25% savings in bus fuel costs mean to a country such as ours? *This information is available at: http://www.dpna-digital. com/dpna/200704?pg=66#pg66 and is dated April 2007.

- For the Overnight Delivery Industry, a UPS package truck was developed through a partnership between the EPA, Eaton, UPS, International Truck and Engine Corp. and the U.S. Army. The truck used a high-efficiency 6.0 L International VT365 V8 diesel that was combined with hydraulic launch assist. In this version the conventional transmission and driveshaft were replaced. This hydraulic-diesel hybrid technology has achieved a 60 to 70% improvement in fuel economy and more than a 40% reduction in carbon dioxide emissions in initial laboratory testing. The EPA estimates that the technology has the potential to save more than 1000 gallons per year for each of the delivery trucks. At $3.50 per gallon, they would save over a million dollars per year for every 300 trucks they used it on. I think they have more than 300 trucks, you do the math. By the way, do you think you will see a reduction in shipping costs? I have seen fuel surcharges, odd isn't it. *This information is available at: http://www.dpna-digital.com/dpna/200704?pg=66#pg66 and is dated April 2007.

You may have never heard of this technology before, even though it has been around for over a decade, but that doesn't mean it is not true. It just means you never heard of it. There are households that spend over $500 per month for gasoline. Don't forget all the adult kids who now live back with their parents, which could mean three cars for those households. Assuming the EPA wasn't lying, if a household could get 80 mpg that would be 3 times better than most vehicles today. Based on that assumption the household spending $500/mth would now be spending $167/mth. That is a savings of $333/mth, which achieves the goal.

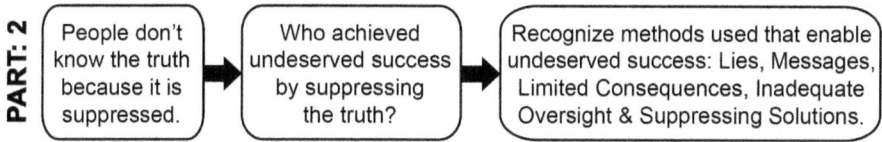

| PART: 2 | People don't know the truth because it is suppressed. | ➡ | Who achieved undeserved success by suppressing the truth? | ➡ | Recognize methods used that enable undeserved success: Lies, Messages, Limited Consequences, Inadequate Oversight & Suppressing Solutions. |

Who is suppressing the truth about hydraulic launch assist and why? I think the "who" is pretty obvious. Any company that deals in the oil industry does not want to see vehicles that get 80 mpg.

How has this technology flown under the radar for so long and why do so many people in our country believe the only solution to higher gas prices is to drill for more oil? It comes down to messaging. The oil industry funds a marketing campaign filled with misleading messages. It is designed to make people believe the oil industry is your friend and it is the life blood of American energy.

You see the ads on television all of the time. The commercials talk about how the oil industry creates American jobs and how people with mutual funds are probably sharing in the profits that oil companies make. Did you ever wonder why they even produce those ads? Do they entice you to apply for an oil industry job or invest more in your 401K? Think about it, why spend millions on advertising when it doesn't even ask you to buy their product? What are they trying to accomplish? Maybe they are trying to make a lie appear to be the truth.

As for oversight and limited consequences, go talk to the people who were actually affected by the recent Gulf of Mexico oil spill and ask them about U.S. protection agencies. If you want to know the truth just go to the source. You now know who, why and how.

PART: 3

| The support system of undeserved success is vulnerable to the truth. | ➡ | Expose the truth by asking the right questions to the right people at the right time, in front of an audience. |

Who are the right people: The President of the United States and the EPA Administrator, those are two good ones to start with. You can also question anyone who developed or is using this technology and can verify the results. You can add anyone in Congress, but it is not the guy down the street or the lady at the supermarket.

How can the world watch it? My suggestion: There are top rated interviewers who have access to the president and I would imagine that means they have access to any public servant. They are Steve Kroft, Matt Lauer, Bill O'Reilly, Diane Sawyer, George Stephanopoulos, and Brian Williams, just to name a few (I apologize if I didn't mention every interviewer's name). They have all interviewed President Barack Obama and they should have no problem getting an interview again. These interviewers are all respected in their industry and have millions of people who follow what they say. Another possibility is for them or other reporters to be able to ask questions at town forums and press meetings. Can anyone think of a reason why they should not setup an interview and ask the President why we aren't using this technology?

Below are truth exposing questions that should be asked of the President, in what would be one of the most historic interviews of all time. Journalists usually have a goal to get the insights of the person they are interviewing, but in this case what we really want is the truth as soon as possible. An interviewer's option would be to complete the following questions first and then ask questions that will invoke insight and opinion after the problem is fixed. That doesn't mean you can't change the following questions, as long as they follow the basic rules of exposing the truth.

QUESTIONS:

1. Do you think the current gasoline prices are hurting Americans?
2. If Americans could reduce their gasoline costs by 50% would they be better off?
3. If there was a technology that has already been developed and is being used successfully to achieve a 50% reduction in fuel costs, do you think Americans would want to know about it?

4. If there was a plan to use this technology, in a way that would create millions of jobs, do think Americans would want you to enact that plan? Hand them the plan below?

An Actual World Saving Plan:

Employ this technology on as many vehicles as soon as possible: cars, trucks, and buses.

Plan Implementation:

I. Build new cars NOW using HLA technology. The EPA already had a proto-type done several years ago. I would imagine they are smart people and therefore it has been perfected over the last 6 years. At least that is what people do when they have a world saving technology in their hands.

II. Figure out how to retrofit the technology. Retrofit cars, trucks and buses that are currently on the road. Maybe it won't work in 100% of the cars, but we don't need a 100% to have a huge impact. Before you disclaim a retrofit solution (such as a unit that fits in the trunk) ask the people if they would want it. Why don't you find out their answers first, don't make that decision for them. For thousands of dollars a year back in their pocket they just might live with it.

Follow These Rules:

I. Begin now. Even if that means creating a detailed plan. By the way, that can be done in less than a month. If you would like one for free I am sure that can be arranged. The point is, get the plan done and then start implementing it.

II. Don't outsource the manufacturing; we have everything we need in the United States. Do you think American's would agree with this rule?

III. No one gets overpaid. For every company or person that is chosen to implement this plan, the question will be, "Why do the taxpayers have to overpay a company or a person when they could get either one for less money?"

IV. No one gets over charged.

    a. Why do taxpayers have to overpay for a product when the reality is it doesn't cost that much?

    b. If I could prove it would cost less by submitting Request For Quotes to American companies, would you go with the best choice for the least money?

V. No one becomes wealthy because they are someone's relative, friend, contributor, etc. People don't mind if someone works hard, provides value and because of it becomes wealthy. What's irking America is people getting so much of our money for doing so little. So before you dish out the big multimillion dollar contract, we would like to know what it is we are getting for our money first. You want to be fair and honest with the American public, don't you?

I know, some of the readers are saying, "This sounds good, but that will never happen." So I ask, "If we did use these rules, would it work?" Then my next question would be, "So why can't we use them?" The only objections will come from people whose plan is to keep you paying as much as possible so they stay rich and you go poor. If you don't believe it, just look around. This technology could have been used years ago. Why aren't we using it? This proves one of the premises from PART 2, solutions are being suppressed.

5. Are you familiar with a technology developed in coordination with the EPA called Hydraulic Launch Assist? They may or may not know about it, if not give a quick overview of the technology. There is more data at the end of this section or just have someone from the EPA there.

6. If you are questioning the EPA and they say they are unfamiliar with HLA then you say, "You honestly are unaware of HLA and you are the person chosen to manage and direct our country's environmental policies, is that correct?" You can add additional questions.

7. If this plan makes sense, but it needs a little tweaking are you the type of person to kill a life changing idea over something that someone could remedy?

8. Where does the EPA get their funding?

9. So basically this technology is available today because of taxpayer dollars, would you agree with that assessment?

10. Can you think of any reason why the United States cannot begin using this technology to benefit the taxpayers who helped pay for it?

11. Can you give me any reasons why oil companies should make tens of billions in profits while there is a technology available that will actually allow average Americans to keep that money in their own pockets?

12. At this point there may be some legitimate objections. There are many answers to possible objections in the following pages. If there are other objections, use what you have learned to overcome them. Be prepared, have your facts and data with you.

13. Now that you have a plan that could use this technology will you put it aside, because it affects big political donors, or will you choose to help the average American?

14. What will be your first move to get this started now?

15. When will you do that?

16. If you don't follow through and make this technology available to average Americans, what would you suggest they do?

PART: 4

Be prepared for their objections as to why the solution is not possible. ➡ Overcome all of the objections. ➡ Craft your questions so they validate the solution, require commitment and promise consequences.

Hard to believe, but there will be objections. You might even see data disappear from industry and government websites, such as the EPA. Don't believe me, just find the data now and download it to your computer, it will only take a few minutes. They will come up with everything from, the technology has not been tested, to the American car buyer doesn't want this type of car, to it isn't good for the environment and maybe even say legally it cannot be done. I am sure they will have other reasons. Why? It is quite simple; if you were making tens of billions of dollars in profit, would you want someone to stop it?

In early 2012 the Environmental Protection Agency and National Highway Traffic Safety Administration held several hearings, giving the public the opportunity to comment on the joint-proposed Corporate Average Fuel Economy rules, which includes raising the fuel efficiency to 54.5 miles per gallon by 2025. By doing this the EPA estimates, that between 2017 and 2025, there would be more than 4 billion barrels of oil saved and it would cut carbon emissions by more than 2 billion metric tons. And

227

then they did something great, they overcame the objections already and revealed a November survey conducted by Consumer Reports that said 80 percent of consumers would support the 54.5-mpg target and that 83 percent said they would be willing to pay more for a car that offered better fuel economy. UAW president Bob King stated, "The drive to bring fuel efficient cars to the market is transforming existing jobs and creating new ones. These are the automotive jobs of the future." Proponents said the U.S. would benefit in the form of increased automotive jobs, consumer savings and enhanced national security. They are already onboard.

So what do you think now? I have shown you proof that the EPA has access and is using technology that increases gas mileage tremendously and they are touting a goal that is much lower than what they claim they could achieve years ago. Do you see how this issue is getting pushed down the road?

Whatever the objection is, I have shown earlier in this book how to turn it around and put it back on them. Here are examples for this issue:

- So what you are saying is, you are totally sure that the American consumer does not want to save 50% on fueling up their vehicle?
- So in other words, if we could integrate this technology and eliminate the hurdles, you would agree that initiating it as soon as possible would be the best solution for our country?
- Do you believe it is more important for large corporations to make huge profits or for U.S. citizens to benefit from technology their tax dollars helped create?

Why wouldn't anyone want to save the world? Sadly they will give you reasons and they will justify why they make sense. Use the questions below to expose the truth and show that their objections are not valid.

OBJECTION 1: There is no way you could retrofit this technology onto existing cars.
We are a smart country and we can do whatever we set our minds to. Honestly, how tough would it be to create a retrofitted hydraulic braking unit that even fits in a trunk and is attached to the drive train or rear axles? I am willing to bet that an open challenge to the engineers of our country would produce the results within 30-60 days.

RETURN QUESTIONS:

- So what you are saying is, if we can do it, that would be an amazing breakthrough, correct?
- Would you agree that utilizing HLA would be a huge financial win for Middle America?
- If there was an opportunity for a huge financial win for Middle America would it be worth 60 days to see if it could be done?
- So what is stopping us from getting the technology to our best and brightest, maybe even college students, to see who can figure out the best way to retrofit it in cars? If they do not figure it out in 60 days did we really lose anything?

OBJECTION 2: The technology is not ready for passenger vehicles.

RETURN QUESTIONS:

- So what you are saying is, if the technology was ready for passenger vehicles you would be onboard with this plan and begin as soon as possible?
- Let's assume it needs to be reengineered, if I could show you how to get that done in 60 days and cost the taxpayers relatively nothing, would you agree that would be a good alternative? Then use Chapter 29: A Workforce For Good.
- Do you believe there are smart people in our country who could figure out how to retrofit this technology for cars currently on the road?
- If there was any kind of problem with the technology and you could have some of the brightest minds work on it for free, don't you agree that would be the patriotic solution our country is looking for?

OBJECTION 3: It will take a long time to ramp up the production.

RETURN QUESTIONS:

- What do you call a long time?
- So if it didn't take that long you would be on board?
- Don't we have a large number of automobile workers still out of work?

229

- Aren't there automobile parts factories dark (closed)?
- If we could retool those factories to produce this system, do you think those workers would like to have those jobs back?
- Do you think having those jobs back would help revitalize those local communities?
- Can you give me any reason why you wouldn't want to put those people back to work? Wouldn't that save the American taxpayer on unemployment costs?
- So what you are saying is, if there was an energy technology that was proven to work, but took a long time to get it online, then we as a country will not use that energy technology? If they are dumb enough to say yes, then ask why do we spend years and billions of dollars building a nuclear power plant or how long does it take to get gas at the pump from an off shore drilling rig that hasn't even been built yet?

OBJECTION 4: It will kill millions of jobs produced by the oil industry.

I love this one, because I live in New Jersey where they recently closed two regional oil refinery plants. Oh, I thought they "created" jobs, plus we must have so much gas that they really don't need those refineries. Doesn't closing refineries reduce the supply and thus increases the price. Do you think that was their plan?

Here's some math for you. If we use 20 million barrels of oil per day in the United States and let's just say 70% of it goes to transportation (14 million barrels per day). We use this technology and cut our usage by 50%. That would save us 7 million barrels/day. That would not affect one U.S. oil worker's job – we would still have the need to produce the 7 million barrels domestically. We would just import less or possibly none, which solves our Middle East crisis.

RETURN QUESTIONS:

- Are you concerned with American jobs as a whole or are you just worried about oil industry jobs?
- Would you agree that even if people bought less gas, we will still have a need for oil?
- If there were more jobs created with HLA than with oil drilling, which one would you choose?

- Would you agree that oil industry jobs are created in specific locations where the oil is drilled, refined, etc.? In other words, these oil industry jobs are not in every American city, correct? What would be better, have job creation and household income gain in every city or just job creation in a relatively few locations? If they say a few you ask why? Then right it down for the whole world to see.
- So, if the oil industry creates jobs why have they shut down multiple refineries around the country?
- I know there are claims that the oil industry creates millions of jobs, but if I don't believe it could you just show me that data so I can verify it for myself?
- Would you agree, if we manufactured the HLA in the United States it would spur demand for mechanics, sales people, delivery people, etc., across the country for years?

OBJECTION 5: There are legal issues. This technology is patented and the EPA has licensing agreements.

I am sure someone will think of legal reasons why we are stuck with oil.

RETURN QUESTIONS:

- We already agreed this technology does work and would save American drivers billions of dollars a year, right?
- Would you also agree that if the American drivers had that extra money they would spend it in their local communities and produce economic growth?
- So what you are saying is, we have a technology that works and could boost the local economies all across the country, but that's not going to happen because the EPA made contracts against it?
- There is a technology funded by the taxpayers that is benefitting commercial companies and the American consumer gets no benefit, is that what you are saying? Please explain how that is fair?
- Who exactly approved these licensing agreements?
- Wouldn't you think that anyone at the EPA, who knew about this breakthrough, should have told the world they have found the solution to our energy crisis?
- Shouldn't someone have asked the American public if they would like to use this technology before there were any outside licensing agreements?

- Is the EPA a for profit entity of the government? Then why are they licensing technology? Are those licensing fees going back to the American taxpayer since they "invested" their taxes in creating the technology?
- Is it possible to audit the EPA to find out just where the money went and who actually benefitted from these licensing agreements? The reason would be to find out if someone on the inside used their power to help either themselves or someone else instead of helping the American public. If that was true do you think that would be considered a crime?

What Else Could They Object To

There is no way you can honestly object to using this technology, unless that objection is because you want to keep the price of fuel high. I really can't think of any other reason. If this is the case, it won't matter what truth you expose, they weren't planning on fixing it anyway. So make sure everyone knows that.

- It seems like you have a lot of objections. Are you just objecting because you were never going to do anything to fix this problem anyway?

- So what you are saying is, as the President of the United States, you have access to a technology that could fix our economy and you are choosing not to use it, is that correct?

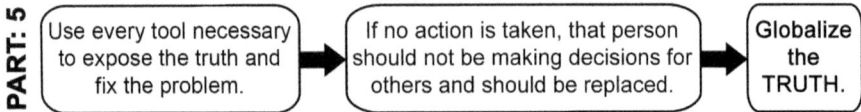

PART: 5 | Use every tool necessary to expose the truth and fix the problem. → If no action is taken, that person should not be making decisions for others and should be replaced. → Globalize the TRUTH.

Add "Additional Ammunition" as needed.

Force Transparency: If they agree to the plan as long as the test will prove it is viable, then those tests need to be transparent. Since these tests are just showing viability and not how the patents work, wouldn't it be better if the whole country could watch as they were being conducted? If there is a cost issue, just ask, "So if I could find someone to provide all of the cameras and pay all of the Internet expenses, would you agree to that?"

Free Workforce: This would be used if there is a question about testing the viability and the costs to do that. So what you are saying is, "If I could find competent engineers to work for free testing and tweaking this technology and it didn't cost the taxpayers a dime, would you be onboard?"

Create A Plan: If you have the resources or skills to create a full plan, try to include all facets from manufacturer to consumer. It would consist of developing a retrofitted version of HLA, then setting up manufacturing and distribution. There would have to be training done on installing the device.

Make It Personal: How many families can you show that are in dire straits right now? Ask "tent city" families if $300 per month would have made a difference for them before they became homeless. Go out and make a short video of Middle America pleading for the President to use this technology that their tax dollars helped develop.

Globalize: Whatever the outcome, show the world. Let them know the truth about our leaders, good or bad. Are they on the side of justice or injustice? Use the power that social media generates when the person refuses to acknowledge the truth, in this case (HLA). The objective is to prove the technology works and to show that the person who has the power to do something about it will not. Use the video as documented proof.

Social media can be used as a campaign to remove people who aren't doing the job they are paid for. If they know the truth, have a solution, but will not use it then the question becomes, "Do we have to have this person in that position if they refuse to do what is right for our country?" If the answer is no, then the next step is to do what it takes to have them removed and get someone else hired or elected who will do what is right.

Chapter 51: Three Technologies That Work

I have added more research on HLA and other available technologies that dramatically increase gas mileage. You can add this information to your arguments.

Hydraulic Launch Assist (HLA)

This technology is called Hydraulic Launch Assist (HLA). The vehicle's fuel savings comes from regenerative braking. It works by taking the kinetic energy from deceleration and uses a hydraulic system to capture it. When a driver steps on the brake pedal, kinetic energy from deceleration drives the pump/motor and forces hydraulic fluid out of a low-pressure reservoir into a high-pressure accumulator. The fluid compresses nitrogen gas in the accumulator to pressurize the system. At start-up or in acceleration conditions, the HLA system switches from pump to motor mode. The nitrogen gas forces the hydraulic fluid back into the low-pressure accumulator passing through the pump/motor, which applies torque to the driveshaft through the clutch. If you want to read all of the details for yourself you can easily Google: Hydraulic Launch Assist.

In 1998 Ford Motor Company created a hydraulic braking energy regeneration system. Tests were made on completely full dump trucks. The dump truck was accelerated to 55 mph and then stopped. The hydraulic system was then used to move the vehicle without any engine assist. They claimed the dump truck was able to get up to 20 mph just reusing the saved energy.

Chrysler is in partnership with the U.S. Environmental Protection Agency to design and develop an experimental hydraulic hybrid power train suitable for use in large passenger cars and light-duty vehicles. The aim is to have a running demonstration vehicle, based on the current minivan, sometime during 2012, which now has been moved to 2013. The technology is over 10 years old, it has been used successfully in a multitude of vehicles for years and now they are going to "try" and adapt it to a mini-van and take a year to get a "test" version. I don't know anyone in the car industry or anyone that is involved with this technology, but I am sure there are enough intelligent people in this country who could figure out how to fit this device into most vehicles.

Hydraulic Hybrid Transmission

There is another technology developed by a Scottish company (Artemis Intelligent Power), which is a Hydraulic Hybrid Transmission system that can double a vehicle's mpg in city driving. Double, that means you spend half the money you used to on gas. Do you think there are cab companies that would be interested in this technology?

The test was done independently and they used a BMW 530i. The results showed double the mpg in city driving. This was compared to the same car with a six speed manual transmission. Besides that, the vehicle had approximately 30% lower carbon dioxide emissions than it had before it was fitted with the system.

So let's see. The Hydraulic Hybrid Transmission doubles the gas mileage and the Hydraulic Launch Assist produced an additional 60-70% fuel economy. These aren't laboratory models, this is happening right now. So I will use my own math, refute it if you like. You spend $300/mth on gas, cut that in half, which gives you $150/mth. Take an additional 60% (the lower amount) from that, which is $90 dollars. Now you are paying $60/mth for the same exact result.

This is a foreign company and they would expect to be paid for their innovation. I wonder if the cost would be less than the savings it will give the car owner? Here is another thought, I wonder what the cost of this transmission is compared to the traditional transmissions used in automobiles today. Maybe someone should look into that. I am willing to bet it is a viable solution.

The Truth About Cars Fueled From Water

One of the best misleading information campaigns has to do with HHO, which is how water and electricity are used to create hydrogen as a fuel. It is incredible how many sides of the story there are; especially for something so simple to prove or disprove that it can be done as a high school science experiment. There is so much information on the Internet stating how it doesn't work; it is not efficient, too explosive, or incomplete research. Use PART 4 and a little Internet research to overcome all of those lies (I mean objections).

Meanwhile one of the largest water to hydrogen plants just came online in California and there are gas stations that have hydrogen fuel pumps that fuel hydrogen cars. Also, SunLine Transit and AC Transit operate hydrogen stations and fuel buses that are used in Palm Springs and Oakland, California. Maybe this is one of the reasons why oil companies are deliberately shutting down refineries; they see the writing on the wall. I wonder when the speculators will get out. What would happen if demand for oil dropped so much that the price fell from $120/barrel to $25/barrel. Someone is going to take a big hit.

Don't believe the people who claim it is not going to work. It's working right now. There is a major university in California that has been fueling their campus vehicles with hydrogen fuel for years. They have their own fuel generator on campus that uses solar panels to create the electricity. That electricity separates the hydrogen molecules from the oxygen molecules in water. Even though HHO is a reality, there are people in the United States that don't even know cars are running on fuel that came from water. That is the power of strong misleading messages.

PLAN: Go to Southern California and look at the University which has been using this technology since 2004. Ask employees who use the technology, "Does this work?" There, now everyone knows there are cars in the U.S. running on hydrogen that is extracted from water using the sun.

Now create the plan to implement it for everyone and get it to the right person. Not the person who will implement it so a few make billions while they overcharge people to use the sun and water. How about a plan to have these generators available for home use. People can use the sun and their own water to create fuel for the vehicles and also for their home. By the way, there are also homes in the united states that use HHO for their energy source. Just because you haven't heard of it doesn't mean it's not happening.

Questions To Ask A Government Official About HHO

- Do we have vehicles that run on hydrogen in the United States?
- Do we have a process that uses solar panels to extract hydrogen from water?
- Is there any reason why we cannot produce more cars that run on this "virtually" free fuel?
- Is there any reason why we couldn't use this technology to heat our homes, heat our water, cook our food, etc.?
- Isn't hydrogen a much cleaner burning fuel than oil or natural gas?

- Aren't there over 100,000 vehicles in the United States currently running on natural gas? Then it is obvious that it isn't that hard to convert a vehicle from gasoline to another fuel type, isn't that correct?

Their main objection will be the explosive power of hydrogen. Your question will be, "So the U.S. is committed to using fuel sources that do not cause drastic explosions, is that correct? When they say yes, just point out all of the natural gas explosions that happen around the country on a regular basis. Also mention all the oil refinery deaths. Bring the news articles with you and ask them why we use an obviously dangerous energy source called "oil".

Chapter 52: Additional Questions You Can Use

You can integrate these during any conversation or interview to help expose the truth.

Questions:

- Would you like to save 80% on the amount of fuel you use in your vehicle?
- If a U.S. government agency had a life-changing solution to one of our country's biggest problems, do you think they should tell the public about it or keep it a secret?
- Can you think of any pending issues that could be more important than saving the U.S. economy and getting Americans back to work?
- Is our country in a financial crisis?
- If you knew of a proven technology, that would drastically improve gas mileage, would you champion that project now or would you wait for someone else to get it done?
- If someone is a Patriot who loves their country and they knew a way to help it tremendously, but didn't, what would you call them?
- If Americans were able to reduce their gasoline costs by 50%, would they be better off?
- Since you understand this critical issue and you are a person of action, who can we contact right now to get this started? I mean make the phone call and setup the meeting right now.
- So what you are saying is, if people who were addicted to oil had a choice, they would choose pollution and toxins?
- As an elected official (leader, decision maker), if you had plans given to you that could turn the economy around right now guaranteed, would you take action now, or would you hire a team to study it for an undetermined amount of time?
- If you had to make a choice between a large corporation making huge profits or boosting the U.S. economy and creating hundreds of thousands of jobs, which would you choose?
- After you leave here and you are approached by corporations/ lobbyist stating that they are going to cut you off and hurt your political career, will you change your mind or will you do the right thing.
- Do you believe the government, mainly the EPA, would charge commercial companies to license a technology that did not work?

- Do you believe the companies using this technology are either lying or are not intelligent enough to know if they are getting better gas mileage?
- If this technology worked and saved the average American driver $100s/mth in gas, but cost the oil industry billions would you say that is a good outcome or a bad outcome?
- Do you think Americans would be upset if they found out the technology they paid for was being held hostage so they could never get the true benefit of it?

Chapter 53: More Benefits And Calculations

When you live in a country that consumes as much as we do in the United States, small changes affecting everyone have a huge impact overall. I want to make sure that everyone understands this. This chapter goes through several calculations related to what will happen when the citizens of the U.S. are able to use this technology.

From the U.S. Census website (www.census.gov), there is a document (12s1096.pdf) entitled "Table 1096. State Motor Vehicle Registrations: 1990 to 2009". The table states that in 2009 there were 246,283,000 vehicles registered in the US, this is commercial, private and publicly owned. The data is further broken down into automobiles (134,880,000), buses (842,000) and trucks (110,561,000). I will use these numbers for my calculations.

There are several different sources that claim how much the average American spends per month for automobile fuel. After researching them I have chosen to use the number $240, which you may think is low. For trucks and buses I am using $1600/mth for fuel consumption.

The EPA states a sedan can get 80 mpg using this technology, which we will assume is 3 times what the average driver gets. That means you can go the same distance on 1/3 of the fuel, which is 1/3 of the cost. The balance of that money goes back into yours or the company's pockets. Let's assume only ½ of the vehicles take advantage of this technology. For trucks and buses, the calculations reflect a 25% savings, which means fuel will cost would be ¾ of what it was before the technology was added.

Automobile

$240 x 1/3 = $80   Savings = $160/month OR $1,920/year

134,880,000 Cars x ½ = 67,440,000 (cars using the technology)

67,440,000 x $1,920/year = $129,484,800,000 in savings per year

Trucks and Buses

$1600 x 3/4 = $1200   Savings = $400/month OR $4,800/year

111,403,000 Trucks and Buses x ½ = 55,701,500
(trucks/buses using the technology)

55,701,500 x $4,800/year = $267,367,200,000 in savings per year

That means the combined savings would be $396,852,000,000/year.

That is almost $400 billion every year. Let's say the EPA is only half right, that is $200 billion a year. Even if these calculations are off, it doesn't matter. There is a true savings that will make a significant difference in the world today. Find someone to deny this, and then ask them why large U.S. corporations keep deploying this technology for their fleets of vehicles if it isn't worth it? Then ask them why they don't want to help people with this technology.

The Daily Oil Consumption Of The United States

Assume we use 20 million barrels a day of oil. Let's assume oil is $100 a barrel. That is $2 billion a day. Let's assume this fuel saving technology only produces a 25% savings. Let's also assume that only 70% of the oil we consume is used for fuel. Therefore, 70% of 20 million barrels is 14 million barrels. So you would take 25% of 14 million barrels, which means we consume 3.5 million barrels less per day. That's a big deal. At $100 per barrel that is $350,000,000 in savings per day. Multiply that by 365 days in a year and we, as a country, will save over $100 billion per year on oil. This is savings for government, business and every U.S. citizen using the technology and that is if the technology is only a fraction as good as they report it to be.

Number Of People Back To Work

All you hear nowadays from politicians is we need to create jobs. Great, this section outlines the solution. How would you like to have millions of jobs created for the U.S. economy without any government stimulus or tax breaks? I would like to see the politician that would publicly say "no" to that question.

Take the retrofit market: installing this technology on cars, trucks and buses that are already on the road. As stated earlier, there are approximately 250,000,000 vehicles in the United States. Let's assume we have a goal to convert only half of them, which would be 125,000,000 vehicles. Another benefit of mass producing any product is that it lowers the cost tremendously.

I am not sure exactly how the installation would work, but I am going to make some conservative, common sense assumptions. Challenge them if you must. Let's assume that one mechanic can complete 2 installations per day. That is 75 million days of work just for the installation. Assuming

260 workdays per year, that would give 288,462 YEARS of work. Or, we can hire 150,000 mechanics and it would still take them nearly 2 years to complete this task. Add to that the manufacturing jobs, the delivery companies, accountants, lawyers, administrators and all the other support positions needed for this endeavor. What will all these new jobs do for local economies? People will have money to spend in their communities, thus fueling the need for local businesses to hire more people. This is how you rebuild the economy; it has to be done locally.

Manufacture New Cars With This Technology

Odd that U.S. car manufacturers were involved with the creation of the HLA technology, yet there are no cars available that have it. Even after a complete melt down of the automobile industry they still did not build a "sure winner". That tells you how strong the "powers to be" are. Most American automobile companies have been making fuel efficient and flex cars for a long time; unfortunately they are for other countries. Once this plan goes into effect, there will be millions of people who would prefer the new Hydraulic Launch Assist cars. It will be a car sales bonanza; they wouldn't be able to keep up with the demand.

Add Hydraulic Launch Assist To Electric Cars

Assume you have an electric car that goes 100 miles on 1 charge. If you can extend that by 40%, that would produce an additional 40 miles per charge. What if you put solar panels on the roof and added magnetic engagement assist (Google that one). That car will easily get 200 miles on one charge, without any gas. What if you charged it at home using solar panels or wind turbines? What if this was possible? No fuel costs and no pollution. Do you think anyone would like to have a car like this?

Apply The Technology To Public Transportation

If the buses and taxies used this technology they would be able to take more profit and simultaneously pass more savings onto their riders. It would be a win-win for those companies. This will increase the incomes of all parties involved. The people who depend on public transportation every day would have more money at the end of the month without doing anything different. The people providing the transportation services will also have more money at the end of the month, because they will be spending less on fuel. This would happen in every community that provides public transportation.

The Real Outcome

- 100,000s of manufacturing, sales and installation jobs.
- Millions of residual and supporting jobs created.
- Drivers get immediate results and start putting hundreds of dollars a month back into their pockets.
- More money in their pockets means they will spend more.
- Cheaper to drive means they will travel more.
- More retail and travel means more revenue and more jobs.
- All this and a cleaner environment, what a great deal.

Who Wins – Who Loses

The winners are simple, every person in the world will somehow benefit from this. Even the oil executives will spend less on fuel costs, not that they care, but it is still a quantifiable benefit. The big winners will be the people who get to go back to work and begin to see the light at the end of the tunnel. There are people who believe that during the recent U.S. economic meltdown, if they had an extra $300/mth, they could have survived through it. That would have been accomplished if this was initiated in 2006.

There is just one problem, when you have winners you also have losers. The savings to one group means it comes out of the hands of another group. They are:

- Oil companies.
- Brake manufacturers.
- Government (would lose the gas taxes and thus their ATM card).
- Politicians who take big contributions from oil companies.

One of the possible reasons our government doesn't want to provide this benefit to citizens is because they have grown to rely on gasoline taxes. This technology could reduce that tax revenue by 30-80%, but the flip side is people will have more money to spend, thus adding new taxes.

How About The War On Terror

There is more than one report that states revenues from oil are used to fund terrorism. So if we stop funding oil overseas wouldn't that stop that particular funding to terrorism? Don't we want to win this war? Can anyone in Congress give me any reason why you would not want to cutoff the funding to terrorist organizations?

243

PART 11:

UNDESERVED COMPENSATION

Chapter 54: Does The Pay Reflect Performance

This has become a hot topic for many Americans who are frustrated with the direction of our country. It is the core of one of the major premises of this book: There are people who have adversely affected others by finding ways to get things they don't deserve. People have become good at this, but some of the people on Wall Street have mastered it. The outrage and anger over this matter is not aimed at people who built their own company and deserve every cent they earn and also lose when their company loses.

Over the last fifteen years there has been a growing belief that earning tens of millions of dollars per year, which is not based on accomplishment or profit, should be the norm. Obviously this belief is strongest with the people who get those millions and supported secondarily by the politicians who get their contributions. These large pay packages are reflective of what an owner of a company would make, not an MBA transport that goes from one firm to another. It would be different if the person taking the huge compensation had invested their life in the company, was the inventor or designer of the main product and had made the initial investments to get the company started, but most of the time that is not the case. So the question is, "How do these people justify multimillion dollar pay packages with little commitment?"

In theory, it should be common sense, the people who pay should have a say. For publicly owned companies, that would be the stockholders. For government jobs, that would be the taxpayers.

Fiduciary Responsibility

The Board of Directors, in every corporation, have the fiduciary responsibility for the decisions they make regarding corporate assets and the rights of stockholders. If you aren't sure just ask these questions:

- Aren't the executives and Board of Directors the stewards of the shareholder's money?
- Do the shareholders expect them to make wise choices with their money?
- What should happen when they don't?

A corporation's board members have fiduciary responsibilities that include:

- Avoiding conflicts of interest in all forms. A conflict of interest may occur whenever the corporation is considering entering into a contract with one of its board members (a lease, an employment contract, sale of stock and so forth).
- Protect the assets of the corporation in all decision making.
- Acting in the interest of the company instead of the board member's personal interest.
- Provide legal oversight for all company business transactions.
- Maintain a sustained oversight system.

Directors are supposed to act in the best interests of the corporation and its members or stockholders, even at the expense of their own interests. This includes:

- Directors must act in the face of a known duty.
- Every board member owes a legal duty of good faith, full disclosure, fair dealing and undivided loyalty to the corporation.
- Not acting in a manner unrelated to a pursuit of the corporation's best interest.
- Directors must positively renounce anything that is unfair.

A breach or violation of the above typically occurs when directors or officers self deal to their own benefit. What you need to understand is, there are legal ramifications if they do not uphold their fiduciary responsibilities.

Chapter 55: Questioning Executive Pay

If the CEO and other executives took less money out of the company, would that mean the company would show a greater profit? I know they base most of their compensation on stocks, but that money has to come from somewhere, if not, then give millions in stock options to the investors. Is it possible that the CEO and other executives could live on a percentage of what they currently take home each year? Isn't one of the main functions of the leaders of a company to produce profits for its shareholders?

- **PROBLEM:** Executive over compensation affects the overall profitability of a company and therefore leaves less for the shareholders.

- **TRUTH:** For the amounts that are being earned, high priced executives can be replaced with cost efficient executives who will be better for the investors.

The questions below are designed to get the public to understand it is their money and they should have a voice when it comes to maximizing their returns. Incorporate these questions into the Problem Solving Process.

1. Who owns a public traded company, the CEO? No
2. Does your company have a wage policy for its employees?
3. Do your employees get raises or bonuses?
4. What are the raises or bonuses based on?
5. If the employees don't adequately perform the duties of their position do they still get a raise and or bonus?
6. Why do you regulate who gets raises or bonuses, why don't you just give them to every single employee? The answer is: That doesn't make sense, the company couldn't afford it, why should someone get a raise/bonus for non or under performance – exactly!
7. What were your yearly earnings for the last 5 years?
8. Were the raises and or bonuses based on performance?
9. If not, what were they based on? They will probably answer, "It was a contract."
10. Who approved this contract?

11. Do you think it is wise and prudent to offer a multi-million dollar contract to a person that states even if they under perform or don't perform at all they still get paid? Do think that is what investors are looking for when they invest in your company?

12. Why should investors be satisfied with an executive that earns millions per year and doesn't perform to the investor's expectations?

13. Should they get rid of that executive? They may answer, "You need to pay that amount for the talent, or they will go somewhere else."

14. So are saying that they can't be replaced? They answer, "Yes".

15. We all agree that the primary objective of an investor is to maximize the return on their investment, is that correct?

16. So if they could be replaced with the same or better talent for less money, then you would agree that would be more profitable for the investors, is that correct?

17. If an investor had the option to have better talent for less money and therefore maximize their returns, do you think they would choose that? Or, do you think they want to see their 401K lose money while a company pays hundreds of millions of dollars to a few top executives?

18. Would you agree that the higher the pay package the greater the performance is for an employee and/or executive? Wouldn't the general "business" rule of thumb be: "Don't payout more than you get back in return"? Isn't that what the company pay policy is all about, you don't pay millions of dollars to front line employees, because their work can only bring in so much earnings for the company?

19. Who decides whether or not an executive should be replaced for performance reasons?

20. What you are saying is, you just can't fire everyone in an investment firm, they are hard to replace, can easily go to other firms and the building will be empty?

21. So if someone could hire intelligent, competent and effective people who produced the same or better results for much less money, would you agree to that strategic move?

22. So if you could find someone who could accomplish the above, they would be considered a great asset to the stock holders. Think about it, the opportunity to save tens of millions of dollars and get the same or better results. Hasn't your business used the same formula in the past when downsizing?

How To Prove They Are Not Indispensable

1. For $10 million in compensation, what did the shareholders get?
2. They answer and you write it down.
3. Show the audience and say to the executive, "Do you believe that without you the company would have not been able to do this (point to what you wrote)?"
4. Would it have been possible for someone else to achieve these tasks?

Question How Executive Pay Is Calculated

- Does the CEO own the company? In most cases no.
- Who owns the company? Stockholders.
- Do stockholders want to maximize their profits? Yes.
- So as owners (the stock holders), isn't watching your expenses a big part of profit management? Yes.
- Who decides how much earnings an executive will make? What is that based on?
- Just because a CEO has a compensation committee does that mean the amount they recommend is correct? What if it isn't? What is the relationship between the committee and the executive, are they subordinates?
- Do these people who decide have any financial interest in the amounts that executives get paid?
- What real-world model is this pay package based on?
- What if the corporate earnings system was corrupt and everyone at the top was just paying themselves exorbitant amounts that were not based on the job performance, do the investors have any recourse?
- Does an investor have the right to question the pay structures for executives since that effects their total return on investment?
- Is there any government agency charged with the fiduciary task of protecting investor's interests?

Why don't they look at replacing the high cost CEO and board members with less expensive, more talented management? If they say it can't be done, no one will work for less. You say, "So what you are saying is, if I can find someone who is better than the current CEO for this company and is willing to work for 1/5 the income, you would agree that would make sense? Then be silent and write down what they say.

By the way, as an owner (stock holder), do people have the right to see how their money is being spent? They might want to know what the actual value is for their Executive Board purchase. Assume a CEO has a $10 million income for the year, which is approximately $200K per week. You can also ask to see what the "perks" are that go along with their compensation package.

Okay, you made $40,000/day last week. You make more in 1 day, then a good portion of Americans make in 1 year. You must be a genius, because let's face it, no idiot would pay anyone $40,000/day if they weren't accomplishing daily miracles. The value you must be returning to your investors has to be in the billions. What great company decisions and breakthroughs did your $40,000/day get us, the owners (stockholders) last week? Write down whatever they say.

Chapter 56: More Arguments That Make Sense

Maybe I am wrong, but maybe I am right. Do you think hundreds of billions of dollars is worth questioning it, or should we just sweep this one under the carpet? I have an idea, why don't we just check it out. Let's see what the owners (stockholders) are getting for their money. If it is not a good value, let's replace the poor performing executives with cost effective executives. Is there anything wrong with people wanting more value for their investment?

Aren't publicly traded company's information available to the public? Why don't we check a few records and question why the executives of a company collectively pull out hundreds of millions of dollars (if not more) from the company, when the company actually lost money and the investors lost money. I understand there are several slick spokespeople who defend the large compensation packages. Someone should find out why they are so eager to defend non-performance pay.

Non-performance pay, isn't that what people are fighting in our federal budget? They want to reduce the entitlement programs, which some people will say is "non-performance" pay, being paid for doing nothing. They will say, "It is not the same." How is it not the same? I give you some money, I want you to perform. If you don't perform, you don't get any money. Find someone who does not agree with this. Our small claims courts are over flowing with cases based on this premise. If you don't do the job, then you don't get the money. How tough is this to understand? Ironically, major corporations have policies in place so they can fire an employee for non-performance. Is that hypocritical?

The American public doesn't mind paying companies for services rendered. Companies are supposed to make a profit and the people who invest in them should share proportionally in those profits. The concerns arise from the fairness of that proportionality. What the American people are tired of is getting the short end of the stick time after time, while others make fortunes for delivering no or negative value. How anyone gets paid millions of dollars for delivering subpar returns is beyond the belief of most Americans.

If you could get the same exact value and service for 1/10 the price you are currently paying, would you do it? Let's say it was the difference of

$30,000,000 and $3,000,000. That would give you a profit of $27,000,000 instantly. If you were getting the same result, can you think of ANY reason why you wouldn't take the $3 million option?

We need to find competent executives who will be paid on performance at a rational pay scale. It needs to be shown that the argument they use for over compensation is hypocritical and makes no sense. Don't expect government regulators to take care of it. There is more than one example where tens of billions of dollars have been taken while the regulators were at the wheel.

PART 12:

RELEASE THE KRAKEN

Chapter 57: Question Everything

There are a lot of unanswered questions in the world. Now that you have the skills to expose the truth, nothing is off the table. Question everything. Whether the truth is good news or bad news, let's just verify it so we can move on. One thing I have noticed while writing this book, is the more I wrote about fixing problems, the more problems came to mind. Obviously, I can't write about fixing every problem in one book, but I can list several of them and get you started.

So if you are ready, the next chapter has issues that probably deserve some research and a little bit of the Problem Solving on Steroids. I started the "fixing" for you by writing key questions and in some cases added research and analysis. The plan is to show you there is no limit to what you can fix. I also want to show that you can expose the truth with just a few good questions. Anyone can take what I started and expand on it with what they have learned in this book. They can find the truth, make a plan, and delivery it to the right person, in front of an audience. Some of the issues need to be proven. I am not saying they are true or false. How hard is it to take a camera and live stream an experiment over the Internet?

Since these are highly charged issues, it would be smart to "bind" a person to their statements before you expose the truth:

1. Get the statement: What are they claiming?
2. Clarify: What exactly does that mean?
3. Verify: Are you absolutely sure about that information?
4. Commit them on camera: So what you are saying is…?
5. Add consequences: If it turns out that you are wrong,
    a. Would you stop trying to convince the country that it is true?
    b. Would that mean you weren't telling the truth?
    c. Would that mean you don't know what is going on?

This questioning sequence alone could change the outcome of any interview where someone is trying to deliver a misleading message to the world.

Chapter 58: Issues Someone Should Question

In this chapter is an alphabetical list of problems, solutions and issues. Read them, find the truth and then go question someone as to why it is happening that way. If it needs to be fixed, you know what to do.

1. Artemisinin

The premise: Artemisinin is a chemical compound extracted from the wormwood plant, Artemisia annua L. It has been shown to selectively kill cancer cells. Is this true or not?

Google: site:nih.gov Artemisinin cancer

Questions:

- Ask the National Institutes of Health (NIH) why they even chose do studies using Artemisinin for dealing with cancer?
- Are these follow-up studies because the initial studies had positive results?
- Has Artemisinin ever been used to treat malaria?
- If there was therapy for cancer that costs 100 times less than chemotherapy and worked better with no side effects, would you recommend it to your patients?
- Would anyone hide a cure for breast cancer, letting our mothers, wives, daughters die a brutal death?
- If there were tests done many years ago that successfully cured breast cancer, but have since gone under the radar to the general public, would it be worth it to rerun those same tests to see if it was true, especially if the tests were extremely simple and inexpensive to perform?

Plan: Get the Artemisinin, use cancer cells from a biopsy, setup a streaming webcam, put the Artemisinin in with the cancer and let the world watch to see what happens. There you go, a one sentence plan to possibly cure cancer without spending millions of dollars. If nothing happens then we can start saving millions of dollars on all those tests the National Institutes of Health is conducting with Artemisinin.

Do you think all of the mothers who will die this year from breast cancer would like to have someone at least check it out? Maybe do a transparent study, so if the results come back positive nobody could hide or change the results. What harm could come from a transparent study? Especially since the money they would use would probably be donated.

Maybe it is true or maybe it isn't, but woman die every day from breast cancer. Would you like to be the research doctor, pharmaceutical executive or FDA director to tell her kids that, "Oh yes… there is a possible cure that looks very promising, but we can't make any money on it, so we didn't want to tell her about it… sorry… my bad."

2. CDC (Centers for Disease Control and Prevention)

- Do you believe it is good or bad for people to take medication that they do not need - or will not help them?
- What happens to all of the pharmaceuticals after Americans ingest them and then get them out of their bodies through urine and fecal waste? Is it now in our drinking water?
- Why did the CDC advocate using the 2-shot flu plan in 2009, when they knew that double shot wasn't even for the strain of flu that was the problem that year?
- Did a pharmaceutical company (Baxter) ever make a mistake by sending the H1N1 virus instead of the vaccine to be administered to people in 18 European countries? Google it.
- If there was a choice, would it be better for the human body to build its own immune system or should it be done artificially?

3. Clean Drinking Water

How come you still hear about millions of people unable to get clean drinking water around the world? There have been several inventions that take polluted water and make it drinkable. As for people on an island or near the coast isn't there a simple solution? What would happen if you had a collecting area for sea water with a dome? The evaporated water could condensate and run down the sides to provide fresh drinking water? Is this really that tough? I might be missing something here, but I imagine there are people who can figure out the details.

Look up U.S. Patent #:3,351,536, it is called Lens-Dome Solar Distillation Unit. Wow, someone finally figured it out; let's go get them some fresh water. Wait, look at the date on the patent, it says November 7, 1967. That was 45 years ago. I guess there is no money in having the sun create fresh water for everyone. I do find it amusing that they can't figure out how to provide fresh water, but they have no problem administering vaccines in the same remote regions.

258

4. Cow's Milk

Here is the question: Does the human body have to have cow's milk to survive, grow, and be healthy? If so, how do people around the world survive and grow strong without it?

Here is the mother of all proofs that mammals do not need dairy for strong bones and muscles. The strongest land mammal is the great ape and the largest mammal is the whale shark, neither has been on a dairy diet since birth. Even then, that dairy was made especially for them, it didn't come from another species. So how did they get the calcium needed for their bodies? Just Google it.

There is a successful messaging campaign that has convinced 100s of millions of people that cow's milk is necessary for a healthy, human diet. There is a side effect from drinking cow's milk so obvious that it could not be hidden. The message became, "It's not the cow's milk, it's you. You are lactose intolerant." People bought this completely and they never thought the milk was the problem. How do you label someone intolerant to something when they're not supposed to have it anyway? You can prove this in 10 seconds by asking any executive in the dairy industry, "Is the human body supposed to have lactose from cow's milk?"

If there were multiple studies done that linked dairy to terrible diseases such as diabetes and leukemia, wouldn't an intelligent nation at least repeat the studies to verify they weren't harming their own children? I am not saying it is true, but what if it is and someone already proved it? Do your own research on this. Just Google words like milk or dairy with words such as: disease, diabetes, sick, leukemia, etc. See what you come up with.

This subject can stir a huge controversy, so why don't we just prove it one way or the other. A transparent lab test so anyone can watch the results. If it turns out cow's milk is great for humans, it will be a bonanza for the dairy industry.

5. Credit Cards

How tough is it to make a fraud proof credit card? I don't know about you, but I would have no problem having my picture show up at the cash register every time my card was swiped. In return for this money saving breakthrough, I would expect a significant reduction in my interest rates. I don't know if everyone would do this, but if the trade-off was worth it, I think a lot of people will.

Another simple solution is for people who try to use your information to open up new lines of credit. Why can't the credit agency have an automated phone system call your cell phone whenever this is happening? Google does it every time someone wants an email account. Why are these CEO geniuses making so much money in these banks? Can someone tell me what they are actually doing on a day to day basis?

Lastly, I recently heard that criminals are stealing children's social security numbers even before they are born. Solution: Run a credit check at the hospital before giving a social security card to the parents.

6. Department of Defense (DOD)

What if it turned out that military expansion around the world was designed to benefit contractors? Military bases are built, they load in personnel, arm them with weapons and support teams. It would be the perfect marketing plan: unlimited funds from taxpayers who have no say, a market that is easily grown by poor economic conditions in the U.S. and around the world, lawmakers benefitting through campaign contributions to keep the scheme going and a message of patriotism to the masses just in case someone wants to question the validity of military expansion. Not saying this is true, I am just saying what if.

As a country, the U.S. is very patriotic; they have proven it time and time again. When they know there is a real threat, they have no problem fighting. Do you think Americans should fight if they can prove there is no threat?

Questions:

- Why do we have troops in Japan, Australia, Columbia, etc.?
- Do the citizens of the United States want to pay the DOD to be the world police?
- Do Americans want to feel like they are being spied on by their own government?
- Do U.S. citizens have the right to question the DOD?
- Do Americans want to invade other countries, setup bases and keep troops there indefinitely?
- Do people think that we are overspending on defense?
- Do Americans get upset when they hear that $60 billion is unaccounted for in Iraq and then the same thing happens a few years later in Afghanistan? Do they wonder if someone is duping them? Do they think the money obviously went somewhere and someone obviously knows where?

- Since we are in a financial crisis, why don't we all become patriots and pass a bill that completely outlaws war profiteering?
- Why does the DOD spend millions of taxpayer dollars sponsoring Nascar? Could that money be used to benefit veterans returning from the Middle East?
- If there was corruption within the upper ranks of the military, how would anyone find out and how could anyone prove it if information is withheld from the public?
- If a major majority (say 80%) of U.S. citizens wanted to stop the military from doing something, do they have that right or power?
  - If the answer is yes: How exactly would they go about doing that?
  - If the answer is no: Are you saying that we now live in a country where if a branch of the government does something that the overwhelming majority of its citizens don't want, there is nothing the citizens can do about it?

Poppy – Afghanistan

This was brought up in the early years of this war and believe it or not the U.S. Government had a reason why we should protect the farmers while they grow poppy. Therefore if you are going to attack this problem make sure you do your research and put together a great plan with all the objections pre-answered. FYI Poppy is the plant responsible for heroin.

Questions:

- How much money do the farmers make for their crops?
- What if we paid those farmers that money not to grow poppy and we destroy the crops?
- If there are no crops can there be heroin from that region?
- If the farmers get the same money anyway, what did they lose?
- Can we just track where all those drugs are sold and follow the money to the terrorists?

Benefits:

That would eliminate drug money that is used for terrorism and take dangerous drugs off the streets, save lives, save families, etc. Can anyone tell me why we can't do this?

7. Education

I know there is a lot to question here, but I have one that nearly everyone could agree on and would literally save millions of dollars. It has to do with the school books that are continuously purchased at staggering prices. Who approves this?

Questions:

- How often do we have to rewrite history?
- Have the principles of K-12 math & science changed?
- Has spelling and grammar for K-12 changed?
- Why do we have to keep buying more books to teach the same material?
- If these new books and processes are designed to better educate, how come the students are less educated now?
- Why don't we take math books, digitize them and let all the schools download them for free. I bet we could find people who will volunteer that service, because then the school budget could actually go down.

8. FDA (Food and Drug Administration)

What if I have higher standards for my family than what the FDA sets for me? What if the government's standards are wrong? What if lobbyists were behind the rating of these standards and it was set that way to benefit the company instead of the people the agency was designed to protect. I am just saying what if.

Questions for the FDA:

- Are you aware that the Surgeon General states there is no minimum level of cigarette smoke that is acceptable for human beings?
- Do you think the Surgeon General is unintelligent?
- Do you think the Surgeon General doesn't know what they are talking about?
- Do you agree with the Surgeon General's statement?
- Would one of your reasons for agreeing be because the chemicals that are inside cigarette smoke adversely affect the human body? If not, then why?
- So if there are chemicals that adversely affect the human body and the Surgeon General states a zero tolerance policy, why does the FDA have allowable limits on chemicals in human consumption products that are known to adversely affect the human body?
- Can you tell me what level of arsenic is good for the human body?

I just saw a news story about lead being used in lipstick. Guess what the FDA says about the safety? You guessed it, it is okay. I thought lead was one of the most dangerous toxins that could enter the human body. Isn't that why we banned lead paint? How tough is it to do a transparent study and trace the lead from the lips through the bodies of these women.

Lead Lipstick Questions:

- Who exactly from the FDA stated that the lead in lipstick is safe?
- Where did they get that "expert" knowledge?
- How much lead is good for the human body?
- If lead got into a developing fetus what could happen to that baby?

Ironically they state this is okay, but they put out warnings about exploding toothbrushes. How about just letting the women know they are putting lead on their lips.

9. Flu Mutation

This has been the pharmaceutical mantra for the last decade. The scary message is that the flu virus is mutating and getting stronger. You would think after a hundred years of "getting stronger" it would be a super killer by now. I am not going to question the strength of the flu virus or the reason why parts of the world that don't even take a flu shot never have any kind of an outbreak. My questions have to do with some basic logic of how the flu virus miraculously travels around the globe.

Questions:

- Is it guaranteed that the flu virus will mutate every year?
- Do humans create mutated flu viruses in labs?
- When a flu virus mutates does it send out some type of message, so the rest of the flu viruses know it is time to mutate? The answer is no.
- Is there some type of internal timing mechanism that tells flu viruses when to mutate, this way they all mutate at once? Again, the answer is no.
- So does that mean if the mutation happened in September in Washington State the chances of that strain showing up in Allentown, Pennsylvania in October are pretty slim?
- The truth is, it would have to take a lot of transferring of the virus into acceptable hosts, in order to spread it around the country even in a year. Would you agree with that?

- So, unless the new strain oddly appears simultaneously in major cities across our country, the chance of any kind of epidemic affecting 300 million people is really slim to none.

You can advance this line of questioning by looking at how bird flu, swine flu and SARS was tracked across certain parts of the world.

Questions Concerning The Bird Flu:

- In the US, aren't we told to wash our hands and disinfect our countertops after handling chicken and pork? Why is that? They claim it is because you need to get rid of germs that can cause severe sickness.
- So what you are saying is, that in the US, it is acceptable to sell chicken and pork that may be infected with germs that could cause human sickness, is that correct?
- So why were there news stories about other countries killing thousands of chickens that were possibly infected with the flu virus? Were those chickens disposed of?
- What would have happened if those chickens were slaughtered, frozen and later fully cooked? Would that have spread the flu virus?
- Can someone please explain to me how that is different from the U.S. policy of selling infected foods? Oh, I know. The bird flu virus is more contagious and when all those dead chickens start sneezing they will spread it around the world.

10. Food Pyramid

Can you show me the doctor, nutritionist, FDA employee, or creator of the Food Pyramid who actually believes it is correct? What if you asked this question 2 decades ago, I am sure you can find documents stating that this IS the best diet for people (back in 1989)? Guess what? It has been changed, so that tells me it was wrong. So if it was wrong did it affect millions of people adversely? Our overweight, disease ridden, pill popping society could give you a clue to that answer. But you know what; people knew it was wrong then and even tried to speak up about it. They even had scientific studies and proof, but we still got the wrong chart from our protective government.

So the question becomes, "Is the new food pyramid correct?" There are still a bunch of studies that prove, beyond a shadow of a doubt, that even though it is better, it is still wrong. So let's just say we don't know who is right. We can perform a transparent test to prove to the world the way the food pyramid should be. I think people's lives, their health and their life savings is enough of a reason to do the study and get the right answer once and for all.

Here is another option, why don't we have people who get proven results to tell us what the food pyramid should look like. We listened to the government for over 40 years only to find out that they admit they were wrong. For the tax dollars they are using, wouldn't you like them to get it right. Maybe they should just turn on the television and see the plethora of data about how to eat correctly. The Biggest Loser obviously knows what to do. Let's compare their track record to the government's track record. Again, why is this so hard to do correctly? And the answer is… because government officials and politicians are swayed by the meat and dairy industries, even though people keep proving that a diet limiting these food groups is better for the human body.

I have a good idea, let's find out exactly who the genius is that says THIS new food pyramid is the best way for humans to eat. I want to know what their background is, what research they have to prove it and then ask them, "If you are wrong, would you resign your position for failing the American public, the people who pay you through taxpayer dollars to make the best decisions for them and their families?" Or, try this one if they are adamant, "Why don't you boost the meat and dairy industries by proving your stance once and for all, let's put you on a polygraph and let the world watch. You have no problem doing that, would you?"

11. Germfree Cleaning

I never remember all the cleaning when I was young and I never remember all of the people who constantly got sick. It is amazing how we survived all those years, but now we are safe because we have tons of products that take away all of those harmful germs.

- Doesn't the body's immune system work by finding germs, leaning how to conquer them and that is what builds the body's natural defenses?
- So what happens when we never introduce germs into our bodies? How do our bodies learn how to fight them?

- What about all of those cleaning chemicals getting washed into our water system? I find it hard to believe the water treatment plants clean everything out of our drinking water.
- Is there an alternative way to clean our households that doesn't involve harsh chemicals that leave toxins in our water systems?

Can someone look into sodium percarbonate as an alternative? Why aren't people just using this, instead of chemical products that include sodium percarbonate? Benefits could include: saving money, better for our water systems and less cans and plastics used when buying the other products.

12. Government

I think one of the things people want from their government is to have the right people in the right position, doing the right thing. What if it was proven that a government employee or official was incompetent, inexperienced, and lacked the common sense necessary to do their job, should they be let go?

- Is it okay for the government to lie to anyone?
- Is one of the jobs of the government to protect its people?
- If a government official knowing misleads the public, Congress, etc., what should happen?
- Do you personally know of specific scenarios where the government knowingly overspent taxpayer dollars, in other words they could have got the same value for less money?

How to question overspending in Government Contracts:

- Is this the lowest price we can pay for the same services and benefits?
- Do I have a right as a citizen to question this?
- Is this the best option the taxpayers have?
- Is there any other way to complete this for less money?
- Since you can't seem to track down the money, what if I could find it, would you let me?
- When spending tax payer dollars on earmarks, is congress in total control of our money? Do we have any say at all if we believe it is being done in a non-fiduciary manner?
- How about before you spend billions of dollars on an idea, you just spend a few million and prove that your idea works? Isn't that how all of your venture capital supporters spend their money? They wait for positive results, then add the big money. That sounds intelligent, aren't you intelligent?

Is it legal to buy influence in the government? Then why do we have to pay consultants millions of dollars for a job that could be done for 1/10 the cost? Is the government over-spending taxpayers' dollars?

Local Government Spending:

- Does our municipality have unlimited taxpayer dollars?
- So would you agree that we should be scrutinizing the money that we spend?
- As a public official, do you have the fiduciary responsibility to spend the taxpayer dollars wisely?
- So why do we spend [fill in the unnecessary spending item here]?

13. Growing Food

If technology allows big agricultural companies to grow more food faster and also process it more efficiently, then why is the cost going up. Shouldn't the prices be reflective of the savings they are benefitting from?

- Can anyone put a seed in the ground and grow food?
- Are there any laws against it?
- Why does the government spend millions of dollars on "beautification" plants when they could use the same amount of money and time to plant fruits and vegetables?
- If people grew their own food would they know if toxic pesticides were used?
- What if millions of people started urban gardens, would that help feed a starving nation?

14. Home Testing Devices

It is a shame it has come to this, but it is hard to trust government protection agencies when they say something is safe for you. Just ask some of the first responders of 911, when the EPA said that air was okay to breathe. They just forget that hundreds of stories of asbestos filled buildings just collapsed and the toxic dust was floating everywhere.

We are a country of convenience testing, anywhere from pregnancy tests, to drug testing, to paternity testing. It can all be done from your home. This is one of the best ways of getting to the truth, see it for yourself. If you start finding results that prove people are lying, now you have the tools to do something about it.

267

1. How many people believe that the government tells the truth when it comes to nuclear fallout? Just do some chronological research on the recent nuclear disaster in Japan. As time went on they kept on increasing what they thought the level of radiation was. One of the last reports stated it was 100 times more than they originally thought. So what they are saying is, the Geiger counters they were using in the first few days of the accident weren't reading correctly and as time went on they were able to fix them and now we have the correct readings? I think someone should think of a way to mass produce a device to detect radiation so it can be available to the general public. Maybe some residents who live around nuclear facilities today would like to know the truth.

2. There should be an economical device that every household could have that constantly checks the quality of their water supply. I think the people who are having problems where gas companies are "fracking" would have liked to have this. I wonder how much water they and their children ingested before they realized there was a problem?

3. I just checked and there are several companies selling devices that detect magnetic, electric, and radio/microwave in one package. I am not saying go get crazy with safety, but there are many studies that show humans do not fare well when they live or work around high power lines. The claims are that the incidence of cancer is higher for those groups. Think about it, how can electromagnetic or microwave radiation be good for the human body?

4. Cable speed tester. A little box with a meter that connects between the outside cable line and your computer. It reads the flow and transfer of data rates. Not sure of all the details, but this can't be too hard. There are people who believe they are paying for one level of service and getting another. This could prove it, especially if the device recorded that data so it can be used in court.

There are probably others and the above may already be available. Like I said, it is just another way to learn the truth. If you knew the truth about the water supply and the radiation levels of a particular home you were going to buy, would that be a factor in your decision?

15. Insurance Companies

- Would you agree that the United States has a problem with rising health insurance premiums?

- If these price increases were unjustified do you think a government consumer protection agency should look into it?
- Why doesn't someone subpoena the accounting books for these companies?
- If I could put together a forensic accounting team that would work for free and not cost the taxpayers a dime, what would the government have to lose?
- How much do the top executives, including board members, make per year collectively, including all benefits? Is that realistic when your customers are hurting just to pay premiums?
- What would happen if 5 million people got together and started their own insurance company and didn't pay billions of dollars in executive compensation, commissions, lobbying, and advertising?

Questions For The Overall Healthcare Crisis:

- Why aren't other countries in the healthcare crisis that the United States is in?
- Their answer: We have a much better health care system than they do.
- Your question: What if that wasn't true? What if we were getting the same or less quality care would that mean we are just overpaying for a subpar service?
- Do you think the people of America deserve to know the truth about where all the money goes in healthcare?
- Does it really cost $150,000 for one surgery or $12,000 staying 2 days in a hospital?
- If this is wrong and we could prove it, wouldn't that be good for the struggling American public?
- As a country, would we be better off if our citizens didn't have to go bankrupt because of medical bills?
- If someone claimed they could prove something was wrong would you let them?
- If someone claimed they could fix this crisis would you let them?

Someone seriously needs to find the truth about this industry and expose it to the world.

16. Internet Service Providers

The consolidation of Internet providers has allowed companies to set prices unchallenged for services that cost a fraction of what they are charging. All you have to do is look at their cash flow to prove this. One of the reasons they claim a price increase is necessary is because more and more people are requiring additional bandwidth.

What if there was a technology that can transfer speeds at 26Tbps (that is Terabytes)? Google what Germany did with a single laser transferring data and also look up similar research in the U.S. and Japan. I wonder when that service will be available. I also wonder how much of a discount we will get because there will no longer be a question of not enough bandwidth.

What if a new company was started with this technology and charged a fair price for the service, would that make the other Internet providers think twice before they ambiguously raised their prices?

17. Oil Speculators

Why would you allow speculators to manipulate oil prices and destroy world economies? Has the cost to get oil out of the ground changed over the last 5 years? Didn't Brazil make a huge oil discovery a few years ago?

1. Are people who speculate with millions/billions of dollars intelligent?
2. Do these people who invest millions/billions do so haphazardly or do they research the market and stay abreast of current events.
3. Is oil a commodity, which means it is based on supply and demand?
4. So we are supposed to believe that these intelligent traders are buying billions in oil, because they believe sometime in the future there will be a shortage?
5. So if it could be proven that oil speculators are aware there have been huge oil discoveries in the last 5 years, that have created a large surplus and predicted surplus, what does that say about these speculators?
6. Does that mean they are stupid, didn't study, or know something we don't' know?
7. Could it mean that oil is no longer traded as a commodity and all the speculators are doing is manipulating the price of oil, which in turn devastates the world's economies and makes billions for a few people?

What do you think investors and fund managers will do when they find out that technology will be released around the world making energy virtually free?

What if people wanted cars that had Hydraulic Launch Assist and ran on hydrogen that was extracted from water, using solar panels, cheaply manufactured in China, do they have that option, or are they forced to use what makes oil companies their huge profits?

18. Patriot Act

I am pretty sure that most Americans are unaware of what the U.S. government has done to the rights of its citizens. Just Google Patriot Act and add any key words from the following sentence:

There is a component of the Patriot Act that would allow the military to indefinitely detain terror suspects, including American citizens arrested in the United States, without charge.

Questions:

1. What is the exact definition of a "terror suspect"?
2. How many Americans were detained who were obviously not terrorists and had no rights when it came to proving their innocence?
3. Why do we have the Patriot Act?
4. There was no way to accomplish those goals before the Patriot Act?
5. Is that the ONLY way you can accomplish those same goals?
6. Do Americans want to lose their rights? This is in general; I am not saying to offer this as a trade-off for security reasons. The question is, "YES or NO, do Americans want to lose their rights?"

So we have a problem and the government came up with a solution called The Patriot Act.

- Does the entire country agree with the patriot act?
- What are the "Checks and Balances" to protect Americans against criminal activity by government officials implementing the Patriot Act?
- What exactly does the Patriot Act do to protect American Citizens?
- So what you are saying is, if there was another way to accomplish that without limiting the rights of American Citizens you would do it, correct?

271

- If they say yes: Great I will get the best people working on that today or hand them your premade plan.
- If they say no: So what you are saying is, the government prefers to control its citizens by limiting their rights, even though there could be alternatives that produce the same results?

19. Professionals

This would be doctors, lawyers, accountants, investment advisors, etc., then add to that mechanics, electricians, plumbers and car salespeople. Learn to ask them simple questions that could make a major difference in your life. If you are paying them, don't you have a right to ask a question concerning what you are purchasing?

Questions:

- Is this the best option available to me or anyone else?
- Have you told me all the facts I need to know in order to make an informed decision?
- Do you have the knowledge and experience necessary to make that decision?

20. Reverse Mortgages

One of the ways the Middle Class was able to build wealth in the past was by inheriting their parent's homes. Now due to the market crash and high health care costs these parents are using reverse mortgages as way to survive. If they are fairly treated then fine, but what if they aren't? What if it turns out these deals are really taking advantage of the people involved?

Questions:

- Show me the people who have done this and are happy about their decision.
- Show me the total number of reverse mortgages.
- Show me the number of people who died, the amount received before they died versus the value of their homes.

Take this data and do some simple calculations and let's see how great this program is. This is math that an 8th grader can do, so don't say it will take a 6 month study costing the taxpayers $2.2 million. Tell us where to get the data and I know there are people who will crunch the numbers (correctly) for free.

21. Solar Power

It has been calculated that if only 0.3 percent of usable surfaces in the U.S. had 10 percent efficient solar applied to them, the power generated would exceed U.S. energy needs.

Is energy used while transporting electricity over 100 miles of power lines? Why are solar panels good enough for government to use it for road signs? In case of the BIG terror threat, wouldn't it be better if each household produced its own energy and therefore reduce the threat of a major blackout. It is easy to knock out one power plant, but let me see a terrorist blowup 70 million homes with solar panels simultaneously. It is not going to happen.

- Can someone tell me why solar panels on individual homes does not make sense?
- Can someone also tell me that it makes sense to produce solar energy 100-1000 miles away and transport it? What exactly do you end up with at the end of that "energy" commute? How much energy actually makes it to the final destination?
- I recently read that China is now the largest producer of solar panels and windmills in the world. Every day they are creating products that produce free energy for the life of that product. Ask the U.S. Department of Energy why China is doing that.
- Is it true that solar panels on the International Space Station absorb light from both sides?
- Why does the space station even use solar panels if they don't work efficiently? The answer to this validates the reason for using them, even if they aren't efficient.

This is another issue that the energy companies have spent millions convincing people it doesn't work efficiently, while they continually build solar farms and sell you their electricity.

22. Vaccinations

A new trend is spreading across the United States and parents are opting out of having their children vaccinated and this is being applauded even by doctors. Why is that? Parents don't love their children? They don't want to protect them...or are they protecting them, because someone said, "Hey, this doesn't sound right, let me investigate the facts myself." All I want to know is why did hospital staff choose to leave their jobs instead of getting vaccinated? Google it.

23. Wall Street

I am not on board with people who claim we need the anonymity of investors or the "dark" investors in order to supply liquidity to the market. Are they needed because investors always had a problem getting their money out of the market? Is that what they are saying? Another theory I don't agree with deals with paying high bonuses in order to keep the talent. I bet there is a long line of qualified people waiting to take those jobs at a fraction of what the current pay is. So if cost reduction and profits is the goal for the shareholders, then this is the solution.

Now there is a system used by traders to extract money out of the market and return no value.

- Do firms use a technology that allows them to "skim" money out of the market to the tune of millions of dollars a day, because their trades get in faster than anyone else's?
- Does this produce any value to our economy?
- Can the average investor use this software and make that money also?

Risky Investment Losses

In May of 2012 JP Morgan admitted to losing over $2 billion in a risky investment. Why don't they tell the public how it really works? They put $2 billion in an investment and where did that money go? Did it just disappear? No, it changed hands. Someone else now has that money. Funny how the news is not reporting who gained from that $2 billion.

Questions to ask JP Morgan Executives:

1. Did you lose $2 billion in a risky investment?
2. Just to clarify, you had more than $2 billion in your possession and you transferred it into someone else's possession via an investment vehicle, is that correct?
3. What was the total investment made into that vehicle? $5 billion, $10 billion, etc.?
4. The investment didn't perform well and a part of it equaling $2 billion is gone?
5. Where did it go? Who benefitted from it?
6. Where did the money you invested come from? Was it from millionaire hedge funds, pension plans or mutual funds that the public invests in (or maybe something else)?

Over Paid Positions

1. What is your job?
2. How much do you make?
3. What am I getting for the part of my money that pays you? Write down all of their answers.
4. That's it, nothing else?
5. If I can get the same or better service for less money, why would I pay you? Let them answer and write it down. This alone may show the compensation fallacy to the world.

The point is that businesses have held down wages for years. The reason is because they want to hold down costs to increase profits. So why is that good for them and not good for you? Cut executive compensation. That cuts costs, which would increase profits. Is this a double standard?

24. War On Terror

Have you ever wondered why we are the only country fighting this war? People may claim that it is a global effort, but I challenge you to look at the actual data showing the commitment from other countries and then make your own decision.

Here is a logical questioning sequence that can be asked and expanded.

1. YOU TO A U.S. DEFENSE OFFICIAL: Do you know why people from other countries want to kill Americans as opposed to say Brazilians or Russians or Germans or Japanese?
2. IF THEY ANSWER: The terrorist attack those nations also.
3. YOUR NEXT QUESTION: Then can you tell me why those countries don't have a "War on Terror" like the United States does?
4. Can you explain how a child born today decides they want to kill Americans in 20 years?
5. If that same child was adopted by an American family and raised in the United States would they still want to kill Americans? THE FOLLOW UP TO THEIR ANSWER: So what you are saying is, it isn't any particular nationality that chooses to kill Americans?

This is one of those emotionally charged issues and you can use what you learned in this book to find out what the truth is. Also, be prepared to be labeled.

25. Women In The Workplace

Why is there a discrepancy of earnings between men and their female counterparts when it comes to the work they produce? This issue has already been debated, but maybe there are other reasons that have to do with people finding ways to get things they don't deserve. It is tough to commit large scale fraud with no help. The perpetrator usually has to influence other people to do things they normally wouldn't do, because they know it isn't right. If they could not influence the right people then the scheme may not even get off the ground. Is this why men don't want women to move up the professional ladder?

Here are questions that aren't usually asked when the subject of pay inequality is discussed:

- Is it easier for upper management to immorally influence men than women?
- Do escort services that charge thousands of dollars a night cater to corporate America or the government?
- Are male escorts purchased for woman by companies trying to influence them?
- Do women have business meetings at strip clubs?
- Are men weaker than women when it comes to moral challenges?
- Is it possible that a woman's genetic makeup doesn't allow her to make decisions that adversely affect other people, even if the leading motivator is sex?
- If sex was used as a tool in business and government, would those methods work with women? If not, could this be one of the reasons why some men don't want women in high places?
- If you get a product or service, does it cost less because it was produced by a woman?
- If the job gets done correctly, does anyone care who does it? Ask this question to any supporter of illegal immigration.

If it was ever proven that men would choose sex over doing what is right for people and women wouldn't, this alone would be enough of a reason for women to run the world.

PART 13:

FINAL
THOUGHTS

Chapter 59: You Could Be The One

I have a simple belief and I hope I am right. I believe there are more people who are honest then there are dishonest. I believe there are literally millions of honest people who work in companies, the government or organizations and they know about wrongful or illegal activities. They sit there and watch as money is mismanaged, data is manipulated, and more serious crimes are perpetrated, but because they need that job and are in fear of retaliation they turn the blind eye.

It's a tough decision. I am not sure what I would do in their exact situation, but I do know one thing, it would eat at me every night. Would I be able to stand up and say, "Enough"? Could I take the information to the proper authorities? I would hope for myself, the answer would be yes. There is a term for these people and they are given federal rights of protection. They are called "Whistle Blowers". Think about what that means. Someone sees something so wrong that they need to blow a whistle and say, "Stop, what the heck are you doing?" Whistle Blowers have brought to light information in many industries that affect a variety of issues from the environment, to finance, to medicine, even in the military. I believe when someone stands up for what is right or for the rights of others, then they are heroes.

You can also blow the whistle anonymously, which has happened plenty of times in the last 30 years. You may be in a situation where you know exactly what is wrong and you know how to fix it, but for reasons that we won't question here, you cannot expose the truth yourself. What is stopping you from putting a plan together and anonymously sending it to someone who will do something about it? Use this book to create the questions that need to be asked to a specific person and then get those questions to an investigative reporter who wants to do the right thing. I see these reporters on the news all the time exposing corruption in corporate America and our government.

Sometimes the perpetrators have a change of heart and can't do it anymore. They can't look into their children's eyes and tell them they shouldn't be bad, when they are breaking the law themselves. Maybe their problem is they were drawn into a scheme long ago and can't find a way out. There is always a way out. Doing the right thing is always right. Maybe they start doing the right thing now, make amends for what they have done wrong. Why not? How hard would it really be? If this paragraph is about you, make a change now. Stop convincing yourself that everyone else is doing it, so you can do it also. Everyone else is not doing it. Only a select few are ruining it for the rest of us. Why do you want to be on their side? You may have the information that could set the world right in medicine or energy. Why would you hold that back? Some day it will come out that you knew and your kids will have to look at you knowing, you were the one. You were the person that withheld information that could have helped thousands or millions of people. Do you want to be that person?

Maybe you are not an employee. Maybe you are in a position to effectuate change a lot easier. Maybe it is part of your job description.

- If you are a reporter (investigative).
- If you are a interviewer.
- If you are a government watchdog.
- If you are a Congressperson.
- If you are on a Government Oversight Committee.
- If you are on a Government Committee to Find The Truth.
- If you are an employee of one of the many Government Protection Agencies.

Do the right thing. Use the questioning techniques outlined in this book to expose the truth for the people who need it the most. These are the same people who watch your shows, elect you, and pay taxes so you can have a salary. They need someone on their side; it's called a champion of the people. Not a handout for the people, just the truth for the people.

Make a common sense stand in a way that the world can see, understand and participate. There are tools available to expose the truth, to dig through the rubble and come up with the facts. Yet, the media keeps sensationalizing the "experts" and rarely gets to the truth. We know why, it is all about ratings, money, and the fear of taking a stand themselves. Think about it, you CAN take a stand. If you are a news reporter, is your goal to be a sounding board for influence or do you want to report the truth? Why did you choose that career path anyway?

Or, you can do nothing. You can sit back and watch as the wrong people get rich while taking advantage of everyone else. And that's okay, because it's your choice. Don't get upset when an investment firm misplaces a billion dollars and it happened to be where your pension plan was, because I guarantee you that someone in that firm knows where the money is and they made a choice, just like you, to say nothing. So if you are not the one, maybe you know who the one is. If so, can you get this book into their hands?

Chapter 60: What's Stopping You

Sometimes all you need is just 30 seconds of real courage. There have been times in your life when you were apprehensive about doing something, but the possibility of success gave you the courage to try and for some reason it worked. I don't know how it is for women, but I know a man can muster up incredible courage when it comes to the woman in their life. It happens every day when a young man sees a young lady who he really would like to be with. In his mind he thinks of all the reasons why he wants her and then he thinks of how it won't work. He goes back and forth and sometimes talks himself out of it, but sometimes he doesn't. He walks up to her and says, 'Hi, would you like to go out with me?'' Then it happens, she says yes.

You can probably look back on your life and track where you are today based on a few decisions you made that took less than 30 seconds. That is how life works. You don't need to be on top of your game 24/7. You can ask a few questions in 30 seconds.

What about your kids, wouldn't you stand up for them? Just look at your new born and think about the world they will grow up in. Unless you are in a privileged group, it will be tough for them. I am telling you right now, if things don't change course within the next few years, it will be nearly impossible for people born today to live the American dream. Is this the legacy you want to leave behind? Is this what you want for your family?

What if you could make the difference? What if you were meant to be "that" person who stood up and said, "Enough is enough!" There is a funny thing about courage, it is contagious. People are waiting for someone to take a stand. You will be amazed at how quickly people come to your side when you decide to stand up for what is right. I started writing this book before the Occupy Wall Street movement began and as of now it is unsure where it will go, but they have made an impact. Someone stood up and said, "Enough" and then that little bit of courage became contagious. Others said, "You know what, that's right and I want to do something."

People love a winner. They will also follow a leader. Anyone can be a leader. Sometimes people are leaders and they don't even know it. It happens when one person gets fed up with something and can't take it anymore. They speak their mind and if they are right for their situation, they are probably right for other people's situations. Those other people pay attention because it hits home. A lot of those people will agree and do absolutely nothing, but some of those people will. They will follow you and you are now a leader. What if you don't want to be the leader? That is fine. Maybe you are the catalyst. Maybe you were able to show the leader what needs to be done. They were just waiting for someone like you to teach them.

You might not think you are smart enough or you are too old or too young. The fact is no one is better than anyone else. You may not have the same education, but it doesn't mean they are smarter than you. We already have so-called smart people ruining the world, it obviously isn't the answer. What we need is logic and common sense - do you have that? Can you look at a situation and say that makes sense or doesn't make sense? Can you read a plan and say that will or will not work? It's not as hard as you have been led to believe and you are not as helpless either.

It is great to know the truth, but there needs to be action. There are many different ways to have an impact and you don't have to do it all alone.

- Build communities, do it as a group.
- Use the group you already have.
- Get reporters to ask the questions.
- Get the people you are intimate with to fix the world.
- Have your parents or children make the change.
- Hand out your plans at town hall meetings, government hearings, political rallies,protests, school board meetings, etc.

When I started writing this book I would get in to conversations, wanting to test my questioning techniques. Even though I wrote the questions, I found myself not asking them the way I wanted to, but over time I became better. All you will need is practice. Anyone can ask great questions. You don't need a college degree, it doesn't depend on your religion and it doesn't matter how much money you have. In the United States, you have the right to ask questions, especially if the outcome will affect your life. Why not practice so you can become a master of asking questions. Practice with friends and family, become great at it. Ask yourself your own questions and then answer them. Make up questions based on the issue you will be challenging. Remember to follow the Rules of Questioning in Chapter 14.

Another great way to practice is to watch a news television show and act as if you were on the panel or the interviewer. Listen to what is said and then figure out what the question should have been that could have exposed the truth right there.

So here you are. You know there are problems in the world. You know that the decision makers have ulterior motives for not fixing certain problems. You know it is mostly because of money. You know how to research a problem and get through to the truth. You know how to ask the right questions to expose the truth. So what are you going to do with all that knowledge?

You can be like a lot of people and say nothing, but that is why our world is where it is at today. Ironically, our world is also where it is today because some people did stand up; they fought for what they believed in and what was right. I am asking you to do what is right. Sadly, there are a multitude of issues that adversely affect the general population of the world. Are you the person looking the other way because you have a better job, a nice house and a new car? Or are you going to be the person they speak of 50 years from now and say, "If it wasn't for them taking a stand back then, we probably wouldn't be living this good life we have now."

Chapter 61: Respect The Rights Of Others

Right or wrong, we should respect that people are allowed to believe what they want. This is one of the hardest concepts of living in a society that people need to understand. As long as someone's beliefs don't turn into actions that adversely affect others, why would anyone even care? Worse off, why would they take the time and energy to prove them wrong?

Whether you believe we are a democracy or a republic, the underlying understanding is that the majority rules (usually). Which means you may have beliefs that are in the minority and I am sure at some level we all have those beliefs. Having minority beliefs means you are probably not going to like every rule of the land. As much as you believe something is right or wrong, there is a good chance that someone else has a different belief. Does that mean they should be kicked out of this country? Maybe they should be put in jail or let's threaten them until they believe like us. Is that the country you want to live in? It may sound good when it is going your way, but trust me, you won't like it when you are on the other side.

Once you get good at asking questions you will feel a certain power, especially if you are one of the people who can make things happen. Anyone with the ability to affect major change for millions of people would be considered powerful. Don't let it go to your head. Do the right thing, isn't that what you wanted everyone else to do in the first place? Don't be the hypocrite and have someone else use this book against you.

Don't do anything illegal and use this book as your excuse. My first question to you would be, "So what you are saying is, you had to break the law in order to ask a question?" If it looks a little ridiculous on paper, it is probably ridiculous in real life.

You also need to use your better judgment. If someone looks like they will cause you harm if you continue to question them and you are not in a public place of safety, then save it for another time. Use the same common sense at work. If your boss is going to retaliate, decide if what you are fighting for "really" affects you or others adversely or are you just arguing because you have some new skills. Fixing a problem is better when you're able to enjoy the benefits. Be smart.

Guidelines we all could live by:

1. Everyone has a right to their own beliefs.
2. No one can tell anyone else what they have to believe in.
3. As long as someone else's beliefs don't affect anyone else directly or indirectly, then we will not waste time or public resources debating them.
4. If you want to turn a minority belief into a majority belief then convince people to believe what you believe, don't force them or lie to them.
5. You have the right to your own beliefs; you just don't have the right to act on those beliefs and adversely affect other people in the process.

I am sure you can add other guidelines, but you get the main idea. Don't ruin other people's lives who don't want to live by your beliefs. On the flip side, don't let others tell you what to believe. You have to find a way to live in society where everyone's beliefs are respected. I hope she doesn't mind, but I am borrowing a favorite line from Ellen DeGeneres, "Be kind to one another."

Chapter 62: Tact - Love, Family and Friends

A good definition of tact is: a keen sense of what to do or say in order to maintain good relations with others or avoid offense.

When it comes to world issues, that affect the finances, health and over all well-being of millions of people, I don't believe it is mandatory to be tactful. When exposing the truth, it is possible you will be mad and it will show. This could happen if someone lied to you and you lost your home or someone died because of it. Are there any laws stating you must be tactful when it comes to exposing the truth? Does it mean if someone exposes the truth in an untactful manner they are lying? That is ludicrous and one has nothing to do with the other.

As you become better at asking questions, inevitably it will spill over into your personal life. This could cause some problems if you are not careful. You have to remember that people don't like to be proven wrong. Not your kids, not your spouse, not your boss and probably not you. If you use these new skills to challenge every little thing in the normal course of your day, you might find yourself alienating the ones you love and interact with. That should not be your plan.

So my first advice would be to limit the amount of "situations" you take on to what is really important to you or your family. If it has to do with health or finances then I believe you have a valid reason to question. As a matter of fact, I wish more families would have in-depth discussions when it comes to health and finances.

Here are a few examples of family questions that I think should be asked:

1. Is this the only option we have?
2. Are there other medical treatments available?
3. Why should we make this purchase when we have all these bills?
4. Wouldn't we feel better if we were debt free?

For your children, you can get the point across and drop a little guilt on them in a tactful way:

1. Do you think I would be a good parent if I didn't care about what you did?

2. When you have children, do you want them to do the same things that you are doing now?
3. If something happened to you and I could have prevented it by asking this question, but didn't, how do you think I would feel?

To make the questions easier to swallow you can add a few tactful words. Try adding one of these options in front of the questions you will be asking:

1. I thought that...
2. I am not trying to argue...
3. I know you believe that.... but,
4. First, I want to say I love you and respect what you are trying to do/say...
5. All I want to do is help you, if I am wrong I will take all of the blame.
6. Maybe we should try...

Remember, when it comes to the ones you love, you don't have to win every argument; that is not what this book is for. Think before you question. There is also the possibility that you could just fix whatever is wrong, without even having a conversation. If you know you are right and it will help your family, just do it and don't expect anyone to pat you on the back. Why do you have to have the validation of "I am right" or "I told you so" to do the right thing?

Chapter 63: Before You Attack Me

Writing a book is a long process. You read it over and over again, make changes here and there, move sections around and reword sentences in an effort to get your message across as effective as possible. Even after all of this, I am sure there will be sections of this book I would like to reword and possibly remove.

This book was not written to become a literary masterpiece. I am sure if you are looking for misspellings, grammatical errors or some other faux pas you could probably find them. But my question would be why? All I am trying to do is make the world a better place for everyone and that includes you and your family. Can you think of any good reason why you would want to hinder that? Or, to put it another way, "Do you think people would prefer to listen to a person who uses these techniques to fix their lives or would they like to hear about some irrelevant mistake in this book?"

If there is a part of this book that is challenged, I will think about it and if I was wrong, I will say, "I am wrong and you are right." That will quickly end the discussion. I am not here to be the final answer and I am sure that any one part does not refute the overall premise of what this book is about. So if your life is so limited that you have the need to prove something wrong, please do. I do not have the right to tell you how to feel or what you should do with your precious time.

Inevitably there will be people paid to go through this book word by word and find something that can be taken out of context, twisted and regurgitated to the public. Their goal will be to cast me as someone who is against a certain culture, doesn't like a type of religion, is against capitalism, is not a patriot, hates America, etc. Save it. If you have read up to this section you know I will easily defend any attack, while simultaneously taking your credibility down with it. The truth is the easiest thing to defend.

Before you attack, just answer these questions:

1. Do you believe our world has problems?
2. Would you like to see some of those problems fixed?
3. Would solving global problems benefit you and your family?
4. Can you explain why you would attack something that would benefit your own family?

If you were on the wrong side in the past, you are probably on the wrong side now. So if attacking is your choice, you will have one more problem, too much publicity could bring the issues to the public quicker than this book will. It's easy to fool a few people when they are uninformed, but when the truth goes viral it's going to be a lot tougher. I am not sure a few misleading messages and a few experts on television will convince people after that. What's going to happen when people can't be fooled anymore? What's going to happen when they say, "Show me, because that doesn't sound right"? The best option for you is to fix what is wrong yourself, because it is going to be fixed either way.

For all of the experts, public relations firms, situation framers and spinners who will be paid big money to discredit the logic that lies within this book, I have already prepared for you. My main focus is to show people that our energy crisis isn't a crisis and I will stick to that. Here is a list of questions any honest interviewer should ask if you are on their show discussing this book.

1. Does the high mileage technology discussed in the book actually exist?
2. Is the high mileage technology being used right now?
3. Why is the book wrong for telling people to use that technology?
4. Can you tell the audience what exactly is wrong with the book's logic?
5. Do you not agree that people can make their own decisions if they had all of the information?
6. What are your reasons for discrediting the book?

I could just go on and on:

- What makes you an expert?
- Where did you go to school?
- Do you have any connection to the cause you are defending?
- Are you totally sure that what is written in this book is wrong?
- Can you simply prove your position?
- Would you be willing to take a polygraph to prove your point?

You get the idea. Any smart interviewer would be able to use these questions and make up more on their own. I could be wrong, but I think what an audience looks for is the truth. So why don't we give it to them.

288

I am just trying to find a way to fix the world; do you really want to be the person that stops that? We need people to do the right thing. Even if you are one of the people who are currently enjoying undeserved success, you have to think about the future implications. You have to think about your family in the future and the world you will be leaving them.

I know everything will never be 100% right, but we only need a few major problems fixed and the rest of the struggles will either diminish or not seem so bad. Think about it, if your automobile fuel cost was $100/month, your home utilities were $100/year, and medical costs were cut in half do you think you would have less stress in your life? Do you think you would have more money to enjoy your life? There is a claim that most divorces are caused by financial stress. Maybe even that industry will get a positive bump once we fix the world.

And that is it. Our country, the world, the economy, health care, and financial markets are in the crises they are today because the right questions are never asked to the right people at the right time. Let's change that.

INDEX

E

earmarks, 187, 266
Economic Circular Flow, 204
economic growth, 202, 212, 214
   lopsided, 213, 215
economist, 202, 204, 215
Edison, Thomas, 1
education, 44, 93, 262
environment, 11, 32, 41, 46, 102,
   226-227, 234, 243
EPA - Environmental Protection
Agency, 46, 194, 267
   HLA, 221-222, 224-228, 238,
     240-241
   licensing, 231-232
   mission, 46
escorts, 276
experts, 18, 37-42
exploit, 137

F

Facebook, 20
family, 43, 88, 138, 217, 285-286
   anti, 113
   consolidation, 210
Fiduciary Responsibility, 246-247
finances, 220
   401K, 208, 220, 223
   debt, 202, 208, 217-218
flowcharts
   entire, 148
   Problem Solving Method, 160
   mini, 7, 30, 53, 76, 120
   question, 171
   template, 178-194

flu
   bird, 264
   H1N1, 258
   mutation, 263
   swine, 39, 84, 264
   vaccine, 88, 258
Food Pyramid, 121, 264-265
foreclosure, 208, 218
fracking, 85, 92, 181-182, 268
fraud, 11, 129, 132, 152, 259, 276
freedom, 11, 22, 45, 137
friends, 166, 194, 226, 285-286
fuel, 220-228, 235, 240-243
fund manager, 271
future, 7, 41, 101, 141, 228

G

Galilei, Galileo, 8
genius, 15, 85, 200, 251
germs, 264, 265
Global Truths, 82
Globalize, 33, 150, 162, 233
Google, 11, 18-19, 25, 38-39, 50,
   121, 132, 164, 206, 234, 242,
   257-271, 273
guidelines, 103, 169, 176, 284
guilt, 285

H

harm, 82, 84, 134, 259, 265, 283
health, 220, 259, 265, 285
health insurance, 35, 67, 208, 268
   medical costs, 209
hero, 57, 96, 115, 121, 123, 278
HHO, 235-236
high mileage, improved, 234-235

I

J

ABOUT THE AUTHOR

Joe Fedison has dedicated his life to mastering effective communication techniques with a focus on direct questioning. He was born in Atlantic City, NJ and grew up between there and Las Vegas, Nevada. Interested in math and science, he did well in school and was accepted to the University of Rochester as a Physics major. He graduated with a BS in Optics Engineering and received a Certificate in Management Studies from the William E. Simon Graduate School of Business Administration in Rochester, New York.

Joe Fedison has over 25 years of business experience, encompassing a multitude of fields and skills, which include: Executive Management, Business Development, Customer Relations, Brand Marketing, Project Management, Sales Management, Manufacturing, Importing, Customer Service Training, Public Speaking, Internet Marketing & Analytics, Financial Analysis, Public Relations, Product Design, Distribution, and IT Management.

www.ingramcontent.com/pod-product-compliance
Lightning Source LLC
LaVergne TN
LVHW051455080426
835509LV00017B/1767